# TRACKS TO
# DISASTER

# TRACKS TO
# DISASTER

## Adrian Vaughan

Ian Allan
PUBLISHING

First published 2000

ISBN 0 7110 2731 5

© Adrian Vaughan 2000

Published by Ian Allan Publishing

an imprint of Ian Allan Publishing Ltd, Terminal House, Shepperton, Surrey TW17 8AS.
Printed by Ian Allan Printing Ltd, Riverdene Business Park, Hersham, Surrey KT12 4RG.

Code: 0011/B2

*Half title page:*
Electro-pneumatic operation was installed between Basingstoke and Woking in 1904. Station areas were controlled from signalboxes with power frames and the open tracks between stations were controlled by these semaphores working automatically through track circuits ahead. The gantries were 1,500yd apart and capacity of the installation is equal to that of an automatic, three-aspect colour-light system. *Mike Esau*

*Title page:*
The appalling wreckage at Ladbroke Grove. What can I say?
*Chris Harris / Times Newspapers Ltd*

*Front cover:*
The cost of track rationalisation is seen at Cowden. A trap point and sand drag would have averted this accident, but was too expensive. *Brian Morrison*

# Acknowledgements

The author is indebted to David Collins, Mike Christensen, Martin Fuller, Peter Jordan and John Morris for their kind advice and assistance and also to the photographers Ken Brunt and Brian Morrison for going out of their way to help.

# Contents

# Introduction

It would be as well to remember, when reading this accumulated collection of railway disasters, that you are safer on a train than in your own home. More people are killed per year in fires in their homes than as passengers in British trains.

The driver of a train has the ultimate responsibility to look where he is going, obey the signals and preserve the lives which his passengers have placed so trustingly in his hands. Up to 2000, no matter what safety devices had been provided, and no matter how conscientious a driver was, there was always a chance that he would make a mistake. Rarely, though, does one come across such a cavalier attitude to red lights as that of Driver Bailey of the Eastern Counties Railway. One night in September 1853 an up goods train stopped on the London side of Brandon station, in Suffolk, due to a locomotive failure. The line seems to have been worked by the Time Interval system. This required a 'policeman' to operate a signal. After a train had passed him he put the signal to 'Danger' which meant putting up a red light at night. After a certain length of time had elapsed, the policeman took down his red signal and put up a white light. There were two guards on the goods train. One went to watch the driver mend the engine and the other went back to the station, told the station policeman what had happened and asked him to maintain a red light on the signal at the east end of the station until 10 minutes or so after they had moved off. He ought then to have walked further back along the line to protect the rear of his train himself but relying on the policeman's red light, he too went off to observe events at the disabled engine. It is also likely that, knowing the scheduled timetable, he thought he knew that there were no more trains for an hour or so. Never 'assume' on a railway. Coming up from Thetford was a special cattle train driven by Driver Bailey. He came along the straight and level towards Brandon. There was the station's red light. He saw it and drove straight past, crashing into the rear of the goods train and causing a great deal of damage to wagons, as well as death and injury amongst the poor cattle. He was summoned to appear before the Chairman of the Board of the Eastern Counties Railway, David Waddington. Waddington asked him: 'Did you not see the red light at the end of Brandon station?'

'Yes.'

'Then why did you not stop?'

'Because red lights are not my concern. I am a driver, not a policeman.'

'Have you not read your Rule Book?'

'I have glanced at it, yes.'

Driver Bailey was very properly dismissed from the service.

Driver Bailey's action was what I call a Determined Drive-by or DDB. Were signals passed at danger less frequently in steam and semaphore days than after the widespread introduction of modern motive power and multiple-aspect colour-light signalling? I worked as a semaphore signalman on busy main lines for 15 years from 1960 and I witnessed two incidents, neither of them serious, just slight errors of braking judgement. I reported neither of them. In 1957 the driver of an up goods train

*Left:*
Three-aspect colour-light signals at Purley's Caterham branch platform. The junction indicator is illuminated to prove that the facing points are safely set for the diverging line. Below it is a green light. This signal is equivalent to a 'bracketed' semaphore with lower distant arms. *Author*

*Above:*
On the left of the view, marked by a piece of litter, is a GWR Automatic Train Control (ATC) ramp in the up Salisbury line at Westbury North in 1974. The distant signals to which it applied are on the right. The left-hand arm is for Hawkeridge Junction, the right-hand for Heywood Road Junction. The ramp was placed near — and to the rear of — the distant signal to which it applied, except where the distant was a lower arm to a stop signal, as in this case. It had then to be placed ahead of the signal to avoid the engine coming to a stand with the pick-up shoe standing on the ramp. The diesel is No D1058 *Western Nobleman* on a service from Paddington. *Author*

running on the up goods loop at Swindon, Highworth Junction, took the main-line signals as applying to him, accelerated, ran past the loop signal at 'Danger' and was derailed at the trap point. The same thing happened at Steventon, near Didcot in 1963. In both cases there were trap points: at Highworth a train on the down main was derailed by the wreckage of the up goods fouling the down line; at Steventon the arch of a bridge was filled with wrecked goods wagons, but the quick thinking of the signalman prevented a full-scale disaster. Trap points at the end of a loop are likely to be useful in keeping an over-running train clear of the main line only when the train is travelling slowly, say 10mph maximum.

The acronym SPAD (signal passed at Danger) did not exist in 1960, so far as I am aware, but seems to be an invention of the 1980s when acronyms had become the 'in' thing to use and SPADs began to be more of a problem than hitherto. It may be that, in steam/semaphore days, incidents of passing signals at danger could easily be 'hushed-up' and were not reported to authority whereas, under modern signalling, trains are much more closely monitored and the incident cannot be hidden. But I still think it was a relatively rare event in the 1960s, or earlier. Mr Peter Semmens reveals (*Railway Magazine* January 2000 p77) that records kept by Eastern Region of British Railways in 1960 and 1961 show that there was one SPAD per 3,500,000 train miles. Maybe many more went unreported. In 1970 there were 700 SPAD incidents reported on British Railways; there were less than 500 in 1979, but then the

figure rose annually until, in 1988, there were over 800. But we have no means of knowing how these figures relate to SPADs per train mile.

The term SPAD does not differentiate between the accidental 'passing' of a signal by a few yards, perhaps through some miscalculation by the driver, and what might be called the 'SPAD-with-a-vengeance' incident, or what I described earlier as the Determined Drive-by or DDB. This is when a driver goes through a succession of signals at high speed without attempting to brake. In the days of steam haulage, power brakes and good signalling, when men had served for half a lifetime and been through the mill of hard experience, there were a few, a very few, DDBs.

At Slough on 16 June 1900 a DDB occurred when an experienced top-link driver, in charge of the 1.15pm Paddington-Falmouth — perhaps the most prestigious express on the GWR at that time — drove through at 'Danger' the entire range of signals at Dolphin Junction from the distant to the advanced starting, and then passed at 'Danger' the home signal of Slough East to collide with the rear of the 1.5pm from Paddington, a local passenger train. Not only did he ignore several signals; the express train driver also did not see the signalmen waving from their signalboxes, nor did he hear the detonators going off under his engine. It is possible he was briefly asleep after lunching too well on steak and kidney pie and stout beer — a meal he admitted to having consumed. This accident prompted the GWR to invest in improvements to its vacuum braking system, to make it as quick-acting as the Westinghouse compressed air brake, and to invent its famous system of Automatic Train Control. What is not at all well known is that, in 1910, the GWR refined its ATC to give an absolute and non-cancellable brake application if the driver passed a signal at 'Danger'. The system was experimentally installed between Ladbroke Grove and Paddington, demonstrated to the Board of Trade, then abandoned.

At Crich Junction, 10 miles north of Derby, just after midnight on 17 June 1931, the double-headed 10pm Leeds-Bristol TPO was driven into the rear of a goods train. No less than four top-link footplate men ignored all the signals at Wingfield and all the signals at Crich Junction to collide with the rear of the goods train which was in legitimate possession of the line.

In the small hours of 4 November 1940, Driver Stacey of Old Oak Common was taking 'King' class No 6028 and train westwards along the down relief line from Taunton. This line came to an end at Norton Fitzwarren, nearly two miles away. Stacey normally travelled over the down main line west of Taunton and had got it into his head that he was doing so now and

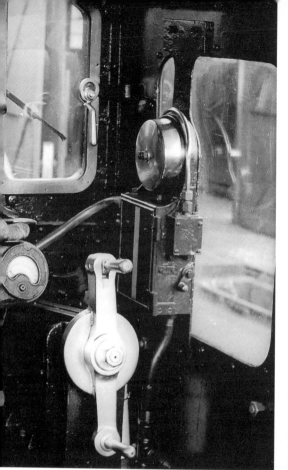

carefully watched the signals on that line. All those signals were showing green for a train which was rapidly overtaking him. Thus, ignoring all the relief line signals he sped along. They were showing green at Taunton West Junction and Silkmill Crossing but the outer and inner distants for Norton Fitzwarren were at 'Caution'. He never saw the amber lights of the relief line distants, although they were quite visible to anyone looking forward. Neither was he brought out of his distracted state of mind when he had to acknowledge the siren for Norton's down relief line outer distant, and then again for the inner distant. One might have expected him to express surprise to his fireman that he had received two 'right side' failures in less than a minute, since, as far as he was concerned, all the signals were showing green. Similarly, the fireman, on whose side of the engine the down relief line distant signals were situated, might have pointed out that they were at 'Caution'. And so Driver Stacey drove through Norton Fitzwarren's down relief line stop signals at 'Danger' with the inevitable consequence that he drove off the end of the relief line, through the trap points, onto 'Olde England'. The train for which the main-line signals were cleared passed as No 6028 and its train were being derailed. Twenty-seven people were killed. This was the first time that anyone had cancelled and ignored the cab warning and the only time that a GWR driver — a conscientious man with long service — cancelled and ignored the ATC warning signals. He had misled himself by reading the wrong set of signal lights, although this distraction might have been due to preoccupation with his own affairs as his home had been bombed a night or two before.

To pass a signal at 'Danger' is, by definition, a dangerous thing to do, but modern cost-cutting policies have increased the number of dangerous situations guarded by fixed signals. I refer to the policy of reducing double line to single track. At about 7.25am on 24 March 1987, a Westbury-Whatley Quarry train, hauled by No 47202 and driven by Mr Noyes, turned right at Clink Road Junction onto the Frome line. The train was travelling at about 15mph, on a double track, down a steepish grade, for about ¾ mile from Clink Road Junction towards signal W312, which guards the exit from the down Frome to the up and down Frome single line. There were no trap points beyond W312 to protect the single line. Frome station was about

600yd further on, situated on the single line. As No 47202 slowly approached the signal, which was at 'Danger', an up Weymouth-Bristol passenger train was coming out of Frome station, running up the hill towards the double-track section. This train consisted of five coaches hauled by No 33032. The Whatley train free-wheeled past W312 and came onto the single track, colliding head-on with the passenger train a few seconds later at 7.33am. The closing speed was perhaps 15mph and no-one was killed, but there were some serious injuries. The guard of the Whatley train was in the leading cab of No 47202. He said at the Inquiry that, just before they passed W312 at 'Danger', his driver yelled 'Where are we going?!' But the driver, when he had recovered from his injuries some weeks later, said that it was the guard who had drawn his attention to the red signal by shouting. The driver humbly admitted his error and could give no explanation. This was the fourth time he had inexplicably passed a signal at 'Danger'. On the first occasion it had been a semaphore; the other three occasions involved colour-light signals.

The most important incentive to safety, for a train driver, ought to be self-preservation, but the fact that the job usually works properly, without incident, together with the feeling of one's own immortality in the routine of the day, has a deadening effect on what ought to be the most powerful stimulus to taking care. A classic example of this deadening effect is illustrated in the events leading up to the Chapel-en-le-Frith crash in February 1957. In this case the driver, John Axon, saw that the main power supply to his only brake was dangerously faulty and was advised by professional railway mechanics that he should 'fail' the engine and prepare another. But he disregarded the advice — in spite of the obvious danger — because it was Saturday and he wanted to get home at the usual time or even a little early; certainly not several hours late as would have been the case if he had had to prepare another engine for the job. In the event he never got home at all.

Brakes, signals — with all their associated safety devices — and the Rule Book are the three tangible components of safety. What is then required is concentration of the mind and a very proper sense of responsibility to apply the Rules. There are the technical aids, the comprehensive knowledge of the situation with which one is involved and the determination of the mind-set to apply everything. To be a safe railwayman involves giving more to the railway than just a shift a day and then forgetting about it for the rest of the time. The job has to become a way of life. This was the old-fashioned attitude and even then there were occasions when, as shown above, short-term imperatives got the better of the best of men. Also corrosive of safety are the commercial considerations: the demands of the public for higher speed and more frequent trains, and a strong desire to save money on the part of the railway's owners. This was as true in the 1880s as it was in the 1980s, and it is the same even today. The pressure for higher speed and greater frequency of trains — being driven closer together with shorter safety overlaps in advance of signals — communicates itself to drivers through the timetable and through 'quality control' techniques to keep drivers 'up to the mark'. And this mark is maybe getting out of reach. Some men and women are working near the limits of their endurance. Drivers who make two and a half 100mph round trips between Euston and Birmingham in one shift tell me of the great mental strain imposed on them. As the stress of driving becomes more intense, the capacity of the signalling safety devices which are provided to assist drivers have not proportionately improved.

To get more trains onto the same length of track, hopefully without delay, the LSWR brought into use at Grateley in July 1901 a signalbox which operated its points and signals by an electro-pneumatic system. Then in April 1903 it introduced, over the 6¼ miles between Andover 'B' box and Grateley, pneumatically-operated semaphore signals which were cleared and put to 'Danger' by means of track circuits in the same way that modern colour-light signals operate. There were five block sections in each direction and, with distant signals below each stop signal, the installation was the equivalent of three-aspect colour-lights — except that their illumination at night-time was not as good. This system was installed between Basingstoke and Brookwood in 1906 and remained in use for 60 years. The maximum permitted speed of trains under these signals was 85mph and, in spite of the absence of cab signalling, there were no accidents due to a driver over-running a signal at danger, possibly due to the restricted line speed.

From 1927 the Southern Railway began to install power-operated three- and four-aspect colour-light signalling, first in the London suburban area and then, from July 1932, between Coulsdon North and Brighton. Electric multiple units ran over the latter route at 75mph. The Southern, short of money for investment, could not install colour-light signalling as well as a cab signalling system and believed that there was a greater benefit to be had from multiple-aspect colour-light signalling. The LMS and the LNER were of the same opinion. The brilliant lights, sharply focused, gave a better degree of protection in the dark, in fog and in falling snow than paraffin-burning lamps on semaphores, and reduced the need for cab signalling. That was the Southern Railway's story, anyhow. The GWR had cab signalling on all its trunk routes by 1930 and in several very congested areas of its territory it had two-aspect colour-light signalling as well. The Southern Railway experienced no accidents caused by the over-running of multiple-aspect colour-light signals at 'Danger'. Dendy-Marshall's *History of the Southern Railway* mentions two collisions which took place on colour-light-signalled lines. Both were shunting movements where a driver had a restricted signal to proceed and, misled by a bright colour-light further off, overlooked the red light at which he should have stopped.

The system of warning drivers of the need to slow down adopted by British Railways was known as the Automatic Warning System (AWS). This had its origins in the 1936 Hudd System installed on, and unique to, the LTSR. This system told the driver whether the distant signal was at 'All Right' or at 'Caution'. The Hudd system used a powerful permanent magnet and a powerful temporary magnet, both laid on the sleepers in the centre of the track about 200yd before the distant signal. There was a receiver on the underside of the locomotive fixed about 4in above the track magnet. The first track magnet encountered by the locomotive receiver was the permanent one with its 'south pole' uppermost. This magnetic field interacted with the field of the locomotive receiver, causing a relay to deflect within the receiver gear on the engine, this movement being used to initiate a brake application, although the vacuum was not immediately invaded by atmospheric pressure. About 40ft further on there was the temporary magnet. If the distant signal was at 'All Right' contacts actuated by the signal arm were closed, sending electricity to energise the temporary magnet, with its 'north pole' uppermost. The locomotive pick-up magnet received this second impulse of opposite polarity which caused the brake valve relay to switch back and thus to cancel the brake application. If the distant signal was showing 'Caution', the second magnet was not energised and, as a result, the first impulse continued unchecked and the brakes were applied.

When the distant signal was at 'Caution', the driver heard a prolonged siren noise from the cab equipment. This was activated by the air rushing into the train pipe to destroy the vacuum. The driver then operated the cancelling lever and took over the process of braking. The action of acknowledging the warning caused a visual display in the cab at eye level to change from an all-black disc, about 4in across, to a series of yellow and black stripes radiating from a central point, like the petals of a flower. Indeed, in this condition the visual warning was called 'the sunflower'. This black and yellow display remained in front of the driver's eyes until he passed a distant signal at 'All Right', when it reverted to a plain black disc. When the distant signal was at 'All Right' the driver heard a brief 'honk' on the horn for as long as it took the engine to travel the 40ft to the second magnet which then cut off the developing brake application.

If he received a warning horn and did not acknowledge it within 15 seconds the brakes were applied so hard that, even if full power was being exerted by the locomotive, the train would be brought to a stand before it reached the 'Stop' signal to which the distant signal applied. The warning had to be cancelled by the driver so that he could take over the braking of the train. No-one ever thought that the driver would ignore the warning. It was utterly taken for granted that a driver would always take notice of the signal and drive in a competent, responsible manner. The AWS or ATC was not there to take away the driver's ultimate responsibility to his passengers, but only to assist him, to make his terrible task easier, especially when it was at its most awesome — in freezing rain, hail storms, falling snow, or on a pitch-dark, foggy night.

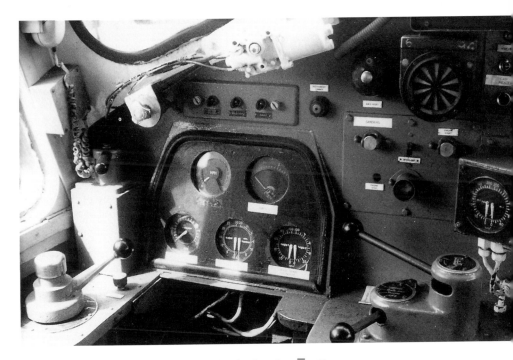

The Hudd system suffered from a lack of technology in as much as the track magnets were very large pieces of metal. During World War 2, owing to the need to develop cathode ray tubes for use in radar, a very powerful magnet in a very small space was required and a new alloy of aluminium was developed. This was capable of holding a far greater degree of magnetism, size for size, than iron. Thus, after the war this new magnet technology found a railway safety application.

The British Railways AWS was an improved version of the Hudd system although, left to themselves, BR's managers would not have included the very important visual display. In the BR AWS system, a distant signal at 'Caution' caused the AWS to sound a sharp, wailing siren, activated by the air rushing into the train pipe, but if the distant signal showed 'All Right' a reassuring, brightly-sounding bell rang. These two features were adopted from the older 'Automatic Train Control' system of the Great Western Railway. On the track, the magnets of the BR AWS were placed 2ft 6in apart and the mechanism controlling the brake valve was redesigned so that the driver had to acknowledge the warning siren within five seconds.

The BR AWS was put on trial in 1950 when track magnets were installed at distant signals from New Barnet to Huntingdon. 'A4' class locomotive No 60026 was fitted with the pick-up gear and cab equipment. As a purely temporary measure, for the purposes of the trial, the Hudd visual display was fitted. This would help the driver to see if the audible indication in the cab agreed with the aspect of the distant signal. The splendid system was still on trial when, on 8 October 1952, the appalling tragedy at Harrow & Wealdstone took place when 112 people were killed and 157 injured. The blame for this crash was laid on the Crewe-based driver of an

up express who had missed seeing a distant signal and two 'Stop' signals and then collided with the rear of a stationary train. Naturally there was a furore in the national press: 'This would not have happened if the ATC or AWS had been installed.' British Railways summoned representatives of the national press to King's Cross on 10 October and showed them over No 60026. Of course, the journalists couldn't understand what they were looking at, but they were very impressed with the visual warning aid and most papers carried a photograph of it, and also a comment that this device was for test purposes only and not part of the production model. There was then another fuss and as a result BR had to adopt the visual warning as standard.

The saving of money has always delayed the installation of safety devices. In the 19th century a *Times* editor wrote: 'Perhaps if a railway director were to be killed in a train crash we might see some progress in safety.' The installation of AWS as standard on all trunk lines was included in the 1955 Modernisation Plan, but at the end of 1958 only 288 miles of track had been equipped.

The AWS was a very capable system for two-aspect signalling with steam engines and well-trained drivers. However, when it became part of the dieselised and electrified four-aspect-signalled railway, where drivers were sitting warm and comfortable, where signals were only 1,200yd apart, and where trains normally ran at 100mph or more, it was not so efficient. As the

14

number of trains occupying the tracks increases, so the likelihood of a signal, or sequence of signals, showing a 'restricted speed' aspect is increased and the AWS warning siren wails with repetitive regularity, its cancellation being required with similar regularity. On 1 August 1963, the driver of a Euston-Liverpool express cancelled and ignored a series of AWS warnings as he approached Norton Bridge, north of Stafford, and cut through a Liverpool-Birmingham train which was crossing the junction. The repetitiveness of the regularly-spaced colour-light signals and their AWS warnings constitute a real risk. Coupled with that is the dullness of mind to risk induced by the relatively luxurious atmosphere in a modern traction-unit cab when compared to the spartan conditions of a steam-engine footplate for which AWS was designed.

The steam-age AWS was, and still is, being used in situations beyond its design capacity. In the late 1960s an experimental 'Signal Repeating AWS' installation was introduced between Southampton and Bournemouth. This had two refinements, the first being a visual display on the driver's console. As the train passed over the magnets on the approach to a colour-light signal, the siren or bell sounded and the aspect of the signal was repeated on the console. A yellow or red signal had to be acknowledged by pressing the illuminated display light. If the driver pressed the wrong button there was no acknowledgement and the brakes were applied. The aspect having been acknowledged, the illuminated button extinguished and the display was transferred to a vertical column of four lights which maintained a 'last aspect passed' indication. The second refinement was of the utmost importance. If a driver passed a red light the system recognised the fact and immediately applied the brakes in a non-cancellable operation. The system was never put into production.

It is vital that drivers have confidence in the signalling system, but this can be undermined by occasional eccentric behaviour on the part of signal aspects. The aspects depend on electrical contacts which can easily be broken. In 1973, I was riding with a former GWR driver in the cab of a diesel multiple-unit between Didcot and Reading. Approaching Pangbourne we both saw the next — entirely-automatic — colour-light signal changing from green to red to green several times. I asked my mate if he was going to stop for safety's sake and to report it. 'No, they are always doing stupid things like that,' he replied, and drove on at 70mph. What had probably happened in that instance was that the electric 'detection' on a set of points ahead of us had been disturbed by the battering vibration of a train passing over the rails. The rapid making and breaking of the detection contacts caused the protecting signal to change between red and green. Semaphore signals did not wave their arms up and down as a train approached had they done 'something would have been said'.

Engine drivers I had known in steam days — men I had travelled with on the footplate, men whose long service, expertise and commitment to the job was unquestionable — told me how monotonous the new signalling had become. They sat in the cab of their 'Western' or 'Warship' and roared away along 'Brunel's billiard table' watching the regularly-placed signals rush towards them at 90mph, while covering 44yd a second. Sometimes the track seemed to be rushing towards them with the train stationary. Linked to this hypnotic monotony at high speed

there is a specific danger attached to four-aspect signalling. The double yellow aspect indicates the point at which a train travelling at 100mph (or an IC125 at 125mph) must start to brake in order to stop at the red. But it also indicates that the next signal will be at single yellow. On first seeing the double yellow he brakes and gets his train under control, but still waits to see the aspect of the next signal. Will it be a single yellow or change to a double yellow? Having reduced speed perhaps from 125 to 80 the driver sees that the next signal is now at double yellow and so he 'lets it roll' and can go on for many miles in a queue of trains all running at 80mph. The AWS warning siren is cancelled every 30 seconds as he speeds along at 80mph approaching a single yellow which in due course turns to double yellow and on he goes.

This is the designed purpose of the four-aspect signalling system; to keep trains moving fast when they are close together, but it does this by inviting drivers to hope that the yellow signal ahead will clear to a less restrictive aspect. The obvious tendency is for drivers to encroach upon their braking distance. The judgement left to the driver is to decide at what point he had better start braking in earnest as he approaches the single yellow because he is getting close and it does not seem that it is going to clear. As the queue bunches up the single yellow takes longer to change to double yellow and the train drivers ease off their power or even brake so as to keep themselves on the right side of a double yellow. The double yellow is an ambiguous signal, in that its aspect may indicate the need to start braking for a stop at the red, 2,500yd further on, or it may not because that 'Danger' signal ahead might — like the chimerical rainbow — be always moving away. This applies particularly to trains travelling at 100mph or more. A diesel multiple-unit moving at 75mph could pass a double yellow without any braking and start to brake only as it approaches the single yellow. The four-aspect system of signals fulfils its role of keeping trains moving at speed and close together only if drivers

*Above left:*
Modern relay interlocking below Westbury Panel, installed in 1985. It was redundant in five years. *Author*

*Above right:*
A 1974 view of a manually-operated, mechanically-interlocked, semaphore signal. Westbury North's advanced starting signal, 4ft arm, on the Trowbridge line with Hawkeridge Junction's inner distant signal below it. The white diamond on the post indicates to train crews that they are occupying track-circuited rails. This combination of arms is the equivalent of a three-aspect colour-light signal. The short post carries a 3ft arm as appropriate for a goods line signal. Through the stone arch, built in 1848 for the broad gauge, is Hawkeridge Junction, which is switched out. Its home signal can been seen, lowered, and this is the 'Danger' signal to which the inner distant signal applies. When Westbury North advanced starting signal is lowered, the distant arm will also lower. There is another distant signal for Hawkeridge, at the correct braking distance, back at Westbury station. A stop signal at 'Danger' can also be seen. This is on the chord line from Heywood Road Junction. *Author*

enter into the spirit of the thing — ie to keep going — whilst remaining very alert to the subtle nuances of the changing aspects. This does not seem to be an entirely safe ethos to adopt. But now that it has been adopted it seems that, on four-aspect at any rate, something more powerful than the AWS is required to guard against human error.

AWS is used for single yellow, double yellow and red aspects, as well as for speed restrictions, but drivers can encounter the wrong AWS magnet if they are travelling on the wrong line during bi-directional working. The AWS magnets are suppressed for the Ladbroke-Paddington section but they are not suppressed between Didcot and Bathampton/Chipping Sodbury. All of that mileage is signalled bi-directionally and trains are put onto the 'wrong' line during normal daily working. In such cases the driver runs over bell magnets 200yd *after* having passed the signal to which the magnet applies, but of course that signal is for the opposite direction to that in which he is running. *His* magnet is coming up and might be for a yellow. There is a confusion waiting to happen here.

A comparison between British and other EU railways shows that in 1974, in Britain, one person was killed per 1 billion passenger kilometres against an average of two persons elsewhere. In 1996 these figures were 0.4 and 0.5 persons respectively.

Automatic Train Protection is a system which continuously monitors and governs train speeds against the aspects of signals or permanent speed restrictions. The system is ultra-complex and can be explained only over-simply here. Each signal has its sleeper-mounted 'beacon' to which it is connected. At most signals, a single beacon is sufficient to transmit all necessary data to the receiver on the train. From signal to beacon to loop, information is passed. On the underside of the train is a downward-pointing antenna which receives the information transmitted by the loop. This information goes to a computer on the train. The on-board computer has to be programmed before the start of the journey with information about the train, including its length and weight and braking characteristics. The database must also contain information regarding the gradients to be encountered on the journey and any permanent or temporary speed restrictions. There are, in this programming, opportunities for human error. Whilst on the move the on-board computer receives speed information from a tachometer driven by a wheel of the power car. This input is subject to distortion from the powered wheel spinning when it loses adhesion with the rail, and also becoming stationary if heavy braking causes it to skid along the rail. But supposing all to be working properly, the driver will receive a warning from the machine if he exceeds the speed limit at any point by 3mph, and should he rise to 6mph over the limit the ATP equipment will brake the train until its speed has been reduced to the proper level. In the case of a train approaching yellow or red aspects, the machine will thus continuously brake the train as it comes ever closer to the signal. The ATP brake application cannot be cancelled until the train has stopped. If a driver drives correctly he will not be aware of the ATP silently monitoring his responses to the signals.

There is also the Train Protection & Warning System (TPWS). If a train fitted with TPWS passes a signal at 'Danger' the device will bring the train to a stand before it reaches the next signal providing that the train is travelling less than 70mph. Since the introduction of Multiple Aspect Signalling in the mid-1960s, steam-age enginemen have commented on the hypnotic effect of miles and miles of signals, a signal every thousand yards. The AWS has become less effective as a safety back-up in this regime of intensive use. In his 1985 Annual Report, the Chief Inspecting Officer of Railways observed that, at some future time, a more powerful system than the AWS would be required to prevent trains passing signals at danger. Between 1986 and 1999 there were 20 railway accidents in Britain causing death to passengers and/or crew. Of those accidents, nine would have been prevented if ATP had been in use and 60 lives would have been saved. In the other 11 accidents, which the presence of ATP would not have prevented, 50 people were killed. This includes the Clapham disaster where 35 people died.

By mid-1988 the British Railways Board approved a plan for a certain type of ATP. There were already standard designs on sale by contractors, and operational elsewhere in Europe, but the BR specification required modifications from the 'off the shelf' ATPs and this increased the costs. The demand for ATP was given greater urgency by the crashes at Purley and Bellgrove the following year, both of which would have been prevented by ATP or indeed TPWS. Pilot ATP schemes were installed on the Western Region, starting in 1991 with the section from Wootton Bassett to Bristol Parkway. Wootton Bassett to Uffington and Uffington to Reading were commissioned in June 1993.

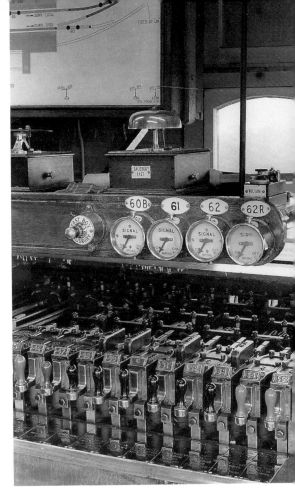

*Right:*
Part of the 63-handle interlocking frame of the electro-pneumatic system in Salisbury West box, seen in 1972. The upright handles are attached to a cam plate, to which are attached two piston valves. When the slide is pulled out, the cam plate opened one valve and closed the other, reversing air pressure to the lineside power cylinder and thus moving the points or the signal. The slides were mechanically interlocked with a vertical tappet machine. Pneumatic operation of the layout at Salisbury (LSWR) through the West and East boxes was inaugurated in November 1902, and the installation was still working perfectly when it was replaced with a 'panel' in August 1981. *Author*

In 1994 there were 358 signals fitted with ATP and the larger part of the installation costs had been incurred. However, on 31 March, just before Railtrack took over, the BRB reported to the Secretary of State for Transport that ATP was not a 'value for money' solution: it cost too much per life theoretically saved. ATP was put 'on the back burner' and there was to be no extension of the existing pilot schemes. But the Heathrow Express trains, custom-built for the route, would be fitted with ATP, so the necessary equipment would have to be installed between Paddington and Milepost 12 where the new lines turned away from the old main line. TPWS was installed between St Pancras and Bedford in 1998 by Railtrack but the trains, owned by other companies, are not fitted with receivers — except for a couple of trial sets.

The demands of commerce, harnessing technology to increase the speed of and frequency of trains, has placed a greater burden on train drivers than ever before. The technology to assist them in their onerous task has not been applied at the same pace. Men and women are expected to adapt and take the strain, something machines cannot do.

The last accident covered in detail in this book is the crash at Southall in 1997, but since then there has been another major accident in 1999 at Ladbroke Grove, West London, in which 31 people died. On 5 October 1999 the 8.6am Thames Trains Paddington to Bedwyn service collided head on at speed with an HST, the 6.3am from Cheltenham to Paddington, at Ladbroke Grove. It is believed that the driver of the Thames Trains Class 165 Turbo diesel multiple-unit had passed Signal N109 by Goldbourne Road bridge at 'Danger' moments before the collision. The Inquiry into this crash continues so it has not been possible to deal with this accident here in the same way as the others covered in the book until we receive the definitive Report from Lord Cullen, who is chairing the Inquiry.

Between January 1967 and October 2000 there were 77 accidents on Britain's railways which produced passenger fatalities (the Hatfield accident happened as this book went to press):

| | Accidents | Fatalities |
|---|---|---|
| 1967/8 | 8 | 72 |
| 1969-79 | 32 | 66 |
| 1979-89 | 21 | 89 |
| 1989-99 | 15 | 64 |

*Above:*
The electro-pneumatic system's lineside cylinder with its two control valves, seen in 1972. Compressed air is admitted to one end or the other of the power cylinder to force the piston to move and thus to operate the rodding to the points. A much smaller, single-action cylinder was attached to the signal posts. *Author*

It was in the steam age that Britain's worst accidents happened. At Quintinshill in May 1915 a signalman's forgetfulness caused a minimum of 224 deaths — the exact total cannot be known because the muster roll of the regiment of soldiers went up in the flames that killed the soldiers. After 1945, the worst years for fatalities were 1947, with 105, and 1952, with 118. There were 90 railway deaths in 1957, 70 in 1967, 38 in 1988, 31 in 1999. These were the peaks, the trend being a continuous reduction in annual passenger fatalities up to 1999. In 1949 and through to 1999, with the above exceptions, annual passenger fatalities never exceeded 20, and in most years never exceeded 10; in 1963-6, 1971, 1976, 1977, 1982, 1983, 1985, 1990, 1992, 1993 and 1996 there were no more than four fatalities per year. It is instructive to recall that road accident fatalities amount to 3,000 per year. The modern, technological railway will install computerised systems to monitor the signals and drivers' reactions to them, to avoid the passing of signals at 'Danger'. Even better carriage design will help to protect passengers when a collision does occur. Eventually, it is to be hoped, computerisation and engineering will make the railway of the future as safe as the Midland & Great Northern Joint Committee's 180-mile network which, between 1859 and 1959 (when it closed), never killed a single passenger, and had only one — non-fatal — derailment.

# Moorgate:
## 28 February 1975

Moorgate station is just within the boundary of the City of London. It was the terminus of British Rail suburban services from St Albans, Luton, Hertford North and Welwyn — via the 'Widened Lines' from King's Cross, as well as being used by Circle Line and Metropolitan Line services. It was also a 'through' station on the Northern Line 'City' branch and the terminus of the Northern Line's Highbury branch. It had 10 platforms: 1-6 were at sub-surface, for the BR, Circle and Metropolitan Line trains; 7-10 were at deep level for the Northern Line.

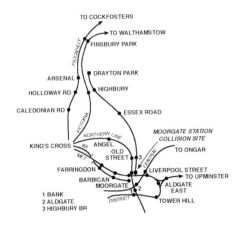

Platforms 9 and 10 formed the terminus of the Highbury branch. A track ran on each side of this platform, No 9 Platform being on the west side. Old Street station was 875yd to the north. For 642yd southwards from Old Street the line fell towards Moorgate station at a gradient of 1 in 150. For the next 233yd the line was level including almost the entire length of the platform. Just before the south end of the platform, a red light mounted on a post in the track marked the end of the line. Immediately beyond the red light was a 36ft-long sand drag with the sand piled 2ft deep over the rails. From the centre of this train-retarding obstacle, the line plunged down at 1 in 80 for a further 66ft 9in to a solid brick wall. Just before the absolute end of the line there was a single hydraulic buffer in the middle of the track. This had never been used in anger and had been allowed to become inoperative.

There was an overall speed limit of 40mph on the branch and a permanent speed limit of 15mph entering the platform at Moorgate. The approaches to the Highbury branch terminus at Moorgate were signalled in the standard manner for London Underground with an installation dating from 1937. The automatic signals were operated by the trains passing over track circuits, and the points and signals in the Moorgate station area were controlled by a signalman at Moorgate. He operated an electric power frame of miniature levers and observed train movements by means of a track diagram on which the presence of trains was indicated by small lights. These became illuminated when a train occupied a section of track. The signals were two-aspect electric colour-lights giving red/green or red/yellow indications. Twenty-five feet south of the south end of Old Street station was a two-aspect signal, A53, operated automatically by the passage of trains over the track circuits. This had two lights and could show either a red or a green aspect. Eight hundred and fifty feet south of this was another two-aspect automatic, A51. The next stop signal was 546ft further on, ND11, the outermost home signal for Moorgate. ND11 signal had a repeater, ND11R. This showed a yellow aspect if ND11 was at red, or a green if ND11 was showing green. This repeater was 166ft on the approach side of ND11. South of ND11 by 409ft was the inner home, ND9/10, and the repeater signal for this signal was fixed below ND11. ND9/10 carried the junction indicator — three white lights at an angle of 45° — which was illuminated when the road was set into Platform 9. There was a

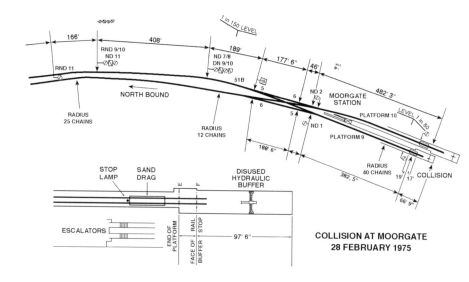

**COLLISION AT MOORGATE**
**28 FEBRUARY 1975**

repeating aspect for ND9/10 underneath ND11, so southbound drivers had warning of the aspect of ND9/10 690ft before they reached it. Passing ND 9/10, drivers could see clearly 600ft to the red light at the extreme end of the platform.

All points on the branch were operated by air pressure activated electrically. The stop signals were fitted with the standard London Underground electro-pneumatic train-stop device. This was fixed to the sleeper end and, when the stop signal (not a repeater signal) was at 'Danger', the arm of the train stop was raised. Once the aspect changed to yellow or green the train-stop arm quietly lowered itself horizontally onto the sleeper. If the train did not stop at a red light, the train-stop lever arm, being raised, struck open a valve in the train's braking system, dumped the compressed air within the train pipe and thus applied the brakes. The driver could not cancel it but had to dismount and close the valve on the outside of the train. This was — and remains — an excellent system, but... The signal at the approach end of Moorgate station could only show a green light when the platform was clear for the train to enter.

The train involved in the crash, Service No 272, was a standard, 1938-built set of 2 x 3-car sets. The total length of the train was 316ft and it weighed 151 tons. The car bodies had little structural strength because of the number and size of the door openings and so the chassis or underframes had to take all horizontal and vertical forces. Accordingly, they were designed to withstand a 50-ton static end-load on the centre coupler without ill effect.

The driver of Train 272 was Motorman Newson. He was 56 years of age and had been employed by London Transport since March 1969. He had fought in World War 2 and had been evacuated from Dunkirk. He was a steady, reliable man. He started as a guard, working out of Barking, until January 1974 when he passed as a guard-motorman. In the next 12 months he had six days' driving experience on 1938 stock on the East London Line and a further 31 days on the C69 stock on the Hammersmith & City Line. After exactly a year of this guard/driving work he was transferred to the Drayton depot on the Highbury branch as a Motorman. His driving instructor here, Motorman Deadman, said that Newson 'was a quiet man, not given to much conversation, and was a particularly cautious driver'. With the exception of Guard Catney, the staff at Drayton depot were not close to Mr Newson, who had no time for smalltalk and banter. Guard Catney had worked with him since 1973. He said he liked a quiet joke and a chat and corroborated Mr Deadman's assessment that Newson was a cautious driver, braking sooner than most men and entering platforms more slowly, never over-shooting the mark. Motorman Bray said the same thing.

Between 23 January and 28 February
Mr Newson drove into Moorgate, either
Platform 9 or 10, 228 times. Between 15 and
28 February No 10 platform was closed and
he drove into No 9 platform 121 times — all
without the slightest incident.

On Friday 28 February Mr Newson was
due on duty at 6.24am but arrived for work
early, as usual, at about 6am. In his bag he
carried the Rule Books and papers required.
In addition to this, he had bound his Rule
Book with a plastic cover to keep it smart and
he also had a personal notebook in which he
had written handy hints on driving technique
and fault finding. This was likewise plastic-
covered to prevent it getting dog-eared. He
was also carrying in his coat £270 with which
he intended to buy a car for his daughter when
he had completed his shift. In the drivers'
cabin he shared his sugar with another
motorman, saying jokingly: 'Go easy on it, I
shall want another cup when I come off duty.'

At about 6.40am the Moorgate signalman, Mr Wade, met Mr Newson and his guard, an
18-year-old, R. P. Harris. Harris made some remark about going camping at the weekend, to
which Newson replied: 'He must be mad. I wouldn't go camping in this weather. I loved it at
Dunkirk, but I would sooner go to a Hotel.' Motorman Newson seemed quite cheerful and in
good spirits. Harris stated at the Inquiry that he was always pleased to work with Newson
because, he said, 'I felt very safe with him'. Harris said that Newson's technique for
approaching Moorgate was slower than other motormen, shutting off power early and coasting
downhill to pass over the crossover at the platform end at 15mph.

Mr Newson made three round trips from Drayton Park to Moorgate and commenced the
fourth from Drayton Park at 8.39am, 30sec late. The distance from Old Street to Moorgate is
750yd. The train set off from Old Street in the usual way and would, therefore, have reached
30mph in about 28sec, having travelled 250 yards, one third of the distance to Moorgate. At that
point he would normally have shut off power to coast for about 15sec before braking gently to
come down to 15mph at the platform end. The train was routed into Platform 9, but instead of
braking Mr Newson put the controller into 'full series', halving the power but still continuing
to accelerate, so that he would have been running at 35mph at the platform end, 56sec after
leaving Old Street.

Unfortunately, Mr Harris was an inexperienced guard and he compounded this by a lack of
alertness. As the train left Old Street on that fourth and final trip, he went into the last car to
look for a newspaper. He found one and was reading the advertisements when he suddenly
became aware that the train was running past the terminal platform at a speed he judged to be
between 30 and 35mph. He said that, had he been aware of this earlier, he would have applied
the emergency brake, but he had no time to do anything and no sooner had he realised his peril
than he was thrown violently to the floor.

A passenger on the train, Mr Holderness, had been passing the time on the journey guessing
which buildings they were passing beneath. At the point where, he judged, they were passing

under Finsbury Square, he suddenly became aware that they had reached the crossings at the entrance to Moorgate station, were running very fast and thought that the driver was 'leaving his braking a bit late'. Mr Holderness then counted and estimated that the train travelled the length of the platform in 7 to 9sec. The platform was 382ft 5in long, so, according to this, the train was travelling at between 30 and 37mph.

Standing on the Moorgate platform were between 20 and 30 passengers and two employees. Railman Andrews was standing one coach-length from the red stop light in front of the sand drag, looking towards Old Street. He realised at once that the train was not going to stop and ran to the Control telephone to report the crash before it happened. Guard Friar, standing near Andrews, was not looking out for the train but turned to look when he heard it approaching; his attention being drawn to it by the noise it was making. It was going far too fast. He turned to look and for a split second caught a profiled view of Driver Newson. He was sitting upright, with his hat on his head, looking forwards. Guard Friar could not see if Newson had his hands on the controls or whether his eyes were open. A passenger, Mr Board, was standing by the red stop light and watched the train come towards him along the full length of the platform. He thought it was travelling at 40mph. He saw the driver sitting perfectly upright with his right hand on the 'dead man's handle' in the centre of the window. His left arm, meanwhile,

reached out towards the left-hand pillar which was obscuring his left hand. Mr Board thought the driver was so still as to be paralysed. Others commented on the 'frozen' characteristic of his posture. Mr Board was the only witness who said he saw Mr Newson's eyes which were 'staring straight ahead and appeared to be larger than life'. This last is probably a figment of Mr Board's shocked imagination. Experiments with slow-moving trains at Moorgate showed that the lighting did not permit an observer to see the eyes clearly, much less the expression in them. The subsequent post-mortem showed that Newson had died with his hands on the controls — holding down the dead man's handle to the last. And this is more than strange because, surely, he would have put his hands up in front of his face, in an instinctive or reflex action, as the runaway train knocked over the red stop light and dispersed the sand drag, sending gravel clattering against or even smashing the cab windows.

Then came the collision with the single-buffer hydraulic ram. This lifted the body of

*Left:*
When the leading carriage hit the wall, the second carriage was forced underneath it, crushing the first carriage against the roof. The roof of the leading carriage has been moulded into and jammed in the roof of the tunnel.
*Daily Mail — Solo Syndication*

the carriage off the bogie and caused the body to impact into the end wall and the roof of the tunnel. The angle of the car and the force of the end-on blow caused the underframe to buckle in three places: a tight 'V', apex uppermost, just behind the driving cab, a downward-pointing 'V' midway and another towards the end. The 52ft-long carriage was reduced to a length of 20ft. The leading end of the second car snapped its massive coupling and drove under the first carriage, crushing the bodywork but doing little damage to the chassis. The rear of the second car was crushed by the third car which suffered relatively little damage. The fourth car sustained a little damage and the fifth and sixth cars were undamaged. The crash took place at 8.46am. The London Emergency Services received the call for assistance at 8.48am. The first ambulance arrived at 8.54 and the first fire engine at 8.58. There were over 300 passengers on the train: 42 were killed along with Mr Newson. A further 74 passengers had injuries which required hospital treatment. The last surviving passenger was not released from the wreckage until 10.05pm, 13hr 19min after the accident took place. It took four days to reach Mr Newson.

The reason for the crash was not established. The post-mortem was carried out by Professor Emeritus Simpson, Head of the Department of Forensic Medicine at Guy's Hospital Medical School, assisted by Professor Cameron, Professor of Forensic Medicine. The cause of death was given as 'shock from multiple injuries'. The Professors examined the organs generally and put samples of tissue under the microscope. They stated that Mr Newson was a perfectly healthy man without any abnormalities of the heart or disease of the brain. The stomach contained no drugs, there was no smell of alcohol and the liver showed no signs of damage from heavy drinking. But an investigation of Mr Newson's blood was undertaken by Dr Ann Robinson, Senior Lecturer in Forensic Medicine at the London Hospital Medical College. Having carried out her scientific tests she formed the view that Motorman Newson had consumed alcohol on the morning of the crash. She estimated that the highest possible level of alcohol in his blood at the time of the post-mortem was of the order of 80 milligrams per 100 millilitres and could have been less. She also analysed the dregs of sour milk found in Mr Newson's bottle and discovered 0.1% weight in volume of ethyl alcohol. She was of the opinion that the alcohol she found in Newson's blood had not arrived there through a process of natural fermentation resulting from decomposition during the four days the body had been awaiting rescue. A layman such as myself will wonder how she knew that the alcohol she found was generated by one means rather than another — alcohol is alcohol, the non-scientific person might say. Dr Goulding, Director of the Poisons Unit at Guy's Hospital, was asked by Motorman Newson's widow to examine Dr Robinson's findings. He accepted her results — that alcohol was present — but 'could not come to the inescapable conclusion that alcohol had been present in Motorman Newson's body prior to his death'. He was unable to state, unequivocally, that no alcohol at all had been consumed before death but was prepared to say that, if alcohol had been consumed, 'it must have been a very small amount'. He also stated it as a fact that as much as 0.2% alcohol can be generated in milk during the process of decomposition. Dr Robinson had found half that amount in the sour milk in Newson's bottle. Following this disagreement between experts, Professor Simpson went back to the Inspecting Officer and advised him that 'it is generally accepted that as much as 80mg/100ml alcohol may make its appearance in a decomposing body after four days in a [relatively] high temperature'.

Clearly, the question of whether or not Newson had been drinking was crucial. Naturally, he was defended by all his workmates. No-one who worked with him would admit to having seen him drinking on that or any other day on duty, nor to smelling any alcohol on his breath. Nonetheless, there is at least one record of an Underground driver having been proved to be drunk at the controls, thereby causing a crash in which he died. In addition, I have been given anecdotal evidence from eye witnesses about staff drinking on duty on the Underground during the 1970s. But that does not mean that Mr Newson had taken any alcohol. The rigidity and uprightness of his posture, upon which so many people remarked, does not sound like a description of a man under the influence of alcohol. Since it was most unlikely that he was drunk, the Inspecting Officer suggested he was 'daydreaming' about the car he was going to buy his daughter but then said that, 'even if this was the case, I would have expected that the lateral accelerations and the noise as the train went over the crossovers would have shaken him from his reverie and, even if it had not, he would surely have come to his senses before that final collision and made an effort to protect his face and head'.

At a loss to find a convincing reason for the crash, the Inspecting Officer wrote: 'The possibility that the collision was the outcome of a deliberate suicidal act cannot be ignored, although there is no positive evidence to support it'. All evidence is positive or it is not evidence.

I do not subscribe to this theory since there is positive evidence against it: Newson was completely normal on the day. He shared a friendly comment — and his sugar — with a mate and spoke of drinking his tea at the end of his shift. He had £270 in his coat to buy a car for his daughter after he finished work and was probably looking forward to doing that. This contented frame of mind, looking to the simple pleasures of the future, is not that of a suicidal person. Nor was his general demeanour bad or sour. And, finally, he did not raise his arms to protect his face at the moment of collision. I do not believe that anyone, not even a suicide, with control of their body could see that wall hurtling towards them and not instinctively throw their hands up at the last moment. Mr Newson's hands remained fixed on the controls.

The best answer to the mystery was put forward by Doctor Raffles, who described himself to the Inspecting Officer as 'someone who had taken a professional, lifetime interest in the factors which may affect people's capacity to do skilled jobs, like driving'. Dr Raffles did not believe alcohol played a part — the level of alcohol found in Newson's blood, however it got there, was within the legal limit for a car driver. Dr Raffles believed that a tiny blood clot had formed in or floated into a blood vessel in the middle of Newson's brain, causing akinesis with mutism — admittedly a rare occurrence but yet a known condition and not as rare as a driver hurtling into a brick wall with a train full of fellow humans. This condition of akinesis causes the muscles to 'freeze' and prevents any movement by the individual. Dr Raffles' theory could not be proved since there was nothing left of Mr Newson's brain to examine.

The signalling on the approach to the Moorgate terminus accorded with standard Underground practice and had never been questioned. If the platform was clear to the buffers, the driver got a green light at signals ND9/10 on the approach to the crossovers. This system was based on the assumption that drivers would always know where they were and act accordingly, and that no driver would ever become incapacitated. After the accident the line was temporarily closed and re-configured to take British Rail Eastern Region suburban services to and from Welwyn and Hertford. Three-aspect signalling was installed, with each signal having the usual Underground ground-mounted train stop. The new trains were similarly equipped so that no train could go very far after it had passed a signal at 'Danger'. At Moorgate, signal ND9/10 giving access to either platform was no longer equipped with a green aspect, but only a single yellow when the line was clear to the buffers, or a red if it was blocked. A special arrangement of train stops was installed, applicable to trains arriving at the terminus. The first was located at the crossovers and was controlled by a track circuit and 'timing-out' device so that, provided the driver had reduced speed to less than 12.5mph at signal ND9/10, the train-stop arm would have lowered by the time he got to it. To prevent a driver accelerating after passing this trip cock, there were two more, both on 'timing-out' devices, along the length of the platform track. They remained raised, ready to engage with the train and put its brakes on if it was running so fast as to arrive at them before they had laid down flat on the sleepers. The death of poor Driver Newson and his 42 passengers brought about such improvements that it seems impossible that such a dreadful accident could ever again happen at Moorgate.

# Taunton Sleeping Car Fire:
## 6 July 1978

Sleeping cars came into use on the Great Western Railway in 1877 when a pair were put into service between Paddington and Penzance. Bigger and better equipped sleeping carriages quickly followed, eventually to become synonymous with romance (literally as well as figuratively) as they stood blank-faced and steam-wreathed in the smoky lamp-light of Paddington station with a mighty 'King' or 'Castle' class engine at their head. They slipped through the night, carrying the most important admirals to Devonport, secretive King's Messengers, famous actresses, along with many ordinary folk. In spite of the galaxy of VIPs who used them regularly, the GWR 1920 and 1936 'General Appendix to the Rule Book' gave no instructions to regulate the actions of sleeping car attendants or the guards of sleeping car trains, although there are dozens of pages of 'Passenger Train Instructions'. The 1960 'General Appendix to the Rule Book' was the first to order that 'corridor and gangway doors should be unlocked so as to provide free access through the train' and 'compartment doors on all vehicles, including sleeping cars, must not be kept locked'.

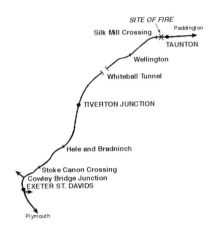

There is particular significance for Western Region in this instruction. After a terrible fire on a train in France in 1844, when the entire trainload of people was incinerated because they were locked into their carriages, doors were no longer locked on French or British railways — except on the GWR. Letters of complaint in *The Times* were answered on the grounds of the company's convenience: the company's servants had to be able to control the movement of passengers to prevent ticket fraud. The 'rail regulator' of the day — the Board of Trade — was timid, but a brilliantly sarcastic letter (see my *Grub, Water and Relief*, p68) from the Rev Sydney Smith gave this Government department the courage to write to the GWR management and demand that one door be left unlocked on every carriage. The GWR responded with its usual insolence towards 'Government officials' and instructed its train guards to leave the offside door unlocked — on the opposite side of the train to the platform. Thus, it was left to the public, via *The Times* letters columns, to teach the GWR its manners. After further protests, therefore, the GWR unlocked all its carriage doors.

When sleeping cars were introduced, it seems very likely that the old practice of locking the door to the platform was used. But once sleeping cars became 'gangway fitted', or formed of corridor stock, it seems to have been common practice to lock the doors between carriages as well. Since there were no instructions one way or the other, the sleeping car attendants did as they pleased and were able to argue that locked-in passengers felt more secure; their persons and possessions were safe from molestation during the journey and no undesirable person could enter from the platform at station stops in the middle of the night. Furthermore, a sleeping car

attendant could point out that if the exterior doors were locked, sleep-befuddled passengers, groping their way to the toilet, could not accidentally open an outer door and step outside. The attendants, having locked them all in, could settle down in their 'pantries' and snooze or, better still, sleep in an unoccupied bunk, if there was one, while the train roared on through the night. The world of the sleeping car train attendant was cloaked in darkness and unintentional — but nonetheless effective — secrecy.

In 1960, when instructions for sleeping car attendants were first issued, they had had 90 years to develop their own system, and there was still no supervision, probably because the trains left Paddington or Penzance so late at night. Fires on sleeping car trains were uncommon when trains were steam-heated, but there were two serious fires. The first was near Beattock Summit in June 1950 and stemmed from the use of an explosive paint based on nitro-cellulose. The second occurred at Huntingdon in July 1951. After these fires, Colonel Walker, Inspecting Officer of Railways, reported: 'Because of the nature of fire, partial measures, resulting from careful calculations of cost and risk, are not good enough; the aim should be no less than to prevent fire happening at all and, where this is not entirely possible, to ensure that every reasonable step has been taken to mitigate its consequences.'

The conversion of sleeping cars from steam to electric heating was gradual, but as more cars were converted the number of fires increased: three in 1974; six in 1975 (including one on Western Region); six in 1976; two in 1977 and five in the first seven months of 1978, one of which was on Western Region.

In the early morning of 5 July the Paddington sleeping car train arrived at Plymouth. The two leading sleeping cars were detached and put into sidings for cleaning and bed-changing. Mr Helen and the attendant from b and c cars went to the same lodgings he had used for years, paid for by British Rail.

Mr Helen had started his career as a sleeping car attendant in 1953. He had travelled with old-hand attendants who had shown him the pantry equipment, how to use the kettle to make tea for the passengers and where the fire extinguishers were, although he had never practised using one. A chargeman had shown him bed-making procedures and how to clean the sleeping compartments. There had been no supervision of his training. For a hundred years attendants had followed the good old ways, handing down knowledge and experience, man to man, for generations. Mr Helen said, following the incident to be described, that it was 'an unwritten law' for the doors to the platform to be kept locked to exclude unauthorised people and he gave the firm impression that this was his practice. He was emphatic that, in 25 years, he had never received a complaint from a passenger about the exterior doors being locked. But he also said that there were 'many occasions' when the exterior doors were not locked, whereupon passengers had complained that luggage had been stolen, or that the wrong person had taken a bunk in a berth. He made his job sound a miserable one, with his concerns for the security of ungrateful passengers, and said the only railway officials that came into his cars were the ticket collectors. He could not remember the last time a supervisor came to check on him, to see if he was doing his job properly, ask how he was or whether he had any problems. Mr Helen's working life had been lonely, nocturnal and unsupervised for 25 years.

About the Rule Book he was vague and evasive. He claimed he had never seen the instructions to sleeping car staff contained in the *Working Manual for Rail Staff* and it is likely that he knew nothing about the supplementary 1960 instructions which were not actually referred to at the Inquiry. Mr Helen recollected that, three or four months before the fire, he had been told 'in a roundabout sort of way' that he should not lock exterior doors. He was unsure who had told him, but thought it might have been Mr Richards.

Mr W. Richards had been Assistant Area Manager at Paddington since 1972. Very surprisingly, he denied ever having told Mr Helen to keep the doors unlocked. One would not have thought that a manager would have denied carrying out supervision of the Rules. The impression one gets from Mr Richards' evidence is that he was unaware of the practices of sleeping car attendants, but left them to get on with the job, assuming that they were experienced, responsible people who read, knew and followed the Rules.

The Area Manager for Paddington, Mr Gronow, appeared to have had no more idea of the working practices of sleeping car attendants than Mr Richards. Mr Gronow was an engineer from the Royal Navy, an expert on large diesel engines, who joined the railway and became Shed Master and Depot Manager at Bristol Bath Road before being transferred in 1968 to an alien world — that of Traffic Department Superintendent at Bristol. He took over at Paddington only two months before the Taunton fire, and sleeping car attendants were far from his mind. He did not know how matters were arranged with sleeping car staff, nor did he know any of the attendants, as he was responsible for 1,540 staff and had not yet had time to meet them all. It is difficult, for me at any rate, to imagine a manager, no matter how many years he had been at the station, going there late at night or in the small hours to have a chat with a sleeping car attendant. As it was, Mr Gronow left all such matters to the local supervisors. He did not know that exterior doors on sleeping cars were kept locked when the train was in motion. He had used sleeping cars on many occasions and had never seen a door being unlocked, nor had he ever found an exit door locked because he had never checked.

Mr Hopkins became Assistant Area Manager at Plymouth a couple of months prior to the Taunton fire. He had been a railway Traffic Department operator all his working life and moved from Operations Manager at Westbury to Plymouth. He had no more idea about sleeping cars than Gronow or Richards. At the Inquiry he implied that he was not responsible for sleeping car attendants. He told the Inquiry that he was not on duty for the departure of the sleeping car in the early hours of the morning but believed his staff had responsibility for sleeping car attendants. He knew nothing about the practice of locking the exterior doors of sleeping cars and no-one had ever complained to him about it. The emerging picture suggests that the world of sleeping cars was *terra incognita* to even the most experienced and responsible of managers. It is possible, therefore, to sympathise with Mr Helen over the lack of official interest in him and his work: the Paddington Assistant Area Manager had, after all, gone so far as to deny mentioning Rules to him!

In spite of Mr Helen's complaint about the lack of management interest in his work, on the one occasion when (he said) he was spoken to, he had ignored the instructions as he deemed it 'completely unworkable' to have doors to the platforms locked while a train was in a station, and then to unlock them just before the train moved off. Having responsibility for two sleeping cars meant he would have to insert his carriage key in four separate doors. He also believed that a sleepy passenger in the corridor might put his hand out of an open drop-light in an exterior door, turn the handle and fall out. The idea that he might patrol his corridors and make sure that drop-lights were closed did not occur to him. Nor did the possibility of a freezing draught jolting a sleepy passenger back to wakefulness. Mr Helen had amassed 18 years' experience of working Mk 1 sleeping cars which were introduced in 1960, but became confused when asked to say where the bell switches were located in his 5ft x 6ft pantry.

On the night before the fire, Mr Helen had worked down from Paddington to Plymouth with sleeping cars B and C. When these were examined after the fire it was discovered that the passenger call bell, situated in the pantry, and by which means occupants of sleeping berths could call for his attendance, had been disconnected. This was not a regular practice to give the attendants a quiet time, but rather an unfortunate malfunction. Mr Helen said that the bell 'had been ringing continuously' on the way down from Paddington and passengers had complained. It must, therefore, have been a very loud bell. He had disabled the bell himself for the convenience of passengers but did not report the fault to the Carriage & Wagon Department at Plymouth. By coincidence, the jumper cable between sleeping cars B and C was not connected, so the passenger call bell from coach C could not have sounded in Mr Helen's pantry in coach B.

The clean linen for bed-changing at Plymouth came from the central store at Old Oak Common. Four bags of it were carried in the vestibule at the leading end of sleeping car B. The dirty linen was bagged, put in the leading vestibule and carried back to Paddington for transfer to Old Oak Common. The electric heater, on the vestibule wall at floor level, was thus effectively covered. This posed an obvious fire risk should anyone forget and turn on the heater. Prior to May 1977 the clean and dirty linen had been carried safely in both directions in the brake van marshalled between the engine and sleeping car B, but after this date removal of the van left staff with no choice but to put the linen in the leading vestibule of coach B.

On 6 July 1978 the 9.30pm Penzance to Paddington 'Sleeper' slipped away from the ancient terminus on time and headed eastwards through the dusk into the night. The locomotive had a heavy train for the Cornish gradients, consisting of six sleeping cars — D, E, F, G, H and J — behind which came two passenger carriages, the guard's brake van, two more carriages and a general utility van.

At Plymouth North Road, the engine from Penzance was taken off and Class 47 No 47498 brought three vehicles to the front of the train: an eight-wheeled passenger brake van and two sleeping cars, B and C. Attendant Mr Helen.

The linen could have been stowed in the van, but instead was still stacked in the vestibule, covering the electric heater. This heater was turned on by a two-way switch in Mr Helen's pantry in coach B. By means of the switch the attendant could turn on either the pantry heater, the vestibule heater or both. Mr Helen was unable to explain to the Inquiry the working of this switch. The electric heaters as originally fitted in Mk 1 stock were so hot that they scorched the timber wall in which they were placed. As a result, a heat deflector was fitted above the heating element and, where such heaters were fitted in a guard's van or a brake van where passengers' luggage or other cargo might be stored, a grille was fitted to the front of the heater. But heaters placed in corridors or in the vestibule at the end of a carriage were not fitted with grilles because it was thought that passengers would not normally put their luggage against the heater.

When the Plymouth sleeping car portion was attached to the 9.30pm from Penzance shortly after midnight on 6 July, the electric heating was switched on from the engine at about 12.15am and the train left on time at 12.30. The guard of the train to Exeter was Mr King. He did not patrol the sleeping car section and did not try the door between the ordinary and sleeping section of the train to see if it was locked or free. Sleeping cars were indeed a world of their own. As the train rolled slowly into Platform 5 at Exeter St Davids, it was watched from the track, from the nearside, by the Carriage & Wagon Examiner. After the tail had gone by and the train stopped, he walked along the whole length of the offside. He found nothing amiss. On the gloomy platform the station staff loaded and unloaded mail to and from the front brake van within feet of sleeping car B which remained, to all practical purposes, invisible. There was no reason why a porter loading mail should look at a sleeping car.

The train pulled away into the night bearing its precious cargo of human life asleep in all innocence on beds of polyurethane foam, with pillows of the same material. It passed the signalmen in Exeter Middle box, Cowley Bridge Junction, Stoke Canon Crossing, Hele & Bradninch, Tiverton Junction, Whiteball Tunnel and Silk Mill Crossing — Wellington box was switched-out. None of the signalmen saw anything wrong with the train, but the bags of dirty linen piled in the leading vestibule against the electric heater were growing hotter and hotter.

Mr Helen arranged his tea trays for the passengers' morning cups of tea after the train left Plymouth, and by Newton Abbot he had nothing left to do. After Newton Abbot he wrote out his journal (a fairly brief entry, I imagine), refreshed himself with a cup of tea and then, because the pantry was cramped and unpleasant, he went to the lavatory and then into the leading berth in car C for a wash and brush-up. He thought all this might have occupied him for as long as 25 minutes. He had no clear recollection of the journey between Exeter and Taunton and, when questioned at the Inquiry, betrayed the fact that he had not noticed that the train had stopped three times for single-line working and had passed six or even seven exceedingly noisy and brightly-illuminated track tamping machines. Well might the Inquisitor, Major King, report to the Minister of Transport that 'the attendant was not as alert as he should have been and might quite possibly have been asleep'.

Mr Helen said he was in the lavatory in car C when he smelled burning rubber. He emerged from the lavatory, made his way towards his pantry at the leading end of car C and saw smoke pouring under the door from car B. He was unsure where the train was in the dark but thought it had 'just left

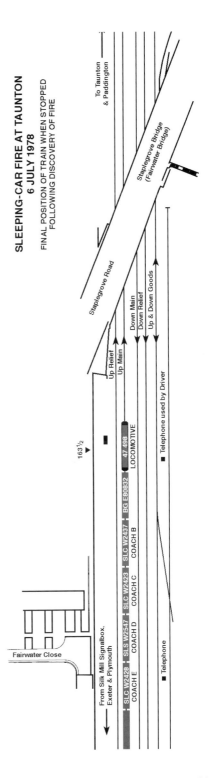

SLEEPING-CAR FIRE AT TAUNTON
6 JULY 1978
FINAL POSITION OF TRAIN WHEN STOPPED FOLLOWING DISCOVERY OF FIRE

Whiteball Tunnel'. Asked why he did not pull the communication cord, he said: 'if the train was stopped in the tunnel it would have been more dangerous'. He said he walked along the corridor of coach C, banging on the doors of sleeping compartments and shouting 'Fire!' until he was rendered unconscious by the smoke. In car B people were either dying in their sleep of cyanide poisoning or were aware and trying to get out and choking to death on the smoke.

Sleeping car attendant Ferro-Lamazares was in charge of cars D and E. He had been on the railway for less than two years. He said he became aware of the fire just after coming out of Whiteball Tunnel, not because he heard the yells of 'Fire!' from Mr Helen, who was in the next coach, but because he smelled smoke. He walked back through his cars, D and E, away from the strongest smell, met Attendant Kelly, spoke to him, found nothing wrong, and so walked forward to the gangway between D and C. It was then that he saw the dense smoke and at once pulled the communication cord. Having pulled the cord he went along the smoke-filled corridor of car C, banging on doors and shouting 'Fire!' until he tripped over the body of Mr Helen. By now the train was at a stand. He grabbed Mr Helen by the ankles and dragged him back into coach D, and unlocked and opened the nearside door, leaving the unconscious Mr Helen by it before going back into car C to help passengers evacuate. He was unable to get into car B because of dense smoke, and was eventually so affected by smoke that he was ordered to leave the scene.

Ferro-Lamazares had pulled the cord as the train approached Silk Mill Crossing at 2.39am, by which time Driver Pope was applying the brake for the Taunton stop. This was eight minutes after the train had passed Whiteball signalbox and seven minutes since it left the tunnel.

During that seven minutes the occupants of car B had been fighting for their lives but, as is often the case with fire, those closest to the seat of the blaze survived. The fire had started in the used bed-linen, packed in nylon bags and piled against the unguarded electric heater in the leading vestibule. It had spread along the corridor until it found the open door of sleeping berth 13. The flames entered here and, setting fire to the polyurethane bedding, burned their way back through the bulkheads towards the front of the carriage.

The narratives of those who survived were all more or less dramatic, depending upon how much they could recall. Surgeon Lieutenant-Commander McMillan's statement was the most comprehensive. He said that he normally slept well on sleeping car trains and was woken only by the train juddering to a stop. He heard some 'railway voices' outside and thought he was at a station, but then he smelled smoke and put the light on. He saw a haze of smoke in the berth before the light went out and then heard a fierce crackling noise, like the sound of burning thatch, in the roof space. He rolled out of his bunk onto the floor where there was no smoke. He reached up, opened the door and was assaulted by billows of choking smoke. He put his head and shoulders through the doorway into the corridor and yelled: 'Get out, the train is on fire! Get down on the floor!' There was no light, just pitch darkness with no sign of flames — only the terrible smoke above him and the noise of unseen flames. He thought he was the only person on the train until he heard someone crawling along the corridor and felt the person touch his left arm. This was probably Mr Nightingale from berth 12. Lt Cdr McMillan told this person to hold on to his ankle and to keep on the floor, and then they both crawled along the corridor. At the end, McMillan raised himself to his knee to open the window in the door but could not breathe at that height and fell to the floor again. At that point someone walking upright in bare feet kicked him — accidentally — in the face. This must have been Miss Drummond. After that he and the person holding his ankle crawled over the steel floor of the gangway and lost consciousness. McMillan came round kneeling on the ballast with his back to the train. Close by, a man on his back appeared to be dead and, assisted by a lady and a gentleman, Lt Cdr McMillan, so recently returned from near-death, turned the man on his side and began artificial respiration. It was then that he became aware of other people: two railwaymen, a young man wearing a black jacket with a silver disc in the lapel and an older man with a blue hat. He could hear people screaming in car C and saw a sleeping car attendant helping people from this car down to the track. He went to some nearby houses, woke the occupants, asked for a ladder and told them to dial 999 for the emergency services. By the time he got back to the train the first ambulance had arrived, more people had been laid on the ballast and he set to work to revive them. Now that the train had stopped and the doors were being opened, the fire was burning very fiercely.

Driver Pope, once he had reduced speed sufficiently to coast into Taunton, had tried to release the brake but was unable to re-create a vacuum. This was, of course, because the communication cord had been pulled after he had applied the brake and so the train vacuum pipe was open to the atmosphere. Driver Pope was not to know this and was puzzled to find his train grinding to a halt, stopping with his engine opposite Milepost 1633/4, 1,000yd short of Taunton station, at 2.41am. He looked back at the train from his cab window, saw smoke pouring out of the leading sleeping car and climbed down from his engine to telephone Silk Mill box from a lineside phone. His words were urgent: 'Stop everything. Get the fire brigade and ambulances. The Sleeper is on fire!'

Driver Pope's alarm message was taken at about 2.42am by Signalman Darch, a man with 33 years' railway service. The signalbox had no telephone to the outside world so Mr Darch rang Taunton railway telephone exchange in the ordinary way. The telephonist, Miss Carpenter, answered the call with no more than the ordinary promptitude since there was no emergency bell signal, but she answered in less than one minute. The resultant conversation appears confused. Mr Darch told the Inquiry that he said: 'Silk Mill. Would you send the fire brigade and ambulance to Fairwater Bridge as the up sleeping car train is on fire'. Miss Carpenter said he made no mention of location and she did not ask for it; either she went off at once to dial 999 or Mr Darch put the telephone down before she could ask, in order to answer another phone.

The call Mr Darch answered was from the signalman at Taunton West, who wanted to know why the up sleeper had not arrived at the station. Mr Darch told him it was on fire and that the down lines were to be blocked. The evidence to the Inquiry makes no mention of 'Obstruction Danger' — six bells — being sent between the two boxes, and I must suppose that this reference to 'blocking the down lines' refers to the sending of the emergency bell signal. Having dealt with this call, Mr Darch received another from Miss Carpenter asking where to send the fire brigade. By this time there was an ugly glow in the night sky ¾ mile from Silk Mill box in the Taunton direction.

Having made the call to Silk Mill box, Driver Pope went back to his train at about 2.46am and met Guard Barribal, who told him he had put 'shots' down to the rear of the train and that the emergency services had been called. Guard Barribal had been walking towards the rear of the train with another railwayman, a Mr Jago, who was travelling to Taunton to take up another duty. Mr Barribal did not smell the fire until the train was passing Silk Mill Crossing, but then looked out and saw thick smoke coming from the leading sleeping car. The train was already braking, and when it stopped Barribal and Jago got down onto the track on the nearside and hurried to the front. They stopped opposite the gangway between cars B and C and stared in amazement for a moment at the flames and the smoke in particular coming from the leading end of car B. It is not difficult to imagine the controlled panic they felt when confronted with this appalling sight. Mr Barribal was banging on car C with his lamp, calling for people to get out, when Driver Pope appeared with a fire extinguisher. The time was then about 2.47am. Perhaps Driver Pope climbed onto the end of the leading brake van to bring himself level with the broken, leading window of car B. In any event, he discharged the extinguisher into the blazing vestibule while standing next to a door that was so hot the paint on the outside was bubbling and blistering. The flames subsided briefly, but soon burst out again. However, this short respite may have saved the lives of four men — Messrs Nightingale, Morley, Watkins and McMillan — who were lying unconscious on the floor of the corridor at the trailing end of the sleeping car.

Driver Pope and Guard Barribal briefly considered dividing the train and drawing the burning part forward because the fire was beginning to spread, but Pope's inability to release the brake made this impossible. Instead, Guard Barribal climbed up and unlocked the by now hot leading door of car C and opened it. Two men jumped out and another was lying on the floor. Barribal then ran to the rear door, opened it and carried out a little girl. Then he remembered the emergency equipment carried in the leading brake van, ran forward and scrambled in. He handed out two axes and a sledgehammer to his colleagues on the ground, whilst keeping an axe for himself. This he used to smash the central window of car C where he could see a man standing. Then he ran forward again to the leading brake van for a ladder and took it back to the window he had broken and helped the man there to climb out. Driver Pope and Mr Jago meanwhile were working furiously to break windows, unlock doors and extricate passengers when at 2.56am help arrived in the form of four policemen and the first fire brigade officers. The first person to enter the blazing car B was Sub-Officer Sams, a retained fireman stationed at Taunton. Using a short ladder he played a hose through the window and then attempted to open the door, but it was locked. Guard Barribal handed over his carriage key, the door was opened and a 2ft 6in-high pile of laundry fell blazing onto the track. The whole of the vestibule wall area was on fire, producing dense, black smoke. Sams crawled into this, but because of the heat and smoke he was unable to proceed very far and returned to hand over to firemen equipped with breathing apparatus.

The fire brigade and the police had arrived on the scene with 'extreme promptness' and the fire, rendered all the more dreadful because of the confined space it occupied, was fought with great skill and bravery by officers who were forced into its close proximity. Householders bordering the line gave magnificent assistance and cared for the injured, while the selfless actions of Driver Pope and Guard Barribal were recognised by cash awards. The whole saga was wonderfully British: plywood — a less fire-resistant material than that used during original construction — had been used during a 1977 refurbishment. There had been a total lack of training for sleeping car attendants, a lack of supervision, a lack of smoke detectors in the carriages, and a lack of fire precautions and inspections such as were standard in hotel sleeping quarters. All these negative aspects were set against the splendid bravery and resourcefulness displayed by those who had to retrieve the situation.

The occupants of berths 1/2 and 3/4, Messrs Nightingale and Morley, survived. Those in berths 5/6, 7/8, 9/10 and 11/12 perished. The occupant of the single berth 13, Lt Watkins, survived. The man in berth 14 died in the corridor. Miss Drummond in berth 16 survived and the gentleman in berth 17 survived the actual fire but died of a heart attack in hospital. Those that died on the train were killed by cyanide and carbon monoxide poisoning, the products of the combustion of plastic. The verdict of the Coroner's Court on 18 August 1978 was 'Accidental Death'.

# Morpeth:
## *23 June 1984*

Driver Allan was 58 at the time of the derailment. He had started on the LNER as a porter in 1942 and shortly transferred to the footplate side. He became a fireman qualified to act as driver — a 'passed fireman' — in 1952 and became a main-line driver, working out of Edinburgh Haymarket shed, in 1972. He was very well conversant with the route from Edinburgh to Newcastle. He was a big man, weighing 14st, and, as a smoker, had suffered from the chronic respiratory problem of bronchitis with emphysema since 1979. Aged 55 in 1980, he had been examined for general physical fitness and for his eyesight by the railway doctor. Nothing untoward had been detected. He had again been examined in 1982 and passed fit to drive express trains. He was within the standards required. His chronic respiratory problems were not considered to be a danger, either by the railway doctor or his own general practitioner. This was in spite of an incident in October 1981 when Mr Allan had been sitting in his garden and began to cough so violently that his face turned red, swelled up and then turned blue as the coughing continued. At that point he fainted and fell off his chair. He was unconscious for about a minute. This was witnessed by Mrs Allan. She said that she had called the doctor but he never came. At least twice in 1982, Mr Allan had fainted as the result of a coughing fit. In one of these incidents he had fallen down and struck his head on the ground with sufficient force to produce concussion. A similar incident was witnessed by Mrs Allan and her cousin. On this occasion, Mrs Allan wanted to call a doctor but Mr Allan had refused to allow this because he had to go to work the following day. It appears from this that he may have thought his condition so serious that he might be banned from driving trains, at least temporarily. He was right, because Mrs Allan did get the doctor to visit her husband and he signed him off work for three weeks and made him visit the hospital for treatment. But Mr Allan was also told that he could drive

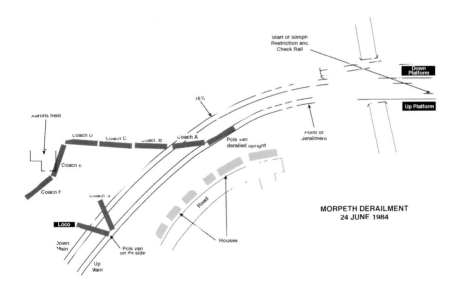

MORPETH DERAILMENT
24 JUNE 1984

his car to keep the appointment, and at no time did any doctor order him not to drive a car or train because of the risk of a coughing fit.

On Saturday 23 June Mr Allan was booked to drive the 1E48 7.50pm Aberdeen-King's Cross sleeping car train from Edinburgh Waverley to Newcastle-upon-Tyne. This was his seventh successive night shift. The train was due to leave Edinburgh at 11.5pm and he left his home at Drem, after a substantial dinner, at 8.50pm. On his way to work he stopped to visit a pub 'down a side street' in Musselburgh. Here, he drank a 1/5th gill of whisky followed by a pint of Foster's lager beer. He left the pub at 9.20pm and arrived at the staff car park behind Waverley goods depot at about 9.35pm. From there, he walked to the shunters' bothy underneath the disused Waverley East signalbox and booked himself on duty by telephoning the time clerk. This was recorded at 9.43pm. Having booked on duty he then walked back to his car to fetch two cans of Tennent's lager, one 'ordinary' and one 'extra strong', both containing just under a pint. He then walked back with them to the bothy and drank them both in seven or eight minutes. He left the bothy at 9.55pm and, he said, 'wandered around the station' until it was time to take over the train.

Station Supervisor Currie was on his way along Platform 9 to Platform 10 (all one platform) at 9.55pm and saw Driver Allan walking through the staff car park towards his platform. Shortly afterwards, Mr Paul, the Train Crew Supervisor who was leaving duty, was walking from the drivers' briefing room down the stairs to Platform 10 when he met Driver Allan coming up the stairs. Driver Allan continued towards the briefing room as if to seek out the Train Crew Supervisor who had just come on duty. The Train Crew Supervisor's job was to ensure that trains were properly manned, and the smell of alcohol on a driver's breath would be enough for the Supervisor to take suitable action. In fact, Driver Allan did not go to the Crew Supervisor, and no-one, after Mr Paul at about 9.58pm, saw him until about 10.50pm, when Supervisor Currie saw him walking along Platform 1 to go to the engine of the sleeping car train. The invisibility of Driver Allan on the station during that 50 minutes entitles one to wonder where he was.

Driver Allan and the guard of the train, W. Brown, met on Platform 1 as they each waited for the sleeping car train to arrive. They did not know each other and did not at first realise that they were both to be working the same train. When the train rolled in behind locomotive No 47452, Guard Brown said 'See you later', then went back to relieve the Aberdeen guard and obtain details of the train's formation and load. He then walked to the engine and told Driver Allan that he had seven sleepers with a 'GUV' at each end and that the first stop would be Newcastle. The train left 'right time' at 11.5pm. The Train Crew Supervisor had not come to check on Driver Allan. The system was flawed because it depended upon the driver presenting himself.

When Driver Allan took over locomotive No 47452 at Platform 1 he had been drinking. How much we do not know but, by his own admission, a tot of whisky and a pint of lager 100min previously, and a further 1¾ pints of lager 70min previously. The maximum concentration of alcohol in the blood occurs between half an hour and two hours after the last drink has been taken, although this varies between individuals. Thus, the amount of alcohol in Driver Allan's blood at the time he drove away might have been as high as 120mg of alcohol per 100ml of blood, or as low as 84mg per 100ml (84mg/100ml). The latter is 4mg over the legal limit for driving a car. Up to 50mg/100ml concentration has no apparent effect on an individual's capabilities, but above that level the effect begins to show and the functions of the brain are retarded in proportion to the amount of alcohol present. Judgement is impaired, powers of concentration are reduced, and, of course, alcohol promotes sleep.

The Class 47 locomotive was in proper working order. The brakes, the AWS and the Driver's Safety Device (DSD) were operational. The DSD is a foot pedal which the driver has to keep depressed. If he releases it and fails to depress it again within 5sec, the brakes start to go on. The line south from Berwick-upon-Tweed to Alnmouth had a maximum speed limit of 125mph, and 100mph onward to Morpeth, with various lower speed restrictions applying to curves or viaducts. After passing over Alnmouth Viaduct, there were two miles at 90mph, 2¼ miles at

80mph and then a limit of 65mph for half a mile around the South Side Curve near Acklington. Running at 100mph was again permitted for 4¼ miles to Chevington, reducing to 90mph from there to Widdrington, and then 100mph again for 5½ miles to Pegswood. The Class 47's top speed was automatically governed to 95mph. From Pegswood, the maximum permitted line speed was 100mph, but it was necessary to reduce this to 80mph to pass over the viaduct north of Morpeth, then to 70mph around Morpeth North Curve, and to no more than 50mph at the north end of the station, ready for the South Curve. The speed restriction indicator for the curve was sited, clear to see, at the foot of

the platform ramp at the north end of the station. The total length of the wicked Morpeth South Curve was 750yd. There was a transition curve of 112yd, with the super-elevation (cant) of the outer rail over the inner rail gradually rising, leading into the main curve which was only 14 chains (308yd) radius, with the outer rail 6in (30cm) above the inner. A guard rail was laid around the curve, close to the inner rail.

In 1969 there had been a derailment on Morpeth Curve due to the driver relaxing his concentration and taking it too fast. To prevent this happening again, an illuminated speed restriction sign was placed at the point north of the curve where a driver would normally begin braking and an AWS magnet was placed 200yd to the north of this sign. Thus, a driver would always get a warning siren as a reminder to begin braking.

The signals were four-aspect colour-lights working automatically or controlled, under Track Circuit Block regulations, by a succession of small signalboxes in which signalmen described the trains forward using the traditional, single-strike bell. The box north of Morpeth was Chevington, nine miles away. The signalman there described the Aberdeen sleeper to Morpeth at 12.31am. The Morpeth signalman, Reliefman J. Earle, described the train to Stannington, lowered the level crossing barriers at Longhirst and then set the route for the train. It passed him at 12.39am. Eight minutes between Chevington and Morpeth was the normal running time for a daytime express, but that was faster than the sleeping car train schedule required and, in that sense at least, Driver Allan was speeding.

Neither the guard nor the Guards' Inspector who was also on the train mentioned rough riding prior to the derailment. Indeed, both said the journey as far as Morpeth was 'uneventful'. Several passengers from the train wrote to the Inspecting Officer with their recollections of the journey. Some of them thought the train travelled uneventfully, but others believed it had been speeding. Mr Mark Barker, Marketing Manager for the Commonwealth Games Organisation, was a regular traveller on the sleeping car train and he stated in writing to the Inspecting Officer that 'the train was travelling far faster than usual'. His coach 'pitched and rolled unusually for 20 minutes prior to the crash, his body slid about in the bunk and his hat slid along the rack above him'. Several other passengers described being thrown about in their bunks, 'rocking like a ship at sea', or of a suitcase falling off the rack, many miles prior to the crash.

How much an experienced driver takes notice of — or needs — a speedometer is open to question, but the speedometer on No 47452 was reading between 3 and 4mph fast and so Driver Allan, if he had regulated his speed by his speedometer, would have been actually travelling at 46mph had the instrument read 50mph on the approach to Morpeth curve. As events turned out, had he been looking at his speedometer as he went through Morpeth station, he would have seen that it was reading 94mph!

In order for the train to be derailed by centrifugal force as it went into — and tried to go around — the heavily-canted Morpeth South Curve, it would have to have been travelling at between 85 and 91mph. A Mk 3 sleeping car coach, given its higher centre of gravity, would have derailed at 85mph; the locomotive, with a lower centre of gravity, would have derailed at 91mph. In order to have been running at this speed at Morpeth, Driver Allan would have had to have been using the full power of the locomotive without interruption after coming off the 60mph speed-restricted viaduct at Alnmouth. This would have entailed going through the 65mph South Side Curve at 80mph, which could account for the sudden eruption of luggage off racks — especially as this curve was lacking 22mm of super-elevation for comfortable passage at 65mph. Taking this curve at 80mph would have increased the lack of cant to 85mm and produced a very rough ride. After this curve there was no speed restriction worth mentioning until Morpeth North Curve. Driver Allan continued to power towards a 90mph section and then a 100mph section. Six miles north of Morpeth, at Ulgham Grange level crossing and on the 100mph-permissible section, Driver Allan saw the lights of a tamping machine on the opposite line and blew his horn as he approached it.

Careful analysis of wheel marks on the rail heads at Morpeth South Curve after the derailment showed that the relatively light and high leading van and the sleeping carriage coupled behind it were the first to derail. They, in turn, brought the engine off. The nearside wheels of the carriages had been lifted off the inner rail 20yd after entering the curve and shortly after that fell over onto their off-sides towards the down main, bringing everything off the rails in front and behind. The front van and sleeping car came to rest 'jack-knifed' into a sharp 'V', lying across the tracks. The next five, still coupled together, shot down the low embankment, falling onto their off-sides with the leading end of the formation ramming into the interior of a bungalow. The rearmost van and the sleeping car coupled to it were derailed but remained upright. It is due to the robust design and construction of the carriages that not one passenger was killed in this high-speed crash; one which left a whole train flung about and rammed into houses. Twenty-nine injured passengers and six train crew members, including Driver Allan, were taken to hospital, but only he and two sleeping car attendants were detained.

Driver Allan was charged at Newcastle Crown Court with the offence of 'Endangering the safety of passengers contrary to Section 34 of the Offences against the Person Act 1861 [in that he] by wilful omission and neglect endangered the safety of persons conveyed upon a railway'. Part of the prosecution evidence was the statement of Professor Rawling, who calculated that, as a blood sample taken from Driver Allan four hours after the crash contained 39mg of alcohol per 100ml of blood, he (Driver Allan) would have had anything from 74 to 90mg of alcohol per 100ml of blood at the time of the crash. Of Police Constable Feltham, who climbed into the crash cab to comfort Driver Allan, Dr Cunningham, who gave first aid in the cab, and Dr Adams, who treated Driver Allan's injuries at the hospital, none smelled alcohol on the driver's breath. The police surgeon, Dr Gardner, visited Driver Allan at Newcastle hospital at 3.55am. Dr Gardner stated that, when he examined him, Driver Allan showed no symptoms of being adversely affected by alcohol, although he could smell alcohol on his breath. An ambulance man, Mr Thompson, also stated that he smelled alcohol. A fortnight later Driver Allan was interviewed by the police at home and there he admitted that he had drunk the earlier stated amount of alcohol. He said that he did not normally drink before or on duty, and that he was not a heavy drinker. When he was asked if he thought that the amount he had consumed that night was a heavy intake and way above normal he replied 'Yes.'

'And consequently your driving ability was likely to be impaired?'

'It could have been,' replied Driver Allan.

The family of Driver Allan offered in his defence the possibility of a sudden attack of coughing leading to fainting which they had seen him suffer in 1981/2 and which, if it happened, would have incapacitated him as he approached Morpeth. If that were the case, while he was coughing he could have shut off power and taken his foot off the DSD to stop the train. The evidence of the crash proves that the train had never been braked, and the passing times at Alnmouth and Morpeth show that for at least 15 miles — 12 or 13 minutes — prior to the crash the locomotive had been on full power, including going round the South Side Curve. Driver Allan had blown his horn at the tamper six miles from Morpeth, so he had been alert to the bright lights, but then the presence of the two sharp curves at Morpeth had escaped his attention.

The Inspecting Officer was of the opinion that Driver Allan had allowed his attention to wander and that he might even, briefly, have been asleep. He had, after all, been out of bed since early the previous evening, it was the last of a long week of night shifts, he had been drinking and could have felt drowsy in the warm cab. But the Newcastle jury gave him the benefit of the doubt; there was the problem of emphysema and the chance of a coughing fit. They found him 'Not Guilty' of the charge.

Driver Allan was very foolish to have taken drink just before and after going on duty. Engine driving work is very tiring as it involves night duty, shifts all round the clock and getting up at all sorts of odd hours. But above all it is a job where one man is entrusted with hundreds of lives. It is work, not necessarily for a young man, but certainly for a physically fit man, and that means one who is clear-headed and who has clear lungs. It is not for a man who has to gasp for breath if he walks too fast. I wonder why, therefore, given the serious nature of his breathing problem, the medical profession had not taken him off the job. The only criticism in the Ministry of Transport Report is of Driver Allan's reckless drinking which was, of course, very wrong, but there is no criticism of the railway regulations, which restrict fitness to drive solely to the non-consumption of drugs or alcohol and so allow a man with such a chronic condition as emphysema, and with a proven risk of incapacitating coughing fits, to take charge of the lives of hundreds of people. The Inspecting Officer made no criticism of the medical profession, nor of the slackness of the railway management, not only in the framing of the Rules, but also in the actual management of crews at Edinburgh and elsewhere.

# Severn Tunnel Junction:
## 11 February 1985

It was a wicked night to be out. There were two inches of dry, powdery snow lying on the sleepers and an easterly wind, as sharp as a whiplash, was driving the ice into every crevice of an overcoat and into every slight gap in the protection of railway equipment. That wonderful invention, the gas-fired point heater, was impotent, its flame extinguished by the wind. It was useless at the very time it was most needed, when wind-driven snow was filling up the space between the switch blade and the stock rail. Brilliant! So once more into the breach came a few human point clearers — those surviving the various cost-cutting purges of the labour force. And these men, as this story shows, were committed to the railway service, willing to put up with hardships, to go the extra mile and generally behave in an opposite manner to machines.

At 11.15pm on Friday 8 February 1985 the Newport Panel Supervisor contacted Mr Bearcroft, the Permanent Way Section Supervisor for Severn Tunnel Junction, and asked for the snowmen to be sent out because the electrically-operated points were becoming frozen and/or jammed due to snow and an absence of point heaters. Mr Bearcroft got the men out (of bed in some cases), and by 1am on Saturday morning they were working in the freezing dark to keep the railway moving. At 3am on 9th Newport Panel could neither use the West Junction points nor contact the clearing gang. The Panel Supervisor woke up Track Chargeman Buffery at his home near the station and asked him to go and find the men and direct them to West Junction. Mr Buffery got out of his warm bed and went off into the freezing night to the windswept wastes of Severn Tunnel Junction to look for the gang members. The track layout extends for a couple of miles, so his search represented a real challenge, but he managed to locate them working at N196 and re-directed them to the West Junction points. Mr I. Hutchinson was in charge, and had lookout men posted to protect the gang. Mr Buffery then went home because he was booked on duty for 7am that morning. He was duly back at work punctually, and worked for 12 hours supervising the various snow-clearing gangs and maintaining the Severn Tunnel Junction complex. The weather was so bad that Supervisor Bearcroft came out to help Mr Buffery, working through from 7.45am until 7pm.

Messrs Bearcroft and Buffery were again on '12 hours' through Sunday, and before Mr Bearcroft went home he left instructions that the night-shift yard gangs were to assist the main-line gangs as required in snow-clearance duties. He left his office open, so that the night-shift men had access to both BT and internal telephones, additional tools, lamps and lookout equipment.

Of the seven staff rostered for the 12-hour Sunday night/Monday morning shift, 10th/11th, five were certified lookout men. I. Hutchinson was in charge of the main-line gang, B. Bushell in charge of the upside Yard gang and T. Watkins the downside yard gang. These three were experienced permanent-way men perfectly capable of taking charge of the men without constant supervision.

The night-shift snow-clearance gang for Severn Tunnel Junction main line booked on duty that bitter night at 7pm. With I. Hutchinson were E. Mustoe and V. Stephens. They went out together to the layout at the east end of the station and worked on the points there.

Mr Hutchinson did not appoint a lookout man. One of his gang held the 'Bardic' lamp to illuminate the work of the other two and this man was supposed to keep a look-out. In doing

## ACCIDENT AT SEVERN TUNNEL JUNCTION
## 11 FEBRUARY 1985

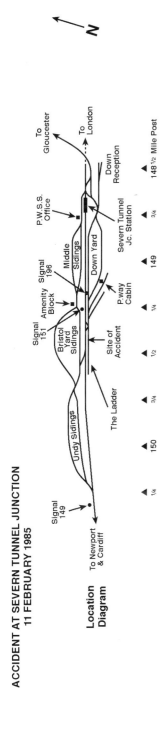

**Location Diagram**

To Newport & Cardiff

Signal 149

Undy Sidings

The Ladder

Signal 151

Bristol Yard Sidings

Site of Accident

Amenity Block

Signal 196

Middle Sidings

Down Yard

P.W.S.S. Office

Severn Tunnel Jc. Station

Down Reception

P'way Cabin

To Gloucester

To London

148½ Mile Post

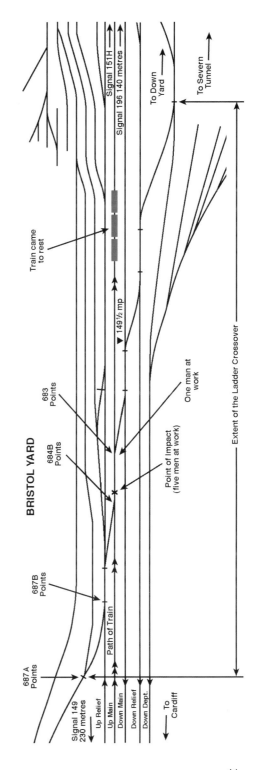

**BRISTOL YARD**

687A Points

687B Points

Signal 149 230 metres

Up Relief

Up Main

Down Main

Down Relief

Down Dept.

To Cardiff

Path of Train

684B Points

683 Points

Point of Impact (five men at work)

One man at work

Train came to rest

149½ mp

Signal 151H

Signal 196 140 metres

To Down Yard

To Severn Tunnel

Extent of the Ladder Crossover

41

this, Hutchinson was in breach of the British Railways Rule Book Section P (1.1), but he was not in breach of the British Railways Civil Engineering Safety Manual, October 1983. In this, the instructions for providing look-out for men working on the track was extraordinarily long-winded and ambiguous. The verbose nature of the instructions can be taken from a heading in large, italic type: *Deciding Whether Lookout Protection Should Be Provided.* This should be contrasted with the ancient Rule 273(f) of the GWR 1904 Rule Book, repeated identically in Rule 234(d) of the 1933 GWR Rule Book and as the same number in the British Railways 1950 Rule Book. The same wording was used in the 1972 Rule Book, still in force in 1985. This was short and unambiguous: 'When work is about to be undertaken on or near lines in use for traffic, the Ganger or Man in Charge *must* [my emphasis] appoint one or more persons expressly to maintain a good look-out'.

The 1983 Civil Engineering Safety Manual Instruction was a sort of 'nudge-nudge, wink-wink' affair which undermined the Rule Book by implying that, if you thought you could do without a lookout man, do so, but *'If there is any doubt* [sic] the only responsible course is to provide it'. This let the management off the hook in case anything should go wrong after a man had been led astray and not provided himself with lookout protection.

Mr Hutchinson and his two trackmen worked for about 90 minutes and then went back to the P-way office for a warm-up, getting back inside at 8.45pm. Mr Hutchinson was a cheerful, gregarious man and decided that, with the weather being so cold and the night ahead so long, he and Stephens would go for a drink in the local inn, and told Mr Mustoe to stay in the office to listen out for the telephone in case they were required by the Panel. Hutchinson and Stephens then went off to the local hostelry.

While Mustoe was sitting alone in the office, Trackman Adams came in on his break and asked where Hutchinson and Stephens were. 'Down the pub,' replied Mustoe, perhaps a little gloomily. Adams also went off to the pub and had three pints with the others. Obviously the others had had at least one more before that. After Adams' third pint, Hutchinson said: 'We must go back now because the Panel [Newport signalling centre] is waiting for us to clear the ladder [a points complex] out.' He and Stephens bought a flagon of cider each and, carrying their bottles, the men returned to their van and to Severn Tunnel Junction P-way office.

The men got back at 10.40pm and came into the office in a noisy, talkative mood. They were very cheerful but Hutchinson was often full of fun and Mustoe did not think he or the other two were drunk.

Having had a good break, Mr Hutchinson got back to business and prepared to go and clear the ladder at the Newport end of the layout. He asked Mr Adams to join him, Mustoe and Stephens and to 'go look-out because it's dangerous down there and we need an extra pair of eyes'. They got into the works van and off they went. Passing the down yard, Adams got out to go and tell his mate, Watson, that he had been called away to help the main-line gang. The others went on and at about 11.15pm arrived at No 687 points. This was the start of the ladder — three crossovers from the up yard to the down yard through the up and down main lines. No lookout men were posted but the man with the 'Bardic' was keeping a watch when not shining the torch on the work. When Adams arrived Hutchinson did not appoint him as lookout after all, but told him to go and fetch two men from the upside yard gang. So there were now six men working on the up main line: Adams, Bushell, Hutchinson, Lord, Mustoe and Stephens. The man in charge, Mr Hutchinson, had been at Severn Tunnel Junction for 17 years. Adams had been at the station nearly two years and the others had been working there for between three and eight years. All of them were wearing their high-visibility vests, all had passed the examination in the Rules and were qualified to be lookout men, while Bushell, Hutchinson, Lord and Mustoe had attended a course specifically on lookout men's arrangements. And still no formal lookout man was posted.

So there they were, six cheerful p-way men, all good mates, doing a rough job in miserable conditions and in the middle of the up main line. They got out of the way of several trains because they saw them coming owing to the bright headlamps fitted to the locomotives, but their luck ran out.

The 12.25am from Cardiff, a three-car diesel multiple-unit passenger train to Newport, continuing to Severn Tunnel Junction as a staff train, was running to time. The driver was C. Davies and the guard G. Davies, who was accompanied by an off-duty guard, J. Purnell. The latter sat in the passenger compartment but was called into the cab by his friend, Driver Davies. Three miles from Severn Tunnel Junction, Guard Davies came to stand in the doorway of the driver's cab. They exchanged a few words but mostly were looking forward at the track. The line ahead was dark except for the occasional flurry of wind-blown snow catching the dim light of the marker lights at the front of the unit. On the approach to Severn Tunnel Junction they got a double yellow, then a single yellow. Driver Davies had braked to 45mph between the two signals. Guard Purnell had worked a Newport-Bristol train earlier and had seen the p-way men clearing the points at the station, so he was keeping a particular lookout. Driver Davies saw nothing until Guards Davies and Purnell both shouted a warning together and, as they were still calling out, the driver caught a glimpse of a high-visibility vest in the track in front of him. He made an emergency application of the brake as the unit struck down the man he had glimpsed. He brought his train to a stand in 180yd, and then he and Guard Davies got down and saw human remains on the front of CH23. Driver Davies hurried to N151 to inform the signalman and Guard Davies put track-circuit-operating clips on the opposite line, the down main.

As the DMU was approaching, its sound was blown away from the ears of the gang by the searing east wind and drowned by their concentration on the job in hand. They had nearly finished what they were doing in the up main and, indeed, Mr Mustoe was already walking towards the down main points and was 25yd beyond where his mates were finishing off. He heard a scream and managed to throw himself clear of the track as the multiple-unit passed him. Mr Adams had his back towards Newport, standing in the 'four foot' and shining the 'Bardic' lamp on the right-hand point blade. He stepped sideways into the 'six foot' space between the up and down tracks and as he did so the DMU swept past his back. He heard a scream, looked to his left and saw his mates being bowled along the track, thrown tumbling forwards by the train.

I. Hutchinson, B. Bushell, I. Lord and V. Stephens were all killed instantly.

It would appear that the BR Civil Engineering Manual was at fault here, by contradicting earlier rules; as a result of this accident, it was recommended that the provision of lookout men be compulsory — a return to the GWR rule of 1904 — and that portable, free-standing lighting be provided for night time work instead of reliance being placed upon the 'inappropriate Bardic', which, powerful though it is, is really only a hand-signalling torch. It was also recommended that all traction units should be fitted with high-powered headlights.

# Colwich:
## 19 September 1986

In the bad old days of the coal-fired railway, before we had the advantages of modern technology, the signalling of junctions was lamentably simple. If the permitted speed over the diverging route at the junction was less than 40mph (for instance, in GWR practice), no separate distant ('Caution') signal arm was provided for the divergence and the lever in the signalbox working the distant signal applicable to the main-line route was mechanically locked in the 'Caution' position when the route was set for the divergence. Thus, the driver was warned to slow down and be prepared to stop at the first 'Stop' signal. If the permitted speed over the junction turn-out was 40mph or more, a workable, 'directing' distant signal was supplied. This was located on a bracket cantilevered out from the main post, to the left or right, depending on the direction of the diverging line ahead. Alternatively, the same arrangement of posts and arms could be mounted on the horizontal beam of a gantry. The directing distant signal could only be cleared to the 'All Clear' position if the junction points were correctly set for the diverging route and the signalman had cleared all the stop signals for the route into the next section ahead. The semaphore directing distant signal told drivers one of two things — 'Go' or 'Prepare to Stop'. There was no possibility of ambiguity. It did, however, leave the driver with the sole responsibility for remembering to slow down to the correct speed for negotiating the diverging junction. This method was unvarying from Land's End to John o' Groats. In prewar colour-light signalling schemes, offset heads were used, mimicking the semaphore system. This semaphore method of signalling junctions was not only efficiently unambiguous, but also the most efficient as an operating procedure because drivers knew, if the 'directing' distant was cleared, that it was safe to drive their train up to and over the junction at the maximum permitted speed.

Beginning in the late 1950s, Multiple Aspect Signalling (MAS) schemes, covering many miles of route and intended, eventually, to control the whole country from a few control centres, were installed. The purpose of MAS is to run more trains, faster, within a given mileage. It costs a very great deal of money to install, usually employs a greater number of technicians than the old system, but removes a very large number of signalmen from the wage bill. The MAS system is a more 'pressurised' one than those it has replaced, and drivers are obliged to become part of a more intensively-used machine. With MAS came a new signalling principle — that no driver should be obliged to pass a red signal on the same post as his own 'Proceed' aspect. This happened routinely in semaphore signalling where there were two or more 'Stop' signals on a bracket or gantry. One arm would be lowered for the driver to proceed but the rest remained at 'Danger' because they did not apply to the route the driver was to take. In this sense, drivers were obliged to pass semaphore signals at 'Danger'. I know of one occasion only when this system caused a problem. A driver, travelling at high speed, approached a junction bracket signal on the main line, with the main-line arm cleared for him and the arm for the diverging route at 'Danger', and did not see his signal at 'Proceed' but saw only the arm at 'Danger'. He very quickly brought his train to a stand. This incident occurred in 1963 at Wantage Road and was witnessed by the Chief Signalling Inspector and the London Divisional Superintendent. The driver had suffered a momentary mental aberration and, coming to the signalbox to complain that the signal had been thrown to 'Danger' in his face, was unable to accept that it was he who had made a mistake and went on his way believing the signalman had worked some trickery on him. This must surely have been a very rare occurrence but it was to avoid such 'one-in-a-million' chance incidents that the practice of having a single post with offset signal heads was abandoned.

The new 'principle' was a bit of fine tuning and might be rather too fussy. More to the point would be a system to prevent drivers from passing red signals at 'Danger', rather than mistaking a green one for a red — and then stopping!

Without the offset signal head — the method chosen to indicate to the driver that he is to take a route diverging from that on which he is travelling — the colour-light signal at the junction is fitted with a 'junction indicator'. This takes the form of a row of five white lights in a cowling which projects diagonally upwards, downwards or horizontally, to the left or right of the signal head. The lights are illuminated only when the route is proved set correctly for the divergence. Only after the indicator is proved to be illuminated does the signal aspect change from red to a 'Proceed' aspect. The junction indicator is generally known to English and Welsh railwaymen as the 'five white lights' or the 'feathers', while in Scotland they call it 'the horn'.

Because it was not possible, under the MAS principle, to give a driver advance warning that he was routed to a diverging line, a system of delayed-action release of the junction signal was adopted when the route was set for the divergence. After the diverging route had been correctly set, the junction signal had to remain at red — even if the line was clear for miles beyond the junction. With the junction signal at red the signals in rear showed double yellow and single yellow to warn the driver to slow down. If the junction signal simply showed a green aspect, then the signals to its rear would also be green and a train could approach a diverging route at full speed with 'greens all the way'. In these circumstances, the driver, lacking any signal to remind him of the diverging route ahead, might forget, with disastrous consequences.

At a junction in an MAS area, prior to 1978, the general rule was that the junction signal remained at red until the approaching train has passed the single yellow aspect in the rear. But after passing the single yellow some variation in the routine of 'stepping-up' the red signal was allowed. If the difference in permitted speed over either arm of the junction was not greater than 10mph the red aspect would clear to the highest aspect permissible as soon as the approaching train had passed the single yellow — sometimes before it came in sight of the driver. If the difference in permitted speed between the main line and the divergence was greater than 10mph, the red junction signal did not clear until the train had been occupying a certain track circuit on the approach to the junction signal for a certain length of time. This length of time was calculated to ensure that the driver would have reduced his speed sufficiently to take the divergence at the correct speed. Then the aspect 'steps-up' to green or some other proceed aspect, dictated by the aspects of the signals ahead.

So, under MAS, junctions were approached while braking continuously, 'coming down onto the red' as it is known, with the driver not knowing whether he had to stop or whether the red aspect would 'step-up'. If there was a train in the section ahead of the junction, or if the junction was not set because there was a train coming along the main line to cross the path of the branch train, the signal aspect would remain at red. More often than not, however, the red light 'stepped-up', but drivers could never be quite sure what the aspect was going to do and they reduced speed as if to stop. The timetable took account of this slowing and thus journey time was extended.

With the introduction of 125mph High Speed Trains (IC125s), this method of signalling the diverging route at junctions became a greater source of delay than before. In order to make full use of the speed of IC125s, and not lose time unduly over junctions, a method of signalling was devised which was intended to approximate to the semaphore signalling system of the 'splitting distant'.

British Railways Board Notice 29775 dated October 1978 explained:

'1. Flashing aspects are to be introduced into the signalling arrangements at certain *diverging* [author's emphasis] junctions. This is an important addition to established signalling practice and this pamphlet has been prepared to explain the meaning and application of the new aspects.

2. The normal practice in colour-light-signalled territory, when a train is signalled to a diverging route through a speed restricted turn-out, is to delay the clearance of the junction signal until after the train has passed the signal next in rear. At the higher-speed junctions where the normal method would be too restrictive to enable trains to take advantage of the permitted speed through the junction, the arrangement is modified to permit the junction signal to display a proceed aspect as soon as the route is set and the line ahead is clear. Although this arrangement has been satisfactory for conventional trains, it does not meet the needs of the new High Speed Trains. To match the higher performance of the High Speed Trains, it is necessary to provide a system of signalling at junctions which will give drivers advance warning of the diversion and so enable them to take full advantage of the permitted speed through the junction while ensuring that the train will not be travelling at too high a speed to negotiate the turn-out safely. In future, where circumstances require, two new signal aspects will be used to give positive, advance indication to drivers that junction facing points are set for a *diverging* route over which speed must be reduced. The new aspects will be: 1. flashing double yellow. 2. flashing single yellow. In such case the sequence of aspects approaching the junction when the facing points are set for the diverging route will be (in four-aspect territory) a flashing double yellow, a flashing yellow, a steady yellow with junction indicator.'

The pamphlet explained 'Meanings of New Aspects'. One flashing yellow light — Preliminary Caution and indication of diverging route ahead of next signal — be prepared to *find the next signal exhibiting one yellow light with junction indicator.* Two flashing yellow lights (vertically displayed) — Advance indication of diverging route ahead of next but one signal. Next signal exhibiting one flashing yellow light.

So, if the yellow aspects are flashing, the driver knows that the junction is set for the turn-out, that he will see a steady single yellow with the 'feathers' in the junction signal and that that aspect will, if conditions of line occupation ahead are suitable, 'step-up' to a steady double yellow or green aspect after his cab passes over the AWS magnet and has thus received the warning siren — which warning must be acknowledged if the brakes are not to be automatically applied.

According to the 1978 Notice, the flashing aspects were to be used at 'diverging' junctions. By this was meant (and was understood by the Inspecting Officer of the Accident and most railwaymen to mean) 'geographical' junctions where two routes diverge. But the very first installation, which was on Western Region, was at the main to relief crossovers at Ruscombe. Another crossover installation followed, and only later was the system installed at a 'diverging' junction — at Wootton Bassett in 1978 for the 70mph South Wales main line from the 125mph Bristol route. The promiscuous use of the flashing aspects could lead to a confusing situation. If a high-speed crossover were closely in rear of a diverging junction, a driver, seeing the flashing yellows indicating the crossover was set for main to relief (or vice versa) could possibly get into a mind-set where he thought that he had a clear road over the diverging junction beyond the crossover. This was especially so as the introductory notice had stated that these new signals were to be used at such divergences and made no mention of crossovers.

On the Western Region, a day course was provided in the method of working with the flashing aspects. During the course, drivers and secondmen were shown a 'cab ride' video, they heard the system explained and took part in a discussion of the system. Presumably similar courses took place on the LMR although some ex-LMR personnel have expressed their doubts about this to me. Driver Shaw of the crash train had not seen the video or the pamphlet. The Inspecting Officer drew attention to the danger of staff cuts when he observed that the number of footplate — or traction — inspectors had been reduced to save money, so there were fewer men to examine the crews, to ask them about their understanding of operating matters, to travel with them on duty, put them right and generally explain things.

On 7 June 1986 flashing aspects were brought into use at the diverging junction of Norton Bridge, north of Stafford, on the West Coast main line (WCML). To quote the Signalling Notice to Drivers, 'The Down Fast signals at Norton Bridge, NB150 and NB148, will show flashing double yellow and flashing single yellow respectively when the route is set from the Down Fast to the recess line (to Stoke-on-Trent) and with signal NB9, on the recess line, showing a proceed aspect'. This was a straightforward, diverging route layout without the complication of a crossover being first encountered to the rear.

Colwich Junction is on the Trent Valley section of the WCML, south of Stafford and north of Rugeley. The diverging route was built by the North Staffordshire Railway and was opened from Stone in 1849. Colwich was a complex junction controlled from a manual signalbox, brought into use on 3 February 1958, equipped with a 1943-pattern, 45-lever mechanical frame. There was — and still is — quadruple track south from Colwich to Armitage. The up and down fast lines are on the outside of the formation. The up and down slow lines, between the fast lines, swing away to Manchester, the down slow crossing the up fast, and going via Stone and Stoke-on-Trent. The up and down fast lines continue as double track to Stafford.

The semaphore-signalled Colwich Junction was re-signalled in 1966, with three-aspect colour-light signals on the Stone line and four-aspects on the WCML still operated by a signalman with manual levers from the existing signalbox. Those points, and their associated ground signals which were closest to the signalbox, were still worked by manual levers but the rather more distant crossovers from down fast to down slow and from down slow to down goods were electrically operated through manual levers. The colour-light signals were either fully automatic, operated by trains passing over track circuiting, or worked by the signalman. The down goods loop was removed in 1977.

On 17 August 1986 at Colwich, flashing aspects were brought into use on the down fast line in signals CH105 and CH103. These

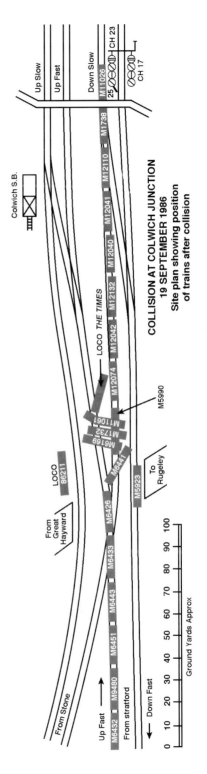

COLLISION AT COLWICH JUNCTION
19 SEPTEMBER 1986
Site plan showing position
of trains after collision

*Above:*
One carriage upside down on the left, four carriages lying side by side across the tracks. The sudden stop at high speed caused the train to fold itself up, concertina-fashion. *Andy Lowe*

signals were on the approach side — in rear — of CH28, which was the junction signal and indicator for crossover No 24 from down fast to down slow. The reason for introducing the flashing aspects here was to permit drivers to traverse the crossover at the full speed permitted — 50mph. For trains on the down fast, this crossover was the point of divergence from the WCML to the Stone-Stoke-Manchester line. When crossover No 24 was set for the route down fast to down slow, signal CH105 displayed flashing double yellows, CH103 a flashing single yellow and the junction signal at crossover No 24 — CH28 — would display a steady single yellow with a junction 'feather' until the approaching train's locomotive had passed the signal's AWS magnet. At that moment — if the aspects of the next signal ahead permitted — CH28 signal aspect would 'step-up' from one yellow to a less restrictive aspect. The speed limit across the fast to slow crossover was 50mph.

About 1,000yd in advance of CH28 was CH23 — the signal protecting the up fast from the train approaching on the down slow. CH23 was 259yd in the rear of the up fast where it cut through the down slow. In semaphore-signalled times this distance would have been 180yd — less than the minimum prescribed safety distance in that situation — and if CH23 were at 'Danger', trains would not have been allowed to approach it without severe restrictions. There was, on CH23, a junction indicator for the crossover from down slow to down fast. This

48

*Above:*
A view from above the down
fast line. The crash is down
the line on the left. Two men
on ladders attend to the
catenary while the road lorry
cranes are busy taking the
carriages off the track and
into the field. The second
track from the camera is the
down slow; the line to Stone
and the points from that to
down fast can be seen in the
foreground. The breakdown
vans are on the up slow.
*Andy Lowe*

crossover was not used as a 'trap' to divert trains from the down slow away from the up main because to do so would prevent a parallel movement from being signalled on the down fast.

The trains involved in the crash were the 1A76 Liverpool to Euston and the 1H20 5pm Euston to Manchester via Stoke-on-Trent. The driver of the latter train was Mr Shaw. He had been issued with the pamphlet giving the formal explanation of the flashing yellow aspects, but he had not seen the video and no footplate inspector had spoken to him about the new aspects — there were too few inspectors to see everyone in a short space of time. However, as an experienced driver he did his best to make sense of the new-fangled gadget and worked matters out for himself. He had never experienced the flashing yellow signals at Colwich, but he had worked successfully with the system at Hanslope Junction, Armitage and at Norton Bridge Junction, and believed he understood it. But the layouts he had negotiated at those places were less complex than the one he would encounter at Colwich. Feeling secure in his knowledge, he honestly admitted to the Inquiry that he had not read the recent Signalling Notices issued on three successive weeks, advising all concerned of the installation of flashing aspects at Colwich. Would Mr Shaw's misconceptions of what the new signalling was all about have changed even if he had read them? The advice issued in those August 1986 Signalling Notices was couched in standard terms in a format unchanged since these Notices started to be issued, pre-1914. They were terms which allow only the baldest statements of fact and, had I been the driver of a 500-ton, 100mph train, I would have liked to have had detailed instructions complete with a diagram, showing how the new system would affect — and be affected by — the Colwich location. Judging from the way the Notices were written, the railway management expected the men to work out such detail for themselves. In the absence of clear instruction and proper supervision, honest misconceptions arose.

Driver Shaw was on his electric locomotive, No 86429, at Euston on 19 September. He was waiting to take out the 5pm to Manchester via Stoke-on-Trent. He had started the day by booking on duty at Manchester (Piccadilly) at 11.50am to work the 12.15pm to Birmingham New Street and, arriving there, he had travelled 'on the cushions' of the 2.18pm to Euston. At Euston he had had some tea, eaten a couple of sandwiches and then walked to Platform 15 where his train was standing. He met his guard, Mr Sharif, who told him that they had 13 coaches for 444 tonnes and asked to carry out a brake continuity test. That done, there was nothing left but to await the 'Right Away'. Shortly before the train left, a young man came to the cab door, knocked and asked Driver Shaw if he could ride with him to Stoke-on-Trent. Mr Shaw thought he was a driver learning the road and, without more ado, let him onto the engine. A few minutes into the journey, this Mr Organ revealed that he was a trainee driver from the Southern Region, based at Brighton, and was travelling with a railwayman's free pass which was invalid on that particular train. They had an uneventful journey and, passing Rugeley at 100mph, Mr Shaw saw the flashing yellow aspects from a considerable distance away. He applied the brakes and had reduced speed to 60mph at the flashing single yellow aspect. Continuing to brake, he went past the CH28 aspect as a steady single yellow with its 'five white lights' or 'feather' and took the fast to slow crossover at 45mph. The turning to the Stone line, crossing the up main about 1,000yd ahead, was also a 45mph turn-out.

The single yellow aspect of CH28 did not 'step-up' as expected and the 'banner repeater' for CH23 remained obstinately horizontal, proving that the actual signal was displaying a red light. Driver Shaw, believing that the flashing yellow aspects he had seen were for the Stoke line divergence, braked some more but nevertheless approached the signal confident that it was 'time released' and would, in due course, step-up to a 'Proceed' aspect. Only as he got within a few yards of it did he realise that it was not going to change and, he said, 'made a full, emergency brake application'. With the brakes allegedly hard on, he passed signal CH23 at 'Danger', and then he and the trespassing Mr Organ saw the up express approaching at 100mph. Realising that the engine was going to foul the up main, both men jumped for their lives out of the left-hand door of the locomotive while it was travelling at 3 to 4mph. The engine stopped smack bang on the 'diamond' where the down slow crossed the up fast.

In the signalbox, Signalman Millward was watching the train from the window while Signal Technician Morgan had his back to the rails, washing his hands at the sink. Mr Millward shouted 'Where's he going?' and Mr Morgan immediately went to the window; both men witnessed the 100mph head-on impact. There was a great deal of noise as the up train rode over the top of the down and a coach came flying through the air to land close to the signalbox wall. In seconds a cloud of dust rose as if there had been an explosion, and obscured the scene. Then, out of the fog of stone-dust came bright blue flashes as the overhead catenary was swept away by tumbling coaches. Prior to the crash, neither the guard of the Euston to Manchester train nor the chief buffet steward were aware at any time of hard braking, although they were aware that the train was slowing down in order to take the crossover from fast

*Right:*
Looking north over the scene from above the up slow line. The white marks are not scratches on the negative but the tangled overhead wires tossed about when the tumbling coaches hit the stanchions. The down train was running on the track marked by the '45' permanent speed restriction sign. While most of the carriages slammed into each other, side-on, and piled across the track, one was forced outwards, in line with the track, and thrown 70ft to the up side of the line. It can be seen just beyond the signalbox.
*Andy Lowe*

to slow. Their first intimation that all was not well was when they were flung about in the shock of the collision.

Signalman Millward ran to his levers, replaced all signals to 'Danger' and alerted the emergency services. Signal Technician Morgan said that the runaway train gave no indication that it was under emergency braking, but was simply gliding past the box, braking normally.

Every seat was taken in the up express from Liverpool and there were passengers standing in the vestibules. The guard was Mr Mason. When the collision occurred he was examining tickets and was flung violently down the length of the central gangway until he grabbed a seat and clung to it as the coach careered over onto its side and shot along the track to the accompaniment of shrieks and yells from passengers and the sound of rending metal.

The train from Liverpool was hauled by electric locomotive No 86211 and driven by Mr Goode. In the tremendous impact he was the only person to lose his life.

Out of nearly 900 passengers — 373 in the down train and over 500 in the up train — only 75 were injured and of these only four were sufficiently seriously injured to be kept in hospital for several weeks. Of the others, 32 were hospitalised for periods ranging from one day to a week. This was bad, of course, but it is remarkable that there were not more casualties, given the nature of the collision. Certainly, the outcome must have been vastly better than one would have expected from a 100mph head-on pile-up on the M6.

Driver Shaw went to the signalbox and said to the signalman: 'You had double flashing yellows and the route was set for Stoke.' To this the signalman replied: 'You passed the red signal.'

Driver Shaw had pointed out to Mr Organ the flashing aspects as they approached Colwich, so one may, perhaps, infer that Mr Shaw was trying to be helpful to the would-be driver. Mr Shaw appears to have become confused. The difficulty arose because the crossover and the diverging route were so close together. There was no flashing aspect for the diverging route, only for the crossover. In his mind he had got it the other way round. He thought the flashing aspects he could see ahead applied not to that crossover but to the diverging Stone route, 1,000yd further on. It was his experience at Norton Junction that flashing aspects meant that he 'had the road' across the junction, and thought that in this case he could proceed towards Stone, subject to the usual speed restriction. As mentioned above, the original Notice issued for these flashing signals in 1978 had said that they would be installed at 'diverging junctions'. Having got this fact into his head, Driver Shaw had to find an explanation for the puzzling red light in CH23 which, according to the way he was thinking, ought to have been at least a steady single yellow. He rationalised the mystery by assuming that it was a delayed-release aspect — as had once been the case at so many junctions.

It is a subtle thing, but, once any person's mind is confidently made up as to a course of action, he or she will conscientiously act accordingly. The original pamphlet issued with these signals said they would apply to 'diverging routes', hence Mr Shaw's understanding of the aspects at Norton Bridge. The close connection between the crossover and the divergence misled him, and he fell into a trap laid by the sloppy thinking of others.

The original notice explaining these signals was misleading and not sufficiently explanatory — but even if it had been perfectly explanatory, Drive Shaw admitted he had not read it. He had received no training, no supervision in these strange new signals. he had successfully negotiated the new system at Norton Junction where the layout was simple and this success gave him the confidence which had misled him for the different situation at Colwich.

Fifteen years have passed since the tragedy at Colwich, but still the promiscuous use of flashing signals at closely-connected junctions is an accident waiting to happen. On 4 February 1998 near Paddington and in mid-February 2000 at Filton, there occurred instances where a train driver was negotiating a complex layout in Railtrack's Great Western Zone exactly the same as that at Colwich. He became confused and ended up passing the junction signal at 'Danger' — luckily without any adverse effect.

The 'flashing aspects' system undoubtedly confused several drivers and this has been acknowledged because recently the old principle of the 'splitting distant' returned to Britain in an improved format. In 1997, for the new railway to Heathrow Airport from Paddington, the signal next in rear of the junction signal at Airport Junction was installed with an offset head. When the junction signal has cleared to its 'Proceed' aspect, the main head of the signal in rear shows a single yellow and the offset head will repeat the aspect of the junction signal. The double yellow signal next in rear has a 'banner' repeater consisting of brilliant lights arranged as a vertical arrow or a horizontal arrow pointing to the left, depending upon which way the Airport Junction points are set. The driver will receive AWS warnings from the various yellow aspects. This system was also installed at Tilehurst East Junction, about two miles west of Reading, in 1998.

# Glanrhyd Bridge :
## 19 October 1987

Nobody would ever think that they could be drowned whilst riding in a train. But then we all live with the perpetual assumption that whatever befalls will befall someone else.

The River Tywi flows from the side of Caron-y-Clawdd, 1,500ft above the sea in the wild, green hills northeast of Lampeter. Tumbling musically down its steep cleft, through woods, over boulders, and fed by many a sparkling mountain brook, it cascades for 15 miles, falling 1,250ft to Llandovery at the rate of 83ft per mile. It sweeps out of the hills here into a wider valley, passing the little town on the west side. It is a powerful river, flowing southwest to Llandeilo, Carmarthen and the sea.

In the 7½ miles of its course from Llandovery to the railway bridge at Glan-Rhyd-Saeson, the river falls approximately 100ft, and on the way is reinforced by a number of potentially-powerful streams, all with their springs in the high hills. Pouring their weight into the Tywi are the Afon Bran, a mile below Llandovery, the Afon Dulais, a couple of miles below that and, at Llangadog, one mile above the railway bridge, no fewer than three rivers: the Afon Sawdde, another Afon Bran and the Afon Marlais. After Llandovery, the river might seem 'mature', broad and meandering in its beautiful valley, but 'mature' is not necessarily 'sedate', and the Tywi has always been well known, locally at any rate, for its sudden and extreme changes of mood.

**GLANRHYD BRIDGE**

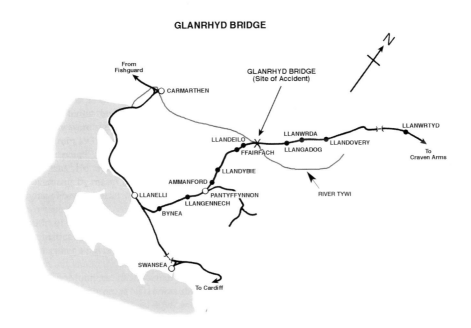

The railway through this part of the valley of the Afon Tywi was constructed by the Vale of Tywi Railway Co and was opened to traffic in 1858. The Glanrhyd bridge, at that stage, was a timber trestle construction, crossing the river at a skew angle of 46°. The Vale of Tywi Co was amalgamated with the LNWR in 1884 and the latter company replaced — perhaps in the 1890s — the timber trestle at Glanrhyd with five wrought-iron, box-girder spans resting on four brick piers and two brick abutments. The spans were numbered 1 to 5 and were 50ft, 56ft, 56ft, 56ft and 49ft in length. The supporting piers were similarly numbered 1 to 4: No 1 close to the Llandeilo bank of the river, No 2 in midstream and Nos 3 and 4 normally founded in dry land. The bridge was inundated on occasions by the river in flood, and records show that one of the piers was undermined in 1929 when the river scoured deep into its bed around the foundations. In 1958, the riveted wrought-iron box girders were replaced with plate girders made of steel. The weight of the new girders was almost exactly the same as that of the old box girders, and no alteration was made to the foundations of the old piers, although cast concrete caps were added to the tops of the piers in order that the bridge be raised an additional 38½ in above the river. This increased the weight on the foundations but no attention was given to strengthening them, and they continued to be at risk from the scouring action of the river. Raising the height of the bridge track put it above the height of the approach track, so that trains ran up a slope to cross the bridge.

Paragraphs 91 and 92 of the Ministry of Transport Report into the accident are very badly written, but they appear to say that the bridge was given a thorough examination by a trained engineer every three years with no intermediate examination, but then, in 1984, this was relaxed (like so many costly regulations) to a thorough examination every six years with an annual look-over.

This six-year inspection entailed the use of a special piece of equipment, commonly known as the 'Gozunda', for examining the girders where they spanned the water and for careful inspection of the piers so far as they were visible below the water line. If there was damage which suggested the need for an underwater inspection team, that inspection would then be arranged, but visible damage might have to be rather extensive before it could be seen above the water. Repairs were carried out in 1970, 1976 and 1982.

During the 1982 inspection the bridge examiner found a hole in the brickwork of the upstream cutwater of the No 2 pier. A diver was sent down and he found a 'deep scour-hole', worn away by the force of the river which was undermining the cutwater. This damage did not extend to the load-bearing pier, but even so the hole was deep enough to contain 'medium-sized trees and parts of trees', and there was debris from 'a metre-square piece of brickwork which had fallen from the [cutwater] pier'. The river could clearly continue to attack its bed here with the scour-hole extending until it engulfed the foundations of the load-bearing pier.

The scour-hole was excavated to a depth of 6ft below the top surface of the river bed down to hard ground, but not down to the level of the foundations of the pier. A wall of hessian bags, filled with concrete to form a coffer dam, was then built up at a distance from — but following the shape of — the cutwater. This bag work was taken up to water-surface level and fastened together with steel rods. The space between the bag work and the cutwater was then filled with poured concrete to a height above the water level existing at the time of the work. The railway civil engineers in charge of the bridge were very capable, experienced men but, as the Report into the accident 'regrets', they had no specialist knowledge of the way powerfully-active rivers work — how the flow of water is affected by obstructions to its passage. The repairs they carried out actually exacerbated the river's scouring effect on its bed around the piers.

A good idea of the river's dangerously erratic behaviour can be gathered from the fact that, at the time the work was undertaken, the water was so low that the road vehicles of the work team were parked on a midstream island, close to the pier receiving attention. One day, while the team was working, a water bailiff came tearing along the river bank with a warning that a wall of water was coming down the river, carrying trees and debris. The men rushed to their vehicles and got them off the island and on the bank seconds before the miniature tidal wave swept past. One heavy tree stump was being tumbled over and over by the advancing wave and this rammed the work, causing damage.

*Above:*
The leading end of the rear coach, seen from the opposite bank. The river level has fallen a little since the bridge piers were undermined but the water is still high enough to give an impression of frightening velocity. One can almost hear the muddy water thundering through and around the bridge and train.
*Western Evening Mail*

The weekend of 17/18 October 1987 in southwest Wales was one of persistent heavy rain. According to the Welsh Water Authority's records, in 27 hours as much as 200mm, or 7½ in, had fallen. The rain was still falling heavily on Monday morning, 19 October. After 60 hours of torrential rain falling on the hills during the weekend, the beautiful River Tywi, engorged by its several tributaries, transformed itself into an ugly, angry monster.

The Welsh Water Authority gauging station, located three miles downstream of the bridge, recorded the river at that point as being 12ft 4in deep from 10pm on Saturday until 1am on Sunday. This was the highest level recorded since the station was opened in 1967. The river was covering about 550yd of its flood plain. The Glanrhyd bridge was right in the middle of the valley and so had water on each bank for 225yd. Welsh Water experts calculated that the centre of the river was flowing at about 6mph, but where it passed between the piers of the bridge the area available for its passage was restricted, so that the velocity of the water was increased to 10.5mph. During the peak period of the flood, between 10pm and 1am, it was estimated by a Welsh Water Authority hydrologist that 17,000 metric tons of mud were carried past the bridge, and to that was being added the bed of the river down to and beneath the foundations of the bridge piers. If the piers had been directly in line with the flow, the force exerted on them by the weight of water would have been zero, but they were at a 10° angle to the water and thus subject to pressure.

In 1980 the Welsh Water Authority introduced a system of graded flood warnings with the impressively military and efficient names of: 'Amber Alert', 'Red One' and 'Red Two'. Only six years after the introduction of the scheme, the Water Authority published a booklet explaining the scheme; what it meant, how it worked and a list of those organisations to whom the booklet was to be issued. 'Red One' was a warning of limited flooding liable to damage fields and buildings. 'Red Two' was the most serious warning, indicating a risk of very severe flooding which posed a threat to life and property. British Rail owned track which ran for miles on the very banks of the river and which bridged the Tywi — or one of its tributaries — 10 times in as many miles. British Rail was *not* one of the organisations listed as a recipient of this informative booklet. This lack of inclusion in a charmed circle of recipients seems to me to indicate the lack of prestige suffered by the railway in the 1980s — Welsh Water never gave it a thought.

A 'Red One' alert had been issued nine times since 1980 but for the first time ever Welsh Water issued a 'Red Two' alert at 7.20pm on Sunday 18 October. These alerts were handed to radio and television but no railway official questioned at the Inquiry mentioned having heard the 'Red Two' warnings broadcast. So, as the weather and the risks worsened, the railway operating people received no alarm messages.

On Sunday 18 October, Driver Rossiter had driven an engineering train up the Central Wales line to Llandrindod Wells. He had taken it to be stabled in sidings at Craven Arms at the end of the job and in the evening he had driven 'light engine' back to Pantyffynnon. The rain had been falling like a monsoon all day but the railway was not threatened until it entered the valley of the River Tywi at Llandovery. Between Llandovery and Llanwrda, around Milepost 26, there was water running through the ballast but it was not up to the rails. At about 9.15pm Rossiter stopped his engine on the Glanrhyd bridge to look at the river. It was thundering below, he could hear the noise and, although it was pitch dark, he could see light reflecting dimly on the roaring, surging water. He thought the river was 3ft below the bridge. He had been driving over the line for 10 years and had never seen the river so powerful and so angry. And indeed, the river was, at 9.15pm, only 45min away from reaching its highest level for 30 years, a mere 18in below the bridge. One wonders how close the bridge was to collapse when Driver Rossiter and his engine were standing on it.

Rossiter eased off the bridge, presumably taking matters cautiously, and found flooding at Milepost 21 with ballast washed out from between the sleepers. Just north of Llandeilo, at Milepost 18½, the valley was only ¼ mile wide and the river was washing over the top of the rails. On arrival at Llandeilo, Driver Rossiter telephoned Signalman Bowen at Pantyffynnon to warn him of the flooding and gave the three mileages where he had seen flooding of the track: 18½, 21 and 26. Signalman Bowen, who had been at Pantyffynnon for eight years, telephoned the 'on call' Operating Manager, Mr Scott, and the local Permanent Way Supervisor, Mr Davies, to pass on this information. The 'on call' Civil Engineer was Mr Andrews of Swansea. He should also have been advised but was not called, probably because he was a remote figure to the signalman, whereas Mr Davies was well known to the signalman and, indeed, a living part of the railway. Mr Bowen closed the signalbox at 10.35pm and went home for a brief rest before returning for another eight hours' duty at 5.30am next morning.

Mr Davies had been employed in the Permanent Way Department of the Central Wales line since 1950 and had been Supervisor of the Llandrindod Wells district for five years. This one man had a district extending all the way south to Llandeilo. He had been working with the aforementioned engineering train, north of Llandrindod, in continuous, pouring rain from

# COLLAPSE OF GLANRHYD BRIDGE ON 19 OCTOBER 1987

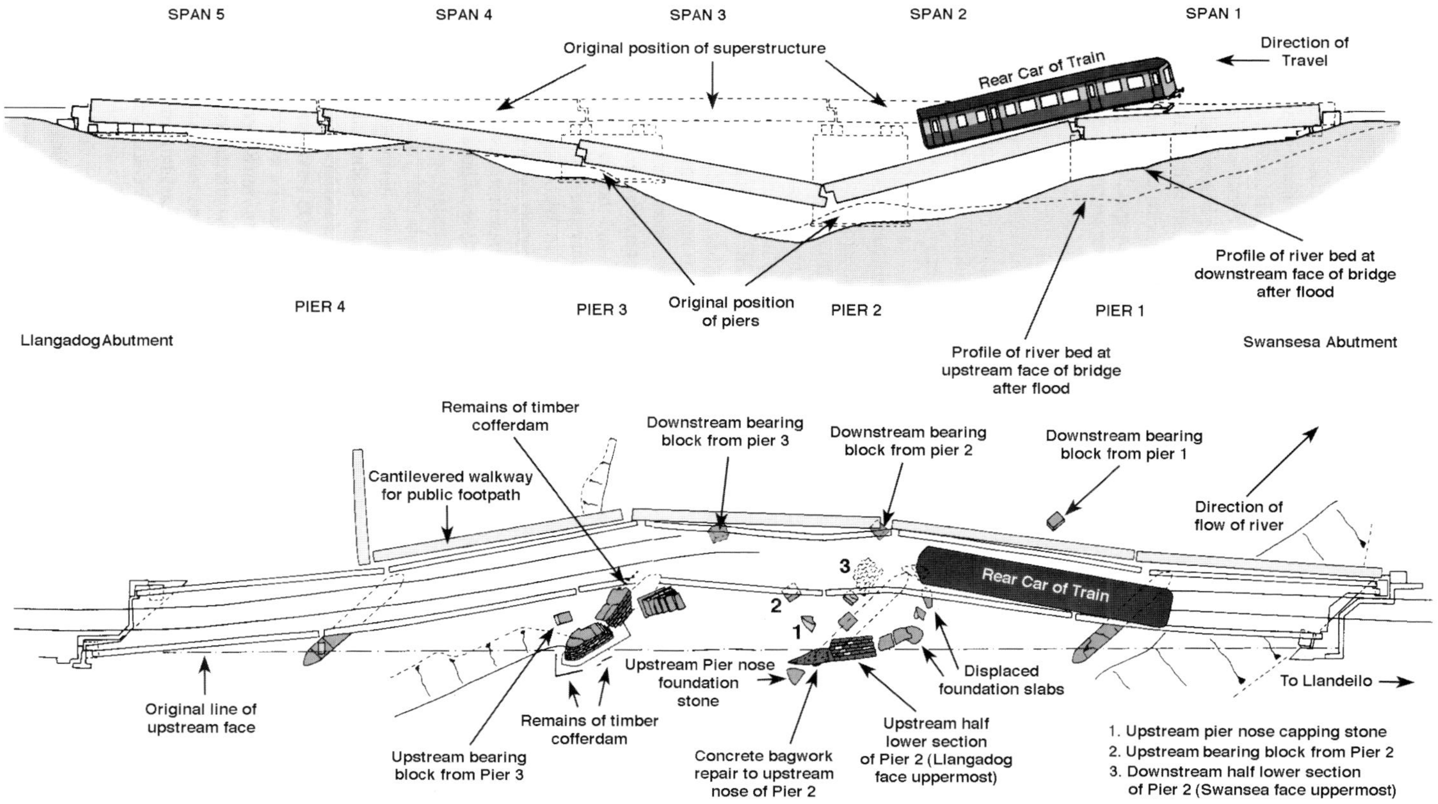

SPAN 5

SPAN 4

SPAN 3

SPAN 2

SPAN 1

Direction of Travel

Rear Car of Train

Profile of river bed at downstream face of bridge after flood

Profile of river bed at upstream face of bridge after flood

Original position of superstructure

Original position of piers

PIER 1

PIER 2

PIER 3

PIER 4

Swansea Abutment

Llangadog Abutment

To Llandeilo

Direction of flow of river

Rear Car of Train

Downstream bearing block from pier 1

Downstream bearing block from pier 2

Downstream bearing block from pier 3

Displaced foundation slabs

Upstream half lower section of Pier 2 (Llangadog face uppermost)

Concrete bagwork repair to upstream nose of Pier 2

Upstream Pier nose foundation stone

Remains of timber cofferdam

Remains of timber cofferdam

Cantilevered walkway for public footpath

Upstream bearing block from Pier 3

Original line of upstream face

1. Upstream pier nose capping stone
2. Upstream bearing block from Pier 2
3. Downstream half lower section of Pier 2 (Swansea face uppermost)

57

## LAYOUT OF LEADING CAR OF DIESEL-MULTIPLE-UNIT TRAIN

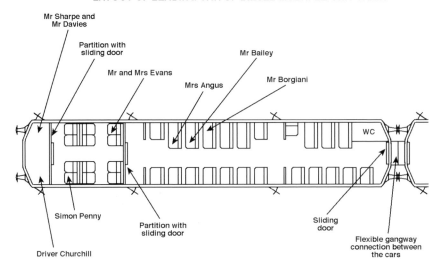

5.45am until 4.45pm that Sunday. He got the call from Pantyffynnon at 10pm, at a time when, I suppose, he had become warm, dry and cosy again, with a good meal inside him, and was thinking of going to bed. His feelings can be imagined, but of course there is no hint of them in the Official Report which states that 'the news did not surprise him'. Given the dreadful conditions Mr Davies had endured all day, and in view of his lifetime experience of the river and its floods, this is a splendid piece of understatement to mask what he really thought. Mr Davies may then have gone to bed. If so, he was woken from his slumbers at 3.45am on Monday morning with a telephone call from Mr Scott and, half an hour later, Mr Davies was back on the road again, in the cold, rain and darkness.

Mr Scott received the telephone call from Signalman Bowen at his home at 10pm on 18 October. The message was that the driver of a 'light' engine had reported flooding of the track in the vicinity of Mileposts 18, 21 and 26, and that the ballast was being washed away. Mr Scott was the 'on call' Operating Manager for the Swansea area. He was supposed to be able to cover the whole of West and South Wales and the Central Wales line. One hears of the 'Thin Red Line' and the 'Thin Blue Line' and wonders what is the colour of an exceptionally thin line of railway managers. Mr Scott had gone to work at around 8am on 18 October, getting home at about 6pm, and so had had about four hours' rest when he received the 'call out' at 10pm. He was then on duty until the evening of 19 October — nearly 38 hours without sleep. At 10pm on 18 October, Mr Scott did not think of calling out the 'on call' engineer but advised the supervisor at Swansea (High Street) that the Central Wales line was under threat from floods and that the 5.27am to Shrewsbury might have to be held back or used to examine the line. He then drove from his home to Llandeilo to see the dangers for himself. Driving through a deep flood at Ffairfach he reached Llandeilo. The Llandovery road just north of the town was deeply inundated. It was clear that he could not take his car through and he tried to walk, but the water was rising so fast that he was in danger of being cut off from dry land. So, he regained his car and drove back to examine the railway south of Llandeilo. He got onto the line between Ffairfach and Llandeilo and, in torrential rain and darkness, began to walk towards Llandeilo. The sound of roaring water was all around, but after a few minutes he met a man out walking his dog along the track! Mr Scott went on and stopped on a bridge over the Tywi. There was scaffolding on the upstream side that was damming the river, piling the water higher on that side than the other. But the places where the river was known to be over the line were six miles away and, in such extreme conditions, he knew he could not walk all that way and turned back. The Report states that he arrived home at 1am where he received a telephone call from the supervisor at Carmarthen to the effect that the station had become engulfed so deeply as to have been abandoned. Mr Scott advised Regional Control at Swindon and then set off to drive to Carmarthen. The floods were so deep he could not get into the town, but with considerable effort he managed to get to the signalbox to the east of the station at Carmarthen Junction. There he found a message asking him to contact Mr Davies, the Llandrindod Section Permanent Way Supervisor. The only way to get hold of him by 'phone was 'on the national' (the BT network). Scott waded back through dark and floods to the road and a public telephone. Davies told him that the line was flooded south and north of Llandeilo and his men were unable to get to any of the sites by road. Scott told him that the 5.27am Swansea-Shrewsbury passenger train would be used to examine the line and that he, Scott, would accompany the train. At about 3.30am on Monday 19 October, Mr Scott finally made it through the floods to Carmarthen station and began to organise a temporary train service according to the resources available — empty coaches being stranded in the wrong place and some staff being physically unable to get into work. He then realised that he would not be able to accompany the 5.27am from Swansea and so, at about 4.20am, he telephoned Mr Sharpe, asleep at his home, and asked him to carry out the examination of the Central Wales line to ensure its safety in view of the reports of flooding at the three locations. Mr Sharpe was the back-up 'on call' manager that day. He held the position of Customer Services Manager at Swansea, the equivalent, I suppose, of the old title 'Station Master'. Previously, he had been Traffic Manager at Woking.

Mr Sharpe must have groaned, but he got dressed, drove to Swansea station, arriving there 'at about 5.5am' and took stock of the situation. At that time he believed that Mr Davies would meet the train at Llandeilo and accompany it as it examined the line on the way north. He did not, therefore, accompany the train from Swansea as there seemed no point. He clearly did not appreciate the extent of the flooding. And so, according to the Report, the train left 'about five minutes after he arrived', which would have been at about 5.10am. But it was not scheduled to leave until 5.27am, so this must be an error in the evidence. At about 6.5am Sharpe heard from Signalman Bowen that the Swansea-Shrewsbury was waiting at Pantyffynnon for some competent person to accompany it through the flooded areas because Mr Davies had been unable to reach the station owing to heavy flooding. Mr Sharpe then told Mr Bowen to hold the train, and that he would drive from Swansea to join it. He got to Pantyffynnon at 6.40am and the train arrived at Llandeilo at about 7.5am. It was a two-car diesel multiple-unit of Class 108, built in 1960.

Daylight was just then beginning to grey the eastern sky as the train pulled out. There were nine people on board: the driver, Mr Churchill; the guard, Mr Anderson and Mr Sharpe, the 'competent person', accompanying it in accordance with Regulation 9, Clause 1(iv) 'Examination of the Line'. There were six passengers: Mr and Mrs Evans and a teenager, Simon Penny, were in the First-class section at the front of the leading car; Mr Borgiani, Mrs Angus and Mr Bailey were in the Second-class seating area, also in the front car.

After the accident, much understandable fuss was made by those who suffered in the crash, by the relatives of the dead and, of course, by the press over the fact that a train conveying passengers should have been used to examine the defective line in such extreme conditions. In steam days, the Regulation governing procedure for examining the line when there was a suspected track defect allowed nothing but an engine to be used for examination. From 1 May 1969 the Regulation was amended to allow a passenger train to be used. In some circumstances there is nothing wrong with this, but it does depend very much on the circumstances. If there had been a report of a railway sleeper having been placed on the line it would be safe to use a passenger train because the sleeper, when found, could easily be removed. If the driver of a train reported a 'bump' or a 'lurch' the line could safely be examined using a passenger train. But if a driver reported a landslide it would not be appropriate to use a passenger train. The Regulation had always been worded very simply and very loosely: 'If it is necessary to ascertain if a line is clear'. Once the Regulation was relaxed to permit a passenger train to be used to search for a track defect, there should have been a tightening of the conditions, but these remained as before, provided the driver could clearly see the track. Thus the use of a passenger train was ruled out in fog, falling snow or where the reported defect was inside a tunnel. There was not, and never had been, even in GWR Regulations, any mention of the specific problem of floods and the peculiar dangers these pose to track and bridges. Until May 1969 this did not matter because no passenger train was used for examination. But when the British Railways Board relaxed the Regulation, it ought to have tightened the wording so as to minimise the risk to passengers when the conditions under which the examination was undertaken were very severe or risky. The relaxation of the Regulation had everything to do with the universal desire for speed, expedition and no delay to daily business. Signalmen can only apply the instructions, word for word. The driver was told that he had to beware of floods just north of Llandeilo at Mileposts 18½, 21 and 26. Glanrhyd bridge was near the 22nd milepost, but had not been included in the warning.

The train set out to examine the line, hoping thereby to continue on its journey without the delay of sending an engine through — under caution — first. Mr Sharpe was riding in the cab with Driver Churchill. Two hundred yards after leaving Llandeilo they were stopped by Mr Davies, the Permanent Way Supervisor, showing the driver a red light from the track. Water was running under the rails between the sleepers. Mr Davies told them to wait and went off, returning, the Report states, with a sleeper which he pushed under the rails where the flowing water had entirely washed away the ballast. Mr Davies was clearly a strong and resourceful man. He then climbed into the cab and gave the driver the order to proceed. That took care of the problem at Milepost 18½. The next trouble spot was near Milepost 21 and Driver Churchill took the train along at around 15mph. As they approached that spot Mr Churchill shut off power and began to brake, but Mr Davies, looking ahead, said, 'That's OK,' so the train coasted on, over brown water running through the ballast. 'The next place is Milepost 26,' Mr Sharpe said to Driver Churchill.

Churchill let the train coast because the Glanrhyd level crossing was not far ahead, over which there was a 10mph speed restriction. Two hundred yards beyond that was the Glanrhyd bridge over the raging Tywi. It is a pity that the railwaymen did not use their imagination to work out what might lie ahead. Back in the passenger compartment Mrs Angus had had a wet morning already. She had waited for the train in the pelting rain at Llandybie and had not expected it to arrive from Swansea because 'the conditions were appalling'. She boarded the train, doubtless grateful to the brave but unimaginative railwaymen who had got through to her, albeit late, so that she could undertake her business trip to Manchester. Now, as the train crept along the line in that most dismal dawn, she felt even more apprehensive. She had never seen flooding like it. At Llandeilo the railway and river are as close as they can be and now, as they left the station, the river was 'a raging torrent', roaring past level with the rails on both sides and washing through the sleepers. It was so bad that, as they stopped to pick up the imperturbable Mr Davies — who had been standing out in the middle of all this — she, along with Mr and Mrs Evans, rose to her feet. They were all 'terrified', and said so to each other. When the train set off again, she tried to take her mind off the appalling scene outside by reading a book.

Farmer Davies and his son Carwyn farmed the land bordering the river close to the Glanrhyd bridge. When they got out of bed at 6.15am to bring the cows in for milking they found the river up to the house and the cows bellowing in the fields. It was still quite dark so they waited until dawn was breaking at 7am to go and investigate. Carwyn Davies went out, crossed the road and entered the field at the far end of which was the railway bridge. He was up to his waist in water which was flowing so strongly that he had to cling to the hedge to avoid being swept off his feet. He could hear the train coming and looked towards the bridge about 400yd away. Normally it seemed quite high above the water, but now it was only just visible in the semi-darkness, barely above the level of the dark water. It was not, however, a dark horizontal line, but a dark 'V'-shaped one. Carwyn Davies was faced with a nightmare. The bridge was down and a train was within earshot. As he tried to run back to the house to call the emergency services, he found he could only run at that terrifying 'nightmare' pace normally associated with dreams because the water was so deep and fast-flowing against his legs. He looked over his shoulder and saw the train come onto the bridge, quite slowly, and the first coach 'take off' then fall into and under the water before bobbing up again and floating. He struggled back to the house and raised the alarm.

The train rode up the slope to the bridge at 10-12mph. Because of the rising gradient those in the cab could not see that the girders had fallen into the river until they were breasting the rise. 'Hang on!' shouted Driver Churchill, and braked hard.

Supervisor Davies saw the collapsed bridge at the same moment as the driver braked. Sharpe looked out of the cab side window and saw there was no escape into the river but, looking back, he saw the carriage rapidly filling with water rising towards the rear coach, which was still attached and approximately horizontal. He was first out of the central door of the cab into the section for First-class passengers. Mr Davies was close behind him and Driver Churchill last. Mr Sharpe had to push open the door between the First- and Second-class sections. Simon Penny had been sitting in the front seat behind the driver and would have been thrown hard against the glass partition, while Mr and Mrs Evans, sitting next to the door into the Second-class area, must have been thrown forward onto the floor when the leading car nose-dived into the river.

Mr Sharpe struggled past them, through the door, up the sloping floor, past Mrs Angus, Mr Bailey and Mr Borgiani, through the gangway, into the rear car, past the guard and within a minute was climbing down onto a bridge girder. Having found a way out Mr Sharpe climbed back into the rear coach and, standing on the level gangway of the latter, he called, 'this way out.'

Mrs Angus testified to the fact that she was thrown hard against the First-class glass partition, at least 6ft in front of her, when the train crashed, so it is reasonable to assume that all those in the car were thrown forward into a heap on the floor. They picked themselves up, because Mrs Angus stated that: 'We all stood there stunned — that is all I can say — for quite a while — time is difficult — it seemed like half an hour but of course it wasn't.' From Mrs Angus's evidence it appears that some of the passengers were shocked and too terrified to move. She heard a voice calling them to come back to the rear but, because the water was rushing between the two cars it seemed as if the water was higher up and so she could not move. Someone she thought was the guard came into the car and tried to persuade them — or her — but this person left and again she was called to come back. After what seemed like 10 minutes, the water was deeper in the carriage and so she half-swam, half-walked up the coach and so reached the safety of the rear car. She left behind her, in the first class section, Mr Churchill, Mr Davies and Simon Penny, and when she finally got through the roaring flood rushing between the two cars she was surprised that they were not behind her.

It seems possible — but the Report does not say — that Mrs Evans was finding it difficult to leave. Mr Davies said he 'encouraged Mrs Evans to leave' and assisted her up the slope to the gangway, but obviously he went through the gangway first. Simon Penny and Driver Churchill were still trying to help Mr and Mrs Evans when the coupling broke, allowing the front coach and all those within it to be swept away by the river.

# King's Cross:
## 18 November 1987

The first 'Underground' railway in London — and the first in the world — was opened by the Metropolitan Railway Co on 10 January 1863. It was not strictly underground but in a covered-over cutting. It ran from Bishop's Road station, on the northern edge of the GWR Paddington station, to Farringdon Street. It was, of course, steam-hauled, so fire was a necessary part of the early Underground. The line was extended into the well-known circular route and extensions were added by the Metropolitan District Railway, with all of these services remaining steam-hauled until 1903. In that year there was a terrible fire at the Couronne station on the Paris Metro which burned or choked to death 84 people and maimed many more. In response to the Paris Metro fire, the British Board of Trade, in 1904, prohibited the use of unsuitable wood in Underground railways. Between 1911 and 1915, 22 escalators were introduced into 10 Underground stations, starting at Earl's Court, between the Piccadilly and District Line platforms. These were made of wood and plywood, the latter's laminated layers being held together with glue and heavily coated in varnish to become almost as inflammable as nitro-glycerine. So, from the days when the Underground was relatively new, its management felt it could ignore fire risk and fire-prevention regulations. There was, on the Underground, even in 1911, a mentality which regarded outbreaks of fire as 'just one of those things' — an occupational hazard. By 1987, fire was regarded by senior management as inevitable 'with a system of this age'. Management went further than this and actually tried to deceive itself that fires did not happen on the Underground. Management insisted that a fire should never be referred to as a fire but by the euphemism 'a smouldering'.

To an outsider such as myself, knowing nothing about the Underground except what is contained in the very extensive and exhaustive Fennell Report, the strong impression is conveyed of an organisation cut off from the rest of the world. Perhaps this is the result of being underground. The various management departments were separate bodies with little communication between them. These separate compartments jealously guarded their independence from each other and the whole lot jealously defended themselves from any outside interference. Where legislation on fire precautions was concerned, they were literally a 'law unto themselves', using a smokescreen of semantics to avoid their obvious duty to the rest of humanity. It is a truly remarkable thing that, instead of being happy to implement fire precautions, London Underground management looked for loopholes to avoid them and turned a deaf ear to the urgings of senior London Fire Brigade officers. At the King's Cross fire inquiry Dr Tony Ridley, Chairman & Managing Director of London Underground, was asked by the Inspector, Desmond Fennell: 'You cannot regard fire as an acceptable hazard, can you? A fire is not an occupational hazard, is it?' To which Dr Ridley replied: 'There have been fires, or smoulderings, on London Underground year in and year out. They are part of the nature of the oldest, most extensive, most complex underground railway in the world. Anyone who believes that it is possible so to act that there are no fires ever, is, I fear, misguided.' The second sentence of Dr Ridley's answer is confusing, but he was understood by Desmond Fennell to be taking the view that there will always be some fires, no matter what is done. Mr Fennell responded by saying, 'That is quite a different thing from concluding that one should not make practical efforts in order to reduce the number of fires.' (Fennell Report into King's Cross Fire, page 237.)

If the Board of Trade 1904 prohibition had been adhered to in 1911 when the first escalators were installed, and then throughout the life of the Underground subsequently, many fires would have been prevented. Excusing negligence by pointing to the age of a system when, throughout all that same age, fire-prevention laws, regulations and the urgings of the Fire Brigade have been ignored seems a lame excuse.

The London Underground workers were keen and railwayman-like with regard to the operating of the system. There were voluntary improvement classes and formal training courses in all matters referring to the signalling and the driving and guarding of the trains, with leaflets, pamphlets and diagrams issued. This was the interesting stuff. But fire regulations? A series of reports from within London Underground and from the London Fire Brigade had repeatedly drawn attention both to the lack of training in emergency procedures and to the fire hazards on the system. The fact that these warnings were repeated must imply that they were not acted upon.

Meanwhile the years passed and scores of fires happened without hurting anyone. The 'catch trays' underneath the top of each escalator were inches deep in thousands of 'dog-ends' at any time between the 1920s and 1980s when it was unusual not to smoke — and also unusual to clear out the catch trays. Burning butts were thrown on the wooden treads of escalators and were dumped, burning, into the catch trays, usually without incident, and if there was a fire it caused no fatality. There were 77 fires on escalators between 1939 and 1944. This high figure, was, I suppose, influenced by the use of the Underground as air-raid shelters by thousands of Londoners. On 24 December 1944 the Bakerloo Line escalators at Paddington were gutted by fire. The cause was attributed to a lighted match or glowing cigarette end.

After the Paddington fire on Christmas Eve 1944 'water fog' equipment was installed, and by 1948 19 escalators had been equipped. Three were installed on the Piccadilly Line escalators at King's Cross. The equipment created a fine spray of water which was turned on late at night for one minute when no-one was on the escalators. This dampened them thoroughly so that anything that might be smouldering out of sight would be extinguished. After a while it was found that the water was causing corrosion in the mechanism of the rising staircases and so it was decided to turn the sprinklers on once a fortnight — to damp down anything which might be smouldering. This was nonsense, of course, and in effect the water-fog system had been abandoned.

Between 1956 and 1987 there were 400 fires on the Underground, of which 42 were on escalators, 32 of these being caused by smokers' materials. Automatic switching-on of the water-fog sprays was envisaged, but that required an efficient smoke detector. The first detector was tried at Tottenham Court Road in 1954, and 10 years later another was fitted at Baker Street. These detectors gave an alarm but were not linked to the water sprays. It was also the case that they gave more false than real alarms. Even as late as 1976, new smoke detectors installed for trial were found to be unreliable. Not until 1986 was a better smoke detector installed, experimentally, at Euston. There was an intention to create an automatic linkage between the detectors and the water-fog equipment. One year, the proposal even got as far as being 'minuted' as going into the budget, but when the debits for the budget were written the alarm/water-fog link was not included. In another year the idea was resurrected but then buried again because — so the argument ran — the escalators were by then so old that it was not worth spending anything on them. But, at the same time, replacement schedules were such that some of the wooden escalators were expected to be in service another 20 years.

Even after the passing of the 1974 Health & Safety at Work Act, Underground safety officers felt they were 'voices in the wilderness', while the urgings of the London Fire Brigade were either ignored or obeyed slowly and reluctantly. The Chief Fire Inspector reported the same problems of litter, grease and faulty electrical wiring in the escalator machine rooms year after year without any action being taken. Not one of the escalator machine rooms had been fitted with a water sprinkler at the time of the King's Cross fire.

The question springs to mind — how was it possible that premises where there were such large and well-known fire risks were allowed to continue functioning? Who issued the annual fire certificate? The Offices, Shops & Railway Premises Act of 1963, the Fire Precautions Act of 1971 and the Health & Safety at Work Act 1974 all required that railway premises be free of unnecessary fire hazards. The 1971 Act stated that it applied to 'railway premises' as defined in the 1963 Act. The latter described 'railway premises' as 'a building occupied by railway undertakers for the purposes of railway undertaking and situated on or near the permanent way'. Given the well-known fire danger inherent in wooden escalators, how was it possible that King's Cross Underground station was awarded a fire certificate? The answer is simple and thoroughly astounding. London Underground did not believe that the station constituted railway premisis within the meaning of the various Acts. The Railway Inspectorate was of the same opinion. So King's Cross Underground station was outside the law and did not have a fire certificate.

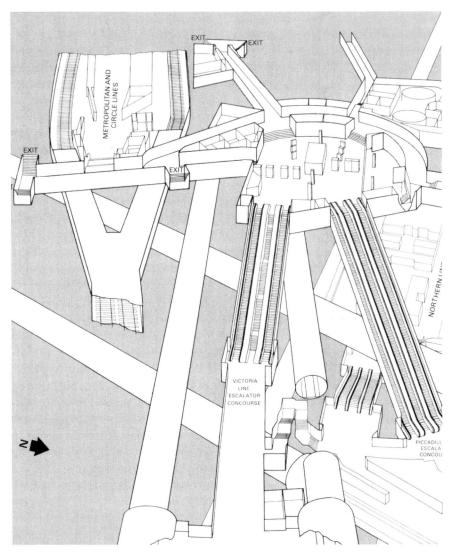

Under the 1974 Act, the Her Majesty's Railway Inspectorate (HMRI) became an Agency of the Health & Safety Commission (HSC). The Chief Inspecting Officer of Railways of HMRI was then able to enforce improvements to safety by issuing improvement and prohibition notices, and, failing any action from the offenders, HMRI could prosecute under Section 3 of the Act. Section 3 laid a statutory obligation on employers that they conduct their undertakings 'in such a way as to ensure that persons not in his employment who may be affected thereby are not thereby exposed to risk to their health or safety'.

The Chief Inspecting Officer of Railways' understanding of the law was that his task was to ensure that railway operating procedures were safe and carried out correctly, and also that railway workers were not exposed to danger. This belief arose because there were earlier Acts, going back into history, which had already laid on railway operators the statutory duty of carrying the public safely. Therefore, if the managers of London Underground had carried out the provisions of those earlier Acts, they would have discharged their duties to public safety as laid down by Section 3 of the 1974 Act. In the view of Desmond Fennell QC, this was a mistaken interpretation of the law. He also stated in his Report that 'in my view, the degree of vigour they — HMRI — applied to enforcement activity on London Underground was insufficient, and so poor housekeeping and potentially dangerous conditions were allowed to persist.'

London Underground senior management had, at least since the 1963 Act, haggled over the meaning of words to avoid the cost and the aggravation of complying with the law. And Parliament itself allowed them to get away with it. The argument was over whether King's Cross Underground station was a 'building' or a 'structure'. If it was the former, it was subject to the law; if the latter, it was not. So London Underground argued that the station was 'a series of passages, shafts and stairways being a collection of interlocking structures'. To maintain this view of the law, London Underground had mentally to fragment its buildings into their component parts. According to the Oxford English Dictionary the two words are synonymous. Lord Goddard in 1946 ruled that 'every building is a structure'. The House of Lords ruled in 1967 that a 'structure covers every kind of building as well as hoardings and erections that could not properly be called buildings 'a structure must be an adjunct of, or ancillary to, a main building'. King's Cross station, being a very extensive and substantial construction in bricks and mortar, cannot be considered, by the proverbial man on the Clapham omnibus, as 'ancillary to a main building'. But it was so considered, and was thus rendered exempt from fire laws by the Railway Inspectorate.

As already mentioned, the 1974 Act makes it the legal duty of every employer 'to conduct his undertaking in such a way as to ensure that persons not in his employment who may be affected thereby are not thereby exposed to risks to their health or safety'. The Safety Manager (Operations), Mr White, agreed that a concern for safety of the railway also extended to a care for the safety of the travelling public. Mr Adams, Senior Personnel Manager (Operations), had written a memorandum to the Operating Management Meeting of August 1987 in which he had urged that 'A safe environment is not one where there is a low number of serious injuries, but is the result of active participation by management and staff in identifying the hazards and then doing something positive about them. The identification, then prompt elimination or control of hazards is essential to the discharge of our duties under current legislation.' But men senior to him — Mr Powell, Safety Manager (Central Safety Unit), and the Senior Personnel Manager, Mr Straker — denied that safety of passengers was part of their duty.

In 1977 the London Transport Executive (LTE) actually applied for a fire certificate for the newly-built Heathrow Central station. The Greater London Council (GLC) then detailed to the LTE various works to be done before the certificate could be issued, including means of escape from fire for passengers, fire warnings and the means to fight a fire. The LTE then passed these requirements to the Railway Inspectorate, which immediately tried to water down the safety measures by pleading the conventional understanding of the law. The Railway Inspectorate wrote to the London Fire Brigade: 'The station platforms and main passenger access passages do not require a fire certificate as the 1963 Act is not applicable to them'. The

*Above:*
The view into a hell-hole.
Looking down the escalator
from the main concourse.
*Denzil McNeelance /
Times Newspapers Ltd*

GLC insisted that the platforms and passageways were an integral part of the station which was an underground building in which persons are employed to work and thus fell within the powers of the 1971 Act. Still the Railway Inspectorate, which was supposed to uphold safety, argued against this GLC reading of the law, and the battle continued for three years until a compromise was reached which left all the Underground, except Heathrow, outside fire laws.

The result of being outside the discipline and control of fire laws is self-evident.

Because the fire problem had been swept under the carpet — or under the escalators — Underground staff were inadequately trained to deal with fire, there were no contingency plans to evacuate stations, there was very little communication equipment and what was available was of poor quality.

Underground staff had always managed to cope with blazing 'smoulderings' without loss of life and so, each weekday in 1987, they operated their system to carry about 2.6 million people on 4,500 trains. During the year 1987/8, London Underground ran 31.8 million miles and carried 800 million people. These people were looked after by about 19,000 staff. It all went along reasonably well with numbers rising, due in part to cheaper fares introduced by the GLC, but as pressure on the system mounted there was no alteration in the attitude of London Underground management towards changing times.

There were six serious fires on the Underground between 1984 and 1987, five of them under escalators. On 23 November 1984 at 9.50pm at Oxford Circus station, a passenger reported smoke on the northbound Victoria Line platform. A Station Inspector investigated and found the contractor's storage area ablaze with flames up to the ceiling. Thirty fire appliances were required to extinguish the 'smouldering', and members of the fire brigade and station staff were trapped by dense black smoke. The whole great station was filled with smoke, trains stalled in the tunnels which were also filling with smoke and 720 passengers had to climb down from the trains and walk along the tracks to escape. The fire was finally brought under control at 1.43am. Fourteen people went to hospital, including a policewoman and nine Underground staff. The cost of repairs came to over £5 million. Some smouldering!

One of the improvements introduced by London Underground as a result of the Oxford Circus fire was a complete ban on smoking within Underground railway stations. If the Great British Public had taken proper notice in 1984, it is conceivable that there would have been no fire at King's Cross in 1987.

The Leicester Square escalator 'smouldered' on 22 December 1984, closing the station for 50 minutes and putting several policemen and station staff in hospital. On 25 January 1985, Green Park's No 3 escalator caught fire. During the Inquiry into this, the Scientific Adviser to London Underground noted that the plywood in the Green Park escalators was 'extremely inflammable'. This was the third 'smouldering' to close a station in six months. The internal Underground inquiry noted that 'although smoking was prohibited beyond the ticket barrier, it was common to see people lighting up as they travelled up the escalator'. Various recommendations were made regarding 'No Smoking' signs, fitting smoke alarms, replacing with metal sheet the wooden skirting boards and panels, more thorough cleaning of escalators and more regular use of the water-fog equipment on escalators. The response of the Underground Lift & Escalator Engineer to the inquiry recommendations was to dismiss, on grounds of expense, the replacement of wooden skirting boards with metal; 'The wood we use is chosen for its fire-resistant properties,' he said. The Engineering Director, Mr Lawrence, does not appear to have seen these recommendations.

On 25 January 1985, escalator No 3 at Green Park 'smouldered' and was extensively damaged. On 22 August 1985 there was a smouldering or fire at Baker Street Underground station. The following day, the Deputy Assistant Chief Officer of the London Fire Brigade wrote a formal letter to Mr Cope, Operations Director of the Underground. This letter stated, in part, that the Head of the London Fire Brigade was 'gravely concerned that, contrary to professional advice, a two-stage procedure has been introduced for notifying the Brigade of fires occurring on the London Underground railway system. Following the recent fire at Oxford Circus Underground station, the Brigade made it quite clear that the Brigade should be called immediately to any fire on the Underground railway network. We are aware that the incidence of fires on the Underground railway network has fallen considerably since the Brigade's advice to reduce the amount of litter. Nevertheless, I cannot urge too strongly that the two-stage procedure be withdrawn and clear instructions be given that on any suspicion of fire the Fire Brigade be called without delay. This could save lives'. Absolutely no notice was taken of this urgent request and the Underground Rule Book (Appendix 8) continued to instruct staff that: 'There are two types of fire [the word 'fire' was used, not 'smouldering'], those that can be extinguished by the use of the equipment available and those that require the attendance of the Fire Brigade. In case of doubt Fire Brigade assistance must be requested'.

Holborn's No 7 escalator burst into smouldering on 23 December 1985 and engulfed the lower part of the station in flames in a few minutes. No inquiry of any kind was held into this incident. And even where there was an internal inquiry followed by a report, there was no trace of evidence that the report was sent to the Directors, nor any evidence that the problems detailed in the report had even been addressed, much less rectified. These same shortcomings were pointed out in reports on these fires from the London Fire Brigade, the Metropolitan Police and the Railway Fire Prevention & Fire Safety Standards Committee. Their recommendations were not properly considered by senior London Underground managers. Indeed, there was no collation of Inquiry Reports and Recommendations, gathered together under one binding, to be circulated to the relevant senior people. When, after the King's Cross fire, senior men were asked if they had seen such a single catalogue of near-disasters and recommendations for improvement, the Engineering Director, Mr Lawrence, said: 'If I had had the reports of previous inquiries I believe I may have dug deeper. I would have read the recommendations about replacing skirting boards, for instance. I think they could have influenced me to cause other action to be taken.' The Chairman of London Underground Ltd, Dr Ridley, was rather more defiant when he replied to the same question: 'I see nothing in the evidence that you have reminded me of... which would have led the Board of London Underground to take a different position.'

Dr Ridley had in 1980 taken over the Chairmanship of London Underground Ltd. He was also the supreme manager of the operations side. He was a big man, an extremely capable engineer with a distinguished career behind him. He had engineered the Tyne & Wear Metro and the tunnelling for the Mass Transit Railway in Hong Kong. While he was in charge of London Underground he also initiated, and drove to completion, the Docklands Light Railway. He was authoritative, tremendously energetic and talked in a loud, Wearside accent. In his garden he ran a 7¼ in-gauge steam railway with beautiful locomotives he had built himself. He improved the efficiency of the London Underground, getting more trains onto the track and getting more people into them by improving the ticketing system and introducing the Travelcard. He was a thoroughgoing engineer-railwayman for whom safety was paramount — but the difficulty was that 'safety' tended to mean train safety. Fire had always been controlled and could always be controlled. In spite of the fires on escalators during his time in charge, his attitude remained unchanged, and in fact he was more worried — as his improvements began to attract more and more people onto the Underground — that an escalator might stop suddenly and kill someone, rather than cause fatalities by catching fire.

There were no more serious fires until Green Park's No 3 escalator caught fire again on 12 June 1987. This was followed on 30 August by a fire on a Central Line escalator at Bank which closed the station for 2hr 37min. In all of these incidents, the station managers, inspectors and railmen did their best with hand-held fire extinguishers and personal courage. They put themselves in very real danger and suffered for it, but they were not formally trained and in some cases did not know how to operate the water-fog equipment, and turned on the wrong valve.

Two weeks before the tragedy, the No 4 escalator on the Piccadilly Line bank of escalators at King's Cross was noted to be 'crabbing', so that a gap had opened on one side large enough to allow a lighted match to be dropped into the running track below. This defect was made worse by the fact that one third of the 'fire cleats' — panels to cover the gap between escalator and wall — were missing. Furthermore, those that remained were plywood, soaked in oil and grease from the running track. The plywood was also coated in varnish and there was a rubber dressguard close to it.

King's Cross & St Pancras Underground station was under the charge of the Station Manager with a Relief Station Manager at peak times to deal with crowd control, particularly in the busiest area known as the 'Khyber Pass', where congestion was extreme at peak periods. The Station Manager was Mr Worrell. His office was a temporary affair at the far end of the Circle Line platform, far removed from the centre of operations. This was against his wishes but he was moved anyway. The two Inspectors who formed his supervisory staff were in offices a long way off. Radio contact between parties underground is impossible, but there was an internal telephone system.

At 7.30pm on the evening of Wednesday 18 November 1987, 23 men and women were rostered for duty but three were absent. Other Underground employees on the station were an automatic-equipment technician and a part-time cleaner. There were 11 staff on the 'Tube' side and 12 on the 'Circle Line' side. There were five booking clerks, two of whom were on the Metropolitan and Circle Lines side, a supervisory booking clerk, three railmen and four leading railmen on the 'Tube' side under Relief Station Inspector Hayes, and four leading railmen on the 'Circle Line' side under Station Inspector Dhanpersaud. They were all there to assist passengers, check tickets, help with crowd control, deal with equipment failures and generally handle whatever befell. But at King's Cross three of the four leading railmen were prevented by ill-health from working anywhere except on the ticket barriers. The Relief Station Inspector, Mr Hayes, had never been to King's Cross Underground station before as an Inspector. In the station operations room at the Underground station were PC Bebbington and PC Kerbey, members of the British Transport Police. Patrolling the concourse of the main-line station were PC Balfe and PC Hanson.

Enjoying a meal break in the staff mess room were Leading Railman Swaby and Leading Railwoman Ord. They usually took from 7pm to 8.30pm, which was standard practice, although only half an hour was officially allowed for a break. (The convention of a 90-minute break had been allowed to develop over the years and was cited in the Fennell Report as another example of poor management.) Their rest was about to be rudely interrupted.

The main concourse of the King's Cross & St Pancras Underground station is approximately horseshoe-shaped. Passages from St Pancras and from King's Cross main-line stations lead into a semi-circular, perimeter subway with stairs down into the concourse for the ticket office and barriers. The 'Khyber Pass' is a passageway from the Euston Road directly into the concourse or into the perimeter subway. From the concourse barrier, escalators 4, 5 and 6 connect with the Piccadilly Line platforms, and 2, 7 and 9 with the Victoria Line, with a set of ordinary steps central between these. That part of the semi-circular concourse to the left (looking down) of the Piccadilly Line escalators had been boarded off by contractors with a temporary hoarding in connection with their work. This hoarding hid a fire hydrant and hose and the London Fire Brigade's cabinet containing plans of the station.

At about 7.15pm, Leading Railman Brickell, working at the ticket barrier, was informed by a passenger, Miss Tolmie, that some paper was on fire at the bottom of the Victoria Line escalator. Brickell was restricted to barrier duties only, by reason of ill-health, but he went down and knocked out the burning fire with a magazine and, having dealt with the smouldering, he returned to the barriers. He did not call the Fire Brigade; the paper was 'out', after all. But what had set light to it in the first instance? Leading Railman Brickell should have called the Fire Brigade, but his Rule Book had informed him that there were 'two types of fire' and he had dealt with one belonging to the first category. The Rule Book had set in motion a disastrous chain of events. Had the Fire Brigade been called at 7.15pm, experienced firefighters would have been on hand when the second fire was reported.

At about 7.29pm, Mr Squire, a passenger, reported to Mr Newman in the booking office that there was a fire on the escalator he had just used. The report does not give the exact words used by Mr Squire to advise Mr Newman of the existence of the fire. It is stated that Mr Newman telephoned Relief Station Inspector Hayes and reported a fire 'on the Northern Line escalator'. The fire was, as we know, on the Piccadilly Line escalator. Possibly Mr Squire had come, originally, from a Northern Line train and so thought that the escalator he had just used was 'the Northern Line escalator'. Or perhaps he had said 'Piccadilly Line'. We do not know.

At 7.32pm, a passenger, Mr Benstead, was the second person to report the fire to Mr Newman. Mr Benstead said that it was on the Piccadilly Line escalator because Mr Newman told the inquiry that, on receipt of this second warning, he had looked out from behind his window towards the Piccadilly Line escalators; 'There did not seem to be any more smoke than when I previously looked out. I didn't think it was very serious so I didn't leave the booking office.' He was in good company; for years top management of the Underground had ignored fire as a serious risk.

Inspector Hayes was unprepared by any training to deal with the situation and, indeed, the

Rule Book did not make clear to him what his actions should be — in spite of the 'grave concerns' of the London Fire Brigade. Inspector Hayes did not dial 999 for the Fire Brigade, nor did he inform the Station Manager that a fire had been reported. Instead, he set off at once, taking Railman Farrell with him, on a wild goose chase (due to the misleading information he had received) to look for the fire and decide which type of fire it was — one that he could extinguish, or one that needed the attendance of the Fire Brigade.

And all the time there was, in the concourse, a fire hydrant and hose. This could have been brought into use so easily, but it had been covered up by the temporary hoarding and forgotten.

While Inspector Hayes was hurrying in the wrong direction — which was not his fault — a passenger, Mr Karmoun, who was riding up No 4 Piccadilly Line escalator, saw the fire above him and also beneath the escalator. There was smoke and a fiery glow showing at the edges of the moving staircase. He must have been carried through the fire zone. When he got to the top he pressed the emergency 'Stop' button for the escalator and yelled down to the people still coming up to go back, to get off. His shouts and gesticulations attracted the attention of Leading Railman Brickell on the ticket barrier and also of PC Bebbington and PC Kerbey. Leading Railman Brickell, restricted to barrier duties due to poor health, and PC Bebbington at once went down Piccadilly escalator No 5 to investigate. They saw a fire on escalator No 4 with flames four inches high above the escalator treads, about one third of the way down from the top. Leading Railman Brickell did not know how to work the water-fog equipment and did not know about the fire hydrant, so he tried to redirect those passengers who were making for the concourse via the burning escalator, away from the fire onto the Victoria Line escalators. PC Bebbington went back up to the concourse and out onto the Euston Road in order to use his radio to call British Transport Police HQ radio to advise of the fire and ask for the attendance of the London Fire Brigade. His call was logged at 7.33pm. British Transport Police

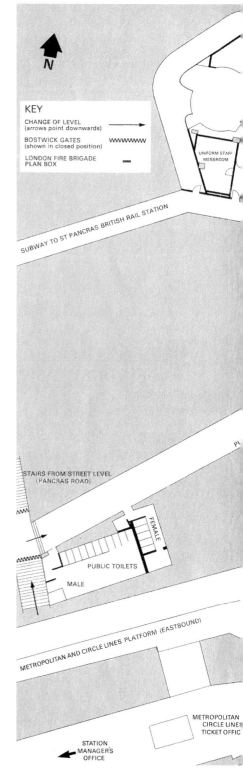

KEY

CHANGE OF LEVEL
(arrows point downwards)

BOSTWICK GATES
(shown in closed position)

LONDON FIRE BRIGADE
PLAN BOX

UNIFORM STAFF
MESSROOM

SUBWAY TO ST PANCRAS BRITISH RAIL STATION

STAIRS FROM STREET LEVEL
(PANCRAS ROAD)

FEMALE

PUBLIC TOILETS

MALE

METROPOLITAN AND CIRCLE LINES PLATFORM (EASTBOUND)

METROPOLITAN
CIRCLE LINES
TICKET OFFIC

STATION
MANAGER'S
OFFICE

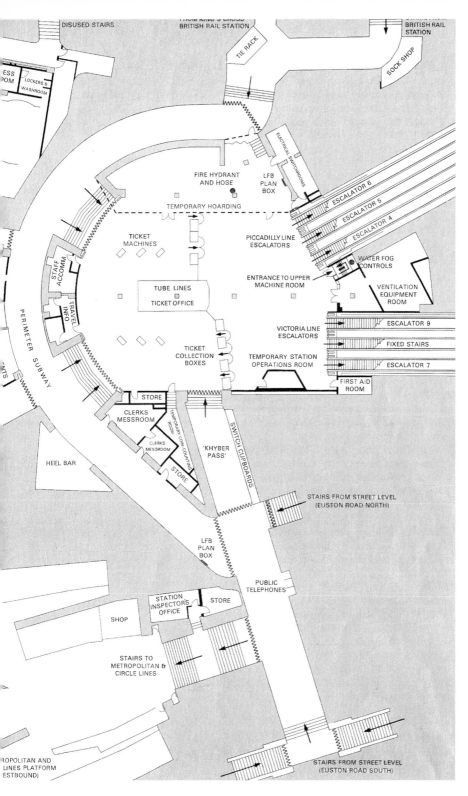

DISUSED STAIRS

FROM KING'S CROSS
BRITISH RAIL STATION

BRITISH RAIL
STATION

TIE RACK

SOCK SHOP

ESS ...OM

LOCKERS & WASHROOM

ELECTRICAL SWITCHROOMS

FIRE HYDRANT
AND HOSE

LFB
PLAN
BOX

ESCALATOR 6

ESCALATOR 5

ESCALATOR 4

TEMPORARY HOARDING

TICKET
MACHINES

PICCADILLY LINE
ESCALATORS

WATER FOG
CONTROLS

STAFF ACCOMM.

ENTRANCE TO UPPER
MACHINE ROOM

VENTILATION
EQUIPMENT
ROOM

PERIMETER SUBWAY

TRAVEL INFO

TUBE LINES
TICKET OFFICE

VICTORIA LINE
ESCALATORS

ESCALATOR 9

FIXED STAIRS

TICKET
COLLECTION
BOXES

TEMPORARY STATION
OPERATIONS ROOM

ESCALATOR 7

FIRST AID
ROOM

STORE

CLERKS
MESSROOM

TEMPORARY CON-COUNTING ROOM

SWITCH CUPBOARDS

CLERKS
MESSROOM

HEEL BAR

'KHYBER
PASS'

STORE

STAIRS FROM STREET LEVEL
(EUSTON ROAD NORTH)

LFB
PLAN
BOX

PUBLIC
TELEPHONES

STATION
INSPECTOR'S
OFFICE

STORE

SHOP

STAIRS TO
METROPOLITAN &
CIRCLE LINES

ROPOLITAN AND
LINES PLATFORM
ESTBOUND)

STAIRS FROM STREET LEVEL
(EUSTON ROAD SOUTH)

71

Constables Hanson and Balfe on the main-line station were alerted to the situation on hearing PC Bebbington's message, and went at once to the Underground concourse. The London Fire Brigade received the 999 call from BT Police at 7.33½.

Euston Fire Station was the one which would normally have answered the emergency, but the appliances there were out on a call and so appliances from Soho and Clerkenwell attended. These engines got to the scene remarkably quickly, given the evening traffic congestion, but, had the Euston engines been available, valuable minutes would have been saved. The first fire engine arrived at 7.42. It was commanded by Station Officer Townley. There was no-one from London Underground to meet him so he had no briefing as to where, in the vast complex, the fire was. PC Dixon was waiting for the Fire Brigade, but at some other place. There was no pre-arranged rendezvous point for firefighters, no London Underground guide, no plan for the Fire Brigade and no London Underground liaison of any sort. The fire had been burning for at least 12 minutes.

Inspector Hayes and Railman Farrell were told by passengers, as they went towards the Northern line, that there was a fire on the Piccadilly Line escalator and so they turned back. They arrived at the foot of No 4 escalator at about 7.35pm and saw the fire about half way up. Inspector Hayes went into the lower machine room of the escalator and, according to Chapter 9 of the Fennel Report, stayed there for three minutes, but, seeing and smelling nothing, he came out at 7.38pm. During the three minutes that Inspector Hayes was in the lower machine room, Railman Farrell joined forces with Leading Railman Brickell to use a skip and tape to cordon off the Piccadilly Line escalators. When Inspector Hayes came out of the machine room and ran up the stairs, Farrell followed him.

Inspector Hayes reached the top of the escalator, turned left and dashed across to the door of the upper machine room situated to the right of No 4 escalator. He unlocked it and went inside, slamming the door behind him and right in the face of the rapidly advancing Farrell. In this room were the controls for the water-fog equipment. Inspector Hayes was aware of the equipment in a general sort of way but he had never worked it or seen it worked — and, considering he was an Inspector, that alone speaks volumes about fire precautions on the London Underground. Forgetting all about the water fog, he ran down the steps below escalator No 5, from where he saw the fire under escalator No 4. He ran back up the steps to the upper machine room, found a carbon-dioxide fire extinguisher and, grabbing this, ran back down to the fire but was unable to get near enough to use the extinguisher.

PC Kukielka and PC Martland were patrolling the King's Cross main-line station when they too heard the emergency call sent out by PC Bebbington. They arrived at the Underground station at 7.37pm. At 7.39pm, the handful of British Transport Police Constables in the overheated, smoke-filled concourse decided to close and evacuate the station. Railman Farrell helped the police officers cordon off the top of the Piccadilly Line escalators until 7.41pm. He was then asked by a police constable to contact the Victoria Line Controller and to ask him to put out an order that Victoria Line trains should not stop at King's Cross. Railman Farrell had to run down onto the Victoria Line platforms to find the necessary telephone.

Up on the concourse, amid thickening smoke, the imperturbable Mr Newman was still selling tickets to passengers. At 7.41pm he was told by the Police to leave the station. At 7.42pm an eastbound Piccadilly Line train stopped and disgorged its passengers, and at 7.43pm a westbound Piccadilly Line train also stopped to set down passengers.

So far it was a soldiers' battle, akin to hand-to-hand fighting. On the London Underground, only the lower ranks knew there was a fire. The British Transport Police constables and their HQ knew, although there is some doubt if they were correctly informed of the actual site of the fire, and the London Fire Brigade knew. At 7.37pm the Piccadilly Line Controller, Mr Hanson, was talking by 'phone to the BT Police 'L' Division information room on an entirely different matter when the fact of the fire was mentioned to him by the police. The manner in which the fire was mentioned is not given in the Report but, from what is written, the police did not give the correct location of the fire, nor did the message convey a great deal of urgency to Mr Hanson. It was 7.39pm before he contacted the Chief Controller of the Underground with the news. This resulted in the Piccadilly Line Traffic Manager being called out at 7.40pm. It was another two minutes before Mr Hanson telephoned the King's Cross & St Pancras Underground Station Manager, Mr Worrell, to ask him 'if he knew of any smouldering in the machine room'. Mr Worrell left immediately to investigate. Sitting in the office with Mr Worrell was the Relief Station Manager for King's Cross, Mr Pilgrim. He was having his meal break, did not regard the reported smouldering as a serious threat and so did not go out with Mr Worrell to investigate. He finished what he was doing and followed two or even three minutes later. Both men, as they emerged, were confronted with astonishing scenes of passengers running through smoke, fire officers and general confusion.

Mr Worrell headed for the Piccadilly Line escalator and tried to persuade those members of the public he encountered to get out of the station. As he was moving towards the concourse the fire on the escalator was rapidly accelerating in intensity. He had reached the top of the steps leading from the perimeter passageway down into the concourse at 7.45pm when he was enveloped in a hot cloud of dense black smoke. He groped his way on, along the passageway and reached the surface at the Euston Road south exit where he assisted with crowd control as an ordinary 'foot soldier'. But he was the Station Manager, and he ought to have made himself known to the London Fire Brigade so as to offer them advice and assistance concerning the internal layout of the station — information they desperately needed. However, he remained in the background, so to speak, for over an hour until he was ordered to contact the fire officers by the Acting Traffic Manager of London Underground. But it is also the case that the London Fire Brigade did not ask London Underground for assistance. I wonder if, perhaps, there was some ill feeling between the organisations, since the latter had ignored the former's advice for so many years?

Mr Pilgrim remained on the Metropolitan Line platforms. Passengers were running from the dense smoke into this part of the station and he assisted in marshalling them onto an eastbound Metropolitan train which arrived at 7.52pm. With the platforms cleared of people, but full of smoke, he took the staff into the mess room for shelter until a special train, sent from Moorgate, arrived at 8.5pm. to carry them away.

The flames of the fire had been burning in — and rising out of — the 'trench' formed by the walls of the escalator. The flames were on the right-hand side (the right-hand side as seen by one looking up the staircase) and rose vertically until they were clear of the top of the trench. Here, they met the main airstream coming up the escalator 'tunnel'. After several minutes, the fire spread to both sides of the escalator and when this occurred the fire was forced by its own physics to 'lie down' in the trench, causing the flames to stretch forwards, low down. At the same time, they were encouraged to rise up the staircase by the steep incline and the fact that heat rises. The wood ahead of the flames was very quickly brought to ignition temperature. The trench-like shape of the escalator concentrated the heat of the fire on the wooden floor, the varnished, oil-impregnated plywood, the rubber dress guards and the handrails. The highly-inflammable materials rapidly accelerated their rate of burn as the flames, channelled between the walls, concentrated and rose up the steep stairway until, after two minutes development, they burst like a bomb blast into the concourse at the top. This was the 'flashover'.

At 7.44pm, Police Constable Hanson was on the Victoria Line escalator, urging people to move quickly upwards and directing them towards the exits, when he became aware of dense smoke in the concourse and went to investigate, moving as quickly as he could through the throng of people heading out of the station. He had got 5ft into the ticket hall/concourse when he saw what he described to the Inquiry as 'a large wall of flame or fire. It was definitely above head height, and immediately following this was a 'whoosh' and a large ball of flame, about head height, that hit the ceiling in the ticket hall. This was followed almost instantaneously by dense, black smoke'. PC Hanson redefined his description of the fireball, saying: 'To be more accurate I would say it was a jet of flame that shot up and then collected into a kind of ball. I saw it shoot up across the top of No 4 [escalator] and collect along the roofing.'

PC Hanson was physically struck, enveloped and knocked over by the fireball and the force of the rush of air accompanying it. Badly burned, he then made his way out, covered by the swirling fire, reaching from his head to the ceiling. The same fireball claimed the life of a London Fire Brigade man, Station Officer Townsley, while he was attempting to save the life of a passenger, Miss Byers. The large number of people around him were also burned and choked by the fireball and smoke. It would be reasonable to suppose that everyone rushing up the Victoria Line escalator through thick smoke would have been terrified, but that does not seem to have been the case. Mr Bates was a Victoria Line passenger who was told to leave the station and came up No 7 escalator with PC Hanson. He told the Inquiry that, when he reached the smoke-filled concourse, he could see flames licking out of the Piccadilly Line escalator shaft — but 'these flames did not appear to present an immediate threat so he continued on into the ticket hall'. Mr Bates sounds like a very cool customer indeed! Accordingly, he was well in line to receive the full force of the fireball when it exploded into the concourse. He heard a 'whoosh' and the flames shot out from the top of the Piccadilly Line escalators to where he was standing. The fireball was followed by dense, black smoke. He crouched down, protected his face with his hands and staggered back to the shelter of No 7 escalator.

Mr Arari Minta, coming off No 7 escalator, saw and heard PC Hanson urging people to get out. PC Hanson was pointing the way to the exit when he became enveloped by the fireball.

Mr Minta dived to the floor and suffered severe burns in a few seconds as he made his way out of the concourse. Mr Brody's clothes caught fire and he rolled on the ground to extinguish them before getting out to the Euston Road with 40% burns. Miss Santello was walking or running with her friend Mr Liberati from No 7 escalator into the concourse when they were caught by the fireball. She suffered very severe burns and her friend was burned to death. Others saw the flames and ran back into the Victoria Line escalator, but still suffered burns to hands and face.

Thirty-one people died in the fire and one has never been identified.

Mr Desmond Fennell states in his Report that the steady reduction in Government subsidy to the Underground, imposed by the Government's 1984 financial objectives, was not a contributory actor to this fire: 'There is no evidence that the overall level of subsidy available to London Regional Transport was inadequate to maintain safety standards.' But what money it did receive was not fully spent. Mr Fennell goes on: 'there has been a tendency in London Underground in the past for actual capital expenditure to be less than the budgeted figure. This may have served to reduce necessary expenditure in safety measures'.

The Chairman, Dr Ridley, denied that there had been underspending as such, but rather that he had had to rearrange his expenditure in response to directives from the London Transport Executive for a reduction of spending throughout the train and bus operation. So a reduction, against the budgeted figure, was made, even if Dr Ridley, in implementing it, was only obeying orders.

The Lift & Escalator Manager, Mr Styles, stated that he did not ask for money to be spent on relocating the water-fog controls or replacement of the varnished plywood on the escalators 'because he felt there was thin chance of the investment being authorised'. It was also the case that the budgeted spending was reduced in respect of escalator cleaning. In five of the seven years 1982-8, actual expenditure on the lifts and escalators was less than budget, and in 1987/8 the underspend had been £1.4 million; Mr Styles admitted that, if the budget had been fully spent, safety in stations would have been better.

At the conclusion of the Inquiry, Dr Ridley resigned his position as Managing Director of the Underground, and became Managing Director of Projects for Eurotunnel in January 1989. In April 1990 he became Professor of Transport Engineering at Imperial College, and in 1995 was elected the 131st President of the Institution of Civil Engineers.

# Clapham Junction:
## 12 December 1988

Barely had the smoke cleared away from the terrible tragedy of the King's Cross fire, than another awful railway shambles hit London. On 12 December 1988, a rear-end collision took place at a point approximately 400yd south of Clapham Junction station, on the up main line from the west of England. The 7.18am Basingstoke was stationary at signal WF47 and this train was rammed in the rear by the 6.14am Poole. At the exact moment of collision, as carriages were being forced sideways towards the down main line, an empty coaching stock train, the 8.3am Waterloo-Haslemere, was passing and was struck by the scattering coaches of the Poole train and was derailed. 1,500 passengers and crew were estimated to have been in the two trains. Thirty-five people were killed, including Driver Rolls on the Poole train.

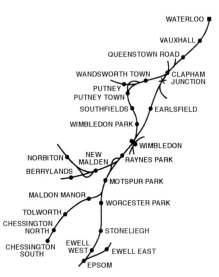

There were two causes for this accident: an initial error made by the Signal & Telegraph Department over two weeks previously and the inability of Driver Rolls to stop his train in time, having been misled by faulty signalling. In the final analysis it was a matter of expense, or rather what is perceived as expensive. Manual signalling is seen as being costly and colour-light, automatic signalling as relatively cheap. Then again, the method of constructing colour-light signalling can be made cheap or expensive. Needless to say, it is made as cheaply as possible. In 1965, when I first came in contact with it, I perceived loopholes in its safety and suggested ways of making it safer. The problem, where I was working, was that trains ran for long distances unsupervised and the lines were unprotected. I suggested that all signals must be capable of being set to 'Danger' by the signalman and all signal aspects must be repeated in the signalbox. These remedies were said by senior S&T Department people to be 'too expensive', given that 'accidents do not happen very often'.

The renewal of the prewar equipment at Clapham was deferred for years because the money was not made available to carry out the work, even though the system was in an increasingly life-threatening condition. It was not, however, the bad state of the wiring which caused this accident. There was a shortage of skilled technicians resulting in overwork for those who were employed and this did have a bearing on the tragedy.

The colour-light signals were operated automatically by the passage of trains over successive track circuits. The great disadvantage — indeed, danger — of the system is that so many of the signals work automatically and cannot be placed to 'Danger' by the signalman should the need arise. This was the case at Clapham 'A' where the automatic signals on the approach to Clapham Junction from Earlsfield could not be placed to 'Danger' by the signalman.

*Above:*
The point of impact between the incoming Poole train and the stationary Basingstoke train: one piled on the other and the westbound empty stock train at bottom left. To the rear of the Poole train, beyond the gantry, can be seen the 6.53 Waterloo to Waterloo via Richmond which Driver Pike managed to bring to a stand in an exceptionally short distance. The gap between his train and the wreck is the distance between a disaster and a double disaster.
*Graham Wood /*
*Times Newspapers Ltd*

At the core of this signalling system lies the track circuit. The length of the circuit can be 20yd or a mile and is determined by dividing the rails with insulated joints. A small current from a battery is fed along one running rail, through the track circuit relay to the other rail and returns to the battery. The current energises the relay's solenoid, causing a set of contacts to close and others to open. Thus, the relay is a switch to put an electric current into a wire and to cut it off from another wire. The relay can, therefore, be used to change signal aspects behind the train — turning a green light to a red, for instance. It can electrically 'lock' points and cause lights to illuminate a diagram to indicate to the signalman the position of the train. Thousands of track circuits, thousands of relays and miles of wiring are involved in a major automatic installation such as that in the Waterloo area.

A four-aspect colour-light signal shows a green light only when the line beyond it — 'ahead of it in the direction of running' — is clear to the far end of the overlap of the third signal ahead. The overlap track circuit extends for 200yd ahead of each signal, and only when a train has passed over and is clear of this overlap can the red signal next but one in rear of the train change to single yellow. So, while the train is occupying the overlap track circuit there will be two red signals to its rear. As the train proceeds over succeeding track circuits, the circuitry brings back the current in such a way as to switch the lights in the first signal initially to single yellow, then to double yellow, then to green. All along the line the signal aspects change behind the train, protecting its rear and always maintaining a safe braking distance between the first and the following train. The noise in a relay room is quite like a chaotic clock, clicking and clattering away, as the relays respond to each other as the train passes over the track circuits.

By 1976 the old Southern Railway installation was still doing its job, but was giving Southern Region signal engineers cause for concern. At 40 years old, the insulation on many miles of electrical wiring had become brittle and was in danger of falling off the wire, thus making short circuits possible. Underneath Waterloo signalbox and at Clapham 'A' in 1979 the wiring looked all right, superficially, but the technicians were reluctant to touch it for fear of the insulation breaking and creating a short circuit. A short circuit can also be called a 'false feed', since current is passed into a circuit where it is not required.

In 1978 a Project Development Paper was put forward by the General Manager of the Southern Region. This plan envisaged the 'essential' renewal of the entire signalling system in the Waterloo area which covered the routes as far out as Wimbledon, Epsom, Leatherhead and Dorking. The General Manager's plan required work to begin in January 1982 and be completed by November 1986. If this timescale were not met, then remedial work would have to be undertaken, piecemeal, to patch up the worst decay. This remedial work would then be swept away when the full-scale renewal later took place.

In spite of the 'essential' nature of the proposed renewal, the plans were deferred on a number of occasions owing to the lack of investment capital for the railways. In 1979 a new Government was elected and the stumbling block remained cost. The new Government had an antipathy towards nationalised industries and in particular towards spending money on railways, but, having said that, it must also be said that it inherited a bad set of economic conditions and there was a financial recession from 1979 to 1981. Money for investment in railways, even such a vitally-important railway as this one, was not easily to be found, although money was found for new roads. A different criterion of 'value for money' applied when recommending funding for new roads.

In May 1981 Southern Region reduced the scope of its Waterloo renewals, and therefore the cost of the scheme, but still there was no money for it. The years passed and the wiring degenerated still further. An enormous risk was being taken with safety because of expense. In May 1983 the Government, specifically the Department of Transport, called the scheme in for inspection by the Secretary of State for Transport. Meanwhile, 'despite increased preventive maintenance, the failure rate of the equipment was increasing and the integrity of the signalling system was at risk' (Hidden Report, para 12.7). It was also becoming more expensive to maintain as it became more dangerous. But authorisation for its renewal could not be obtained. Expenditure on major railway improvements had a low priority in Government policy at that time. The influence of the Treasury may have been brought to bear on the deliberations of the British Rail Committee, but owing to the secretive '30-year rule' this cannot be verified. In September 1984 Southern Region made what might be described as an impassioned plea to the BR Investment Committee. Paragraph 3.4 of this report included the words: 'It is imperative that replacement in some form takes place within the timescale to maintain a minimum standard of safety in the face of deterioration of insulation of internal wiring and corrosion of signal housings. There have been three *wrong-side* signal failures in the past two years and a 26% increase in equipment failure in the same period. To permit further deterioration is completely unacceptable'. (A wrong-side failure is when a signal shows 'Proceed' when it ought to show 'Stop'.)

This urgent appeal opened the purse-strings. On 1 October 1984 the British Rail Investment Committee endorsed the expenditure plan which then went to the Minister of Public Transport for authorisation. He authorised the expenditure of £32.5 million on 19 December 1984. Seventy-four jobs would go saving wages of £737,000 per annum. It had taken rather more than six years to reach this stage. During that six years massive expenditure on new roads and motorways had been authorised. In 1982 £232 million had been spent on major new road projects, in 1983 £429 million, in 1984 £210 million and in the first five months of 1985 £122 million. These are Department of the Environment Roads Policy Division figures. In slightly

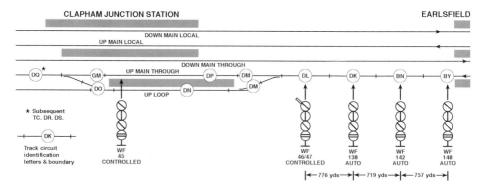

less than six years the London & Southampton Railway to planed, constructed and opened original railway from Nine Elms to Southampton.

The Waterloo Area Resignalling Scheme (WARS) could now get underway and the necessary discussion meetings began on 13 February 1985. The problem was gigantic: how to renew the hundreds of miles of cabling, thousands of track circuit relays and hundreds of signals — and rearrange the track layout too, in places — without interfering with the tremendous tidal flow of traffic in and out of Waterloo. Not only was the condition of the wiring deteriorating throughout this period, but the skilled labour necessary to carry out the plan was diminishing. This last was recognised by paying a bonus to those remaining, keeping them at work, on overtime, for weeks on end. The Hidden Report into the Clapham Junction disaster says this was 'not a safe working practice'. Mr David Rayner, the Joint Managing Director (Railways), stated to the Hidden Inquiry that if there were insufficient staff to do the work, extra time would have to be given. Mr Callander, a Senior Construction Assistant at South Lambeth, had requested an additional six months spread over four of the stages of work, but his request was not granted. The timetable for the project came to be regarded as 'set in stone', and no-one else asked for extra time.

The result of this was that, in the three months before the accident, the central character in the tragedy, Mr Brian Hemingway, a Signal & Telecommunications Technician, had had but one day off work. This was no more than typical of the others working on the job. Supervisors were not supervising but working as technicians because of the shortage, and everyone put an enormous amount of effort into driving the work on to keep up with its very tight schedule. Along with his colleagues, Mr Hemingway was probably glad of the overtime, but it went deeper than that; they were committed and got 'stuck into' the challenge, working towards the very difficult completion of an enormous project.

Mr Hemingway started work for British Rail in 1972 and had been a Senior Technician since 1981. He had worked on the re-signalling of London Bridge and Victoria. He was experienced and well liked by his colleagues and supervisors, a modest man who enjoyed doing a good job for the railway and for himself. He thought he did 'alright'. His work had never been criticised, but that was to be part of the problem.

On Sunday 27 November 1988 a new automatic four-aspect signal was to be commissioned. This was WF138, sited on the up main line from the Basingstoke direction, about 1,500yd on the country side of Clapham Junction station. This signal was to replace a 1936-vintage four-aspect at the same site. It was within the area of control of — but could not be controlled by — Clapham Junction 'A' signalbox. This rested on a steel gantry above the tracks, on the London side of Clapham Junction, a familiar sight to millions of people. The wiring diagram for WF138 had been prepared by the drawing office in Croydon back in August. During the preliminary work, Mr Hemingway discovered that there was no room on the relay racks for

78

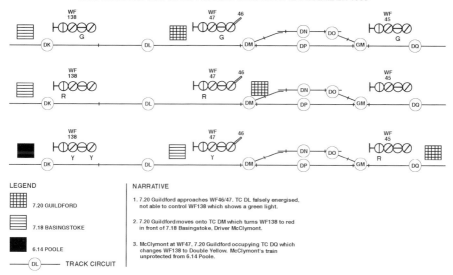

## CLAPHAM JUNCTION FAULTY SIGNAL SEQUENCE 12 DECEMBER 1988

**LEGEND**

7.20 GUILDFORD

7.18 BASINGSTOKE

6.14 POOLE

(DL) TRACK CIRCUIT

**NARRATIVE**

1. 7.20 Guildford approaches WF46/47. TC DL falsely energised, not able to control WF138 which shows a green light.

2. 7.20 Guildford moves onto TC DM which turns WF138 to red in front of 7.18 Basingstoke, Driver McClymont.

3. McClymont at WF47, 7.20 Guildford occupying TC DQ which changes WF138 to Double Yellow. McClymont's train unprotected from 6.14 Poole.

the new relays, so he worked out a scheme of wiring which was approved by the design staff at Croydon. All this was done in the good old informal way, by people who knew what they were doing. But no amended wiring diagram was issued, so the diagram kept in the relay room was inaccurate. None of this had any bearing on the terrible collision, but it is an example of the best railway traditions of getting on with the job in difficult circumstances.

All the necessary wiring between the signal, the location cupboards and the relay room in Clapham Junction 'A' cabin had been laid out during the preceding weeks and now, on 27 November, the new signal had to be brought into use through the various connections still to be made.

Mr Hemingway's Supervisor for the day was Mr Derek Bumstead, and Hemingway's assistant was Patrick Dowd. Brian Hemingway had not worked very much with Patrick Dowd, did not have a high opinion of his abilities and so gave him work to do outside and took on most of the rewiring within the relay room himself.

Derek Bumstead was not supervising but working outside, on the ground, with a gang of S&T men, carrying out the role of a Senior Technician. This left Brian Hemingway to work inside, on his own. The Department was short-staffed and everyone was 'mucking-in' to get the job done.

What Mr Hemingway had to do was not complicated and could have been done in half an hour. There were several terminals on top of track circuit relay TRR DM. He had to remove a wire which connected a terminal to fuse 12-107 and then run a new wire from the terminal to TR DL, and from that to several other connections before returning to fuse 12-107.

Inside the relay room the light was dim, the atmosphere close and surfaces dusty and grimy with the accumulations of the years. Mr Hemingway removed the old wire from the terminal but did not remove the other end from Fuse 12-107. He did not push it away from its old terminal, nor cut it back, nor even tape over the live end. He moved on to the next stage of his work. When he had completed the re-routing he had two other installation jobs to carry out, Nos 111 and 226. At the end of the day, no wiring check was made by his Supervisor, nor did the Testing & Commissioning Engineer, Mr Dray, come to look at what had been done. This of course contravened the Rules and, had these men done their jobs and carried out a wire count, it seems certain that the rogue wire would have been noticed and dealt with. But the men trusted each other; they had worked hard that day and for months. They were tired but

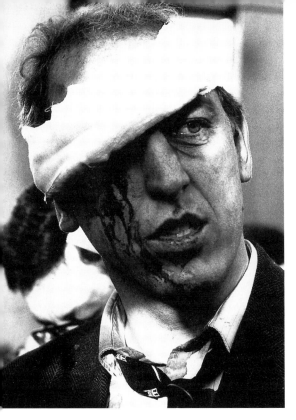

happy enough, with another load of Sunday overtime in the bag. Brian Hemingway left work and closed the door behind him on the dark and antique relays on their dusty racks, with an electric 'sword of Damocles' hovering live, beside a terminal of TRR DM.

Two weeks later, on Sunday 11 December, Brian Hemingway was again working in the relay room at Clapham Junction 'A'. On this occasion he had to replace relay TR DN with a new one. Now these things are heavy, glass-sided cubes, known to S&T men as 'fish tanks'. They are a bit larger and heavier than the average car battery. It was logical that TR DN should stand next to TRR DM on the shelf. From the top of each of the relays several terminals projected with wires, fastened on their terminals with nuts, rising slackly to join the wiring loom, forming a 'tree' with branches as thick as a man's arm. Mr Hemingway had to disconnect TR DN, drag it off the rack and shove its replacement into place and re-connect it. This was 'like for like' replacement and there was no requirement for any inspection of the completed job by a Supervisor. The work done, he left the room.

During his efforts to change TR DN, Brian Hemingway had inadvertently moved relay TRR DM sideways, bringing the old, live wire into contact with a terminal on TRR DM and thus giving a false feed to the relay. This rogue current kept the relay energised when it should have been de-energised by the occupation of the track circuit DL. When a train occupied DL track circuit, signal WF138 was not placed to red to protect the train's rear, but continued to show a green. To make matters worse, the three signals leading towards WF138 were given no aspect control but were all showing green.

When a train running over track circuit DL hit the overlap track circuit DM beyond the next signal, WF47, that track circuit put WF138 to red and the signals to the rear of WF138 took up their correct aspects. Once the train cleared off track circuit DM and was wholly on track circuit DP, signal WF138 was released to a single yellow and, thereafter, signal WF138 and the signals to its rear had their aspects controlled correctly by the train occupying the successive track circuits along the line towards London. When this train had passed three signals on, WF138 was again showing green.

So, to a casual observer on the track it would appear that the signal was working; it switched its aspects from red to yellow and green. The really evil thing about the false feed was that in Clapham 'A' box the track circuit indicators showed 'Occupied' and 'Unoccupied' perfectly correctly, but there was no indicator to show the signal's aspect. Had there been, it seems likely that in the 18 hours or so during which the fault had existed prior to the accident, a signalman would have noticed the wrong-side failure on WF138: the track circuit actually occupied by a train and signal WF138 in rear showing green.

All through Sunday and the early hours of Monday, the interval of time between trains passing signal WF138 was great enough to ensure that the malfunction remained invisible:

17 trains passed between 6.10am and 7.40am, an average of one every five minutes. At about 7.58am, Driver Christy passed Earlsfield with the 6.6am Bournemouth. Signal WF148 was at the London end of Earlsfield platform; 757yd further on was WF142. Both these were showing one or two yellows but both changed to green simultaneously, but then WF142 immediately went back to one yellow. Inspector Meticulous might take the view that Driver Christy should have stopped at once and reported the irregular change, but Driver Christy had seen this sort of thing happen before; it was the sort of thing that happened in the Clapham area. Probably the signalman was altering the road ahead, hence the change of aspect. Indeed, this was the way that many drivers had come to regard colour-light signalling, because that is how it behaved not infrequently.

Following Driver Christy was Driver Priston with the 7.20am Guildford. He passed Earlsfield three minutes later and saw that WF142 was at green, but just as he was about to pass it he saw it change to single yellow. For a moment Driver Priston doubted himself and wondered if the last signal had been a double yellow. He checked his AWS monitor and saw that it was displaying the plain, black disc, proving that the last signal had indeed been a green when he had passed over its AWS magnet. Driver Priston did not make any report of the odd signal aspect, for the same reasons as Driver Christy.

Even if one or both men had reported the signal irregularity, no importance would have been attached to such a report because everybody always trusted the track circuits implicitly. Mr Ivor Warburton, Director of Operations, British Railways Board, stated to the Hidden Investigation: 'If the driver of an earlier train had reported an irregularity the danger was unlikely to be realised immediately because the correct track circuit indications continued to be given in the signalbox.' Everybody trusted the machine — even though it behaved eccentrically. If a semaphore signalman had waved his signals about as a driver approached, matters would not have been taken on trust. There was also a feeling of contempt for the machine, a 'bloody signals, messing about again' sort of feeling.

The interval of time between trains began to shorten from 8am. The trains were running closer together as the morning 'rush' developed. Only four minutes behind the 7.20am Guildford was the 7.18am Basingstoke, 12 cars driven by Mr McClymont, and behind that the 6.14am Poole, also 12 cars, driven by Mr Rolls.

An act of vandalism had caused a derailment that morning, blocking the line between Poole and Branksome, near Bournemouth, so the Poole train had actually started from Bournemouth but was referred to as the 'Poole' train in the Hidden Report. Coming out of Waterloo on the down main line, which ran alongside the up main, was the 8.3am Waterloo to Haslemere empty coaching stock. These were the trains to be involved in the disaster.

Driver McClymont came through Earlsfield, under green signals, at just over 60mph. Rounding the long, sweeping curve he saw WF138 at green ahead. He was then running at 65mph. But just then, passing signal WF47, was the 7.20am Guildford. It now occupied the overlap track circuit DM and this immediately turned WF138 to red. McClymont was about 30yd from the signal. Seeing a green turn to red right in your face is a horrible experience and McClymont slammed his brakes on to the fullest extent. They acted so well that he realised he would stop before he got to WF47 so he eased them and ran up to and stopped at that signal for the purpose of reporting the irregular action of WF138. This proved that a 12-car train could pull up in well under the distance from one colour-light signal to the next if the driver instantly slammed his brakes on.

His train was then standing on track circuit DL, whose operating mechanism — TRR DM — was inoperative due to the rogue wire. McClymont, of course, had no idea that the rear of his train was not protected by the track circuiting and climbed down from his cab intending to use the signal-post telephone (SPT). Signal WF138, behind him, would have been at single yellow due to the presence of the 7.20am Guildford advancing over the track circuits towards Waterloo, but as that train drew further away so the aspect shown by WF138 would become less and less restrictive until it was showing a green. It was a truly horrible nightmare of dysfunctional machines which had entrapped ever-trusting human beings.

Driver McClymont went to the nearest lineside telephone, which did not work. He then went to another, climbing a ladder to reach it. He took it off its rest and was 'almost immediately' answered by Signalman Cotter in Clapham 'A'. McClymont told Cotter what he had seen and Cotter, defending the signalling against the drivers, told him that all his indications showed that there was nothing wrong with the signal. The trouble was, of course, that Mr Cotter could not know that. He did not have an aspect indicator for WF138 or else he would have seen that, even as they spoke, it was showing a double yellow as the 7.20am Guildford continued its progress towards the terminus.

Driver McClymont was a little irritated by Signalman Cotter's response and I suppose it is possible that Cotter was a bit fed up with drivers stopping and reporting irregular signal aspects for which he could see no cause. By stopping 'unnecessarily' they played havoc with punctuality.

Now the moment had come. Driver Rolls with the 6.14am Poole was motoring through Earlsfield at 60mph, or slightly more, the correct speed for the schedule. The line is on a long, gentle curve with a radius of 2,000 metres. Two hundred yards after passing Earlsfield, Driver Rolls would have seen a green signal at WF142 and 15 seconds later WF138 would have come into view. Given the probable position of the 7.20am Guildford, it seems most likely that WF138 was showing double yellow; but it might have been showing a green if the Guildford train had cleared off the last track circuit which sent aspect controls back to WF138.

At the same time, coming through Clapham Junction station, on the down main through, was the 8.3am ECS to Haslemere.

The 8.3am empty stock train was passing WF47 as Driver McClymont finished his conversation with Signalman Cotter. As McClymont put down the telephone he heard a thunderous crash, whirled around and saw his train, with its brakes full on, shoot forward. Realising his train had been rammed in the rear, he immediately got back on the phone and advised Signalman Cotter, telling him that there would be casualties and that he should call the emergency services. Cotter immediately turned his controlled signals to 'Danger'. This put WF47 to red and WF138 to single yellow. He then sent six bells, 'Obstruction Danger', on the single-strike bell to Wimbledon and to West London signalboxes and told the signalmen there why he had sent the signal. Those men put what signals they could to 'Danger'.

What Driver McClymont did not realise in those first few seconds was that the colliding train had spilled coaches into the path of the empty coaching stock train and derailed that, throwing part of it onto the up main local line.

Sitting in the rear guard's van of the Poole train was Driver Flood. The Report states vaguely that 'more than 200yd after Earlsfield' the driver reduced [speed] to about 50 [mph]'. Driver Flood noticed that this was done with a 20psi brake application. This was an ordinary service application, but it was followed by a full emergency application when the full brake power was thrown in. A Mr Staton, travelling in the third coach from the front, described the sensation produced by this second braking as 'violent'. Driver Flood estimated the speed at impact as 35mph.

The time interval between the first and second brake applications is not given in the Report. Because there were two brake applications it seems likely that Driver Rolls saw WF138 at double yellow and braked just enough to bring his train under control. Then, having got closer to the Basingstoke train, he realised that it was stationary in front of him, foresaw the possibility of a terrible collision and 'threw in everything'. Later measurement revealed that McClymont's train had been forced forward 10ft and, from this, careful mathematical calculations showed the speed of the 6.14am Poole at the moment of impact to have been approximately 40mph.

The disaster would have been much worse but for some brilliant railway work from Driver Pike on the 6.53am Waterloo to Waterloo via Richmond, an eight-car service. He had followed the 6.14am Poole from Surbiton and testified that he had passed Wimbledon's last controlled signal, WH70, at green. This was just seconds before the Wimbledon signalman, Mr Spencer, got 'six bells' from Clapham 'A' and turned what signals he could to 'Danger'. Driver Pike

# CLAPHAM: HOW A WORSE DISASTER WAS AVOIDED

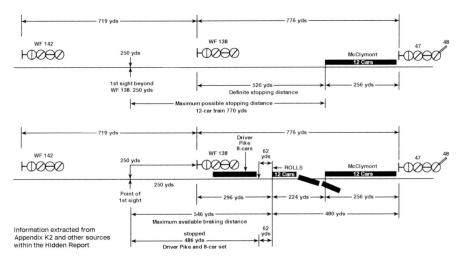

Information extracted from
Appendix K2 and other sources
within the Hidden Report

was passing WF152 at green when 'the juice went off'. This was the outcome of clever deductive work by the Raynes Park Electrical Controller, Mr Ronald Reeves. Driver Pike, unaware of what was happening, thought he had a fault on his train. He sensibly decided not to brake but to coast into Clapham Junction where he could obtain assistance. He went through Earlsfield station at around 68mph and passed WF142 at double yellow. This latter aspect was in response to Signalman Cotter having put WF47 to 'Danger'. Driver Pike was 250yd from WF138, travelling at about 58mph, when the scene of carnage came into view. The rear of the Poole train was about 520yd away. Driver Pike's reaction was instantaneous and had it not been so the tragedy would have been compounded. He stated that 'I immediately applied the emergency braking and just kept my fingers crossed. That is all I could do.' He brought his train to a stand 62yd to the rear of the wreckage.

Driver Pike immediately contacted his Guard, Mr Evans, by the train's 'Loudaphone' link, told him to go back to the rear, see what aspect WF138 was showing and to put down detonators to protect the rear of their train. Guard Evans found WF138 showing a single yellow. On the up local line a Chessington-Waterloo had stopped. Mr Evans got detonators and track circuit operating clips from his driver and walked back to WF142 because he 'could not take it for granted that it was at red'. Sensible man.

Meanwhile, Driver Pike had contacted Clapham 'A' on the telephone at WF138. Signalman Cotter answered and Pike reported that he had passed WF138 at single yellow and that there were trains standing ahead of his train. Signalman Cotter, defending his signals to the last, replied that WF138 was an automatic signal and should be showing a red aspect. According to the Hidden Report, Driver Pike retorted: 'Red aspect be damned,' (and you can believe that if you like) 'there are three trains standing in front of it and it is still showing one yellow.'

The rear of Driver McClymont's 7.18 Guildford train stood 520yd ahead of WF138. It was clearly stated at the Inquiry that the line ahead of WF138 could clearly be seen from a point 250yd to the rear of WF138. Therefore, Driver Rolls had, at most, 770yd —say 700yd — in which to see the train ahead and brake from around 50mph to a stand without hitting the Guildford train. He collided with the rear of the Guildford train at 15-20mph. The rear of the Poole train was then 296yd ahead of WF138. Driver Pike on the following train had a maximum of 250yd plus 296yd in which to stop: 546yd. He stopped in 486yd, 62yd short of the wreckage. It seems as if Driver Rolls was slow to realise the danger he was in otherwise he would have been able to stop in time.

For reasons of pity perhaps, Judge Hidden made no such analysis of the actual cause of the crash but concentrated on the lack of supervision of Mr Hemingway and his shortage of rest to criticise, at great length and in great detail, British Rail policies of man-management and safety. Such a large and detailed Report on a railway accident had not been seen since the Hixon disaster of 1967. At Hixon an entirely new piece of equipment — the automatic half-barrier — had been improperly used and the result was a terrible crash. There was a great need to inform the railways, the police and the public as to the correct way to use these barriers. There was nothing new about the equipment which had been abused at Clapham, nor was this the first time that bad workmanship by S&T technicians had caused a collision. It had happened at Farnley Junction, Leeds, in 1977 and at Shildon tunnel. Both of these accidents, similar in cause and effect to Clapham, got their conventional 20 pages of explanation and recommendation from the Inspecting Brigadier. So what was different about Clapham? Why did it merit 225 pages? Was it because it was an accident involving London commuters?

The response from press and politicians was extreme — a truly 'knee-jerk' reaction. Certainly Hidden became a splendid 'stick with which to beat a dog', and politicians on both sides of the political fence used it to beat their opponents. One lot argued that BR was incompetent and wanted to sell off the railways because that would automatically make them efficient; the other lot meanwhile said that Hidden proved that the railways had been starved of investment for years.

When the Report was published it contained white-hot criticism of BR management and made 93 very important recommendations to improve matters. These had an astonishingly galvanising effect on BR management, equivalent in some rail workers' eyes to 'total panic'. The day after the Report came out every available technician was out on the lineside and underneath signalboxes, checking every single track circuit relay, fitting terminal posts with plastic shrouds and earning several million pounds, in total, in overtime. Testing procedures at the end of essentially-simple installation jobs radically extended the time needed to do the work and, since so much of it was done at weekends, overtime pay soared.

But the implementation of important recommendations, those that cost more than some extra overtime for the men, were not supported by the vociferous politicians. The Automatic Train Protection system was recommended to be installed and was not. And the Rule Book used by Railtrack in 1999 still contains the Rule which obliges a driver who observes a signal giving a faulty aspect to stop at the next signal. Yet this is the very trap into which the railwaymen at Clapham innocently fell. In the light of Clapham, this rule should have been rewritten as 'Stop at the next-but-one signal' after the faulty signal.

# Honeybourne:
## 1989

This is the story of a near miss. It concerns Honeybourne, on the single-track railway between Moreton-in-Marsh and Evesham. Honeybourne station, on the Oxford-Worcester line, is on the edge of the Vale of Evesham, at the foot of the steep Cotswold escarpment. This great geological fault, known as 'The Edge', forced I. K. Brunel to design an incline of 1 in 100 for 4½ miles, finally piercing the Cotswold ridge with a tunnel 887yd long at the top of the 1 in 100 grade.

Honeybourne station was, in steam days, the junction for Stratford-upon-Avon and Cheltenham. It had four platforms, quadruple track and two signalboxes, Station North and Station South. Honeybourne Station North box, with 61 levers, was closed in 1965 and Station South Box, with 57 levers, was reduced to ground frame status on 20 September 1971 when the line was singled. The signalbox was demolished in 1983 after an incident with the electric train token (ETT) and a hut was erected to shelter the ETT equipment. All that was then left at Honeybourne was an unstaffed halt alongside a single-track main line with a connection, facing Evesham, into the three-mile branch line or Long Siding to the military depot of Long Marston. There was also the 'Tip' siding which could be reached by hand-operated points from the Long Marston Long Siding. Wagonloads of spent ballast and other civil engineering debris came here to be dumped. The connection from the main line to the Long Siding was operated by the guard of the train from the two-lever ground frame near the site of the former Honeybourne Station South signalbox.

The main-line block section was from Moreton-in-Marsh to Evesham and was signalled by 'old-fashioned' and 'inefficient' semaphores. To guard against head-on collisions on the single line, the signalmen used the antique but perfectly adequate ETT instruments, one in each signalbox for that section. There was also the Intermediate ETT instrument in Honeybourne ground frame. The 'train token' was an aluminium key, about 6in long, which was locked into or released from the instrument. It is referred to hereafter as 'the token'.

The lever by which the signalman at Moreton operated the semaphore signal giving access into the section to Evesham — the down starting signal — was locked in the 'Danger' position until the Moreton signalman had withdrawn the token from the instrument. He could not do this without the co-operation of the signalman at Evesham. The latter held down a switch to send

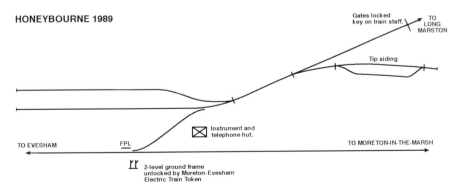

**HONEYBOURNE 1989**

Gates locked key on train staff. TO LONG MARSTON

Tip siding

Instrument and telephone hut.

TO EVESHAM    FPL    TO MORETON-IN-THE-MARSH

2-level ground frame unlocked by Moreton-Evesham Electric Train Token

85

*Above:*
Honeybourne from the road overbridge looking towards Oxford. The Long Marston branch is on the left.
*Brian Druce*

an electric current to the instrument at Moreton. This current energised and released the lock in the token instrument, allowing the token to be turned in its lock and removed. Doing this sent a current to — and released the lock on — Moreton's down starting signal lever. The signalman delivered the ETT to the driver of the train and then lowered his signal.

On a beautiful sunny day, sometime in 1989, a departmental train of civil engineer's wagons, some of which were destined for the Honeybourne 'Tip', left Moreton-in-Marsh. The train was thoughtlessly marshalled. The wagons for the 'Tip' siding were not at the rear of the train. They ought to have been, for then the whole train could have been reversed 'inside', clear of the running line. As it was, there was a wagon for Worcester marshalled between his van and those for the 'Tip' siding.

On arrival at Honeybourne, the train guard, riding in the rear cab of the locomotive, collected the token from his driver, got down to the track, walked back along his train and uncoupled the wagon at the rear. He then walked to the ground frame, put the token into the lock on the lever frame and waved his driver forward until the rearmost wagons were clear of the points. He reversed the points and waved the train into the siding. Once it was 'inside clear' he set the points for the main line, took the token out of the frame, inserted it and turned it into its lock in the intermediate instrument. He then telephoned the signalman at Moreton to tell him that his train was clear of the main line.

With that the guard went from the ground frame to rejoin his train.

As he was walking, the signalman at Moreton was 'getting the road' from Evesham for the 10.30am Paddington. With the token restored to the intermediate instrument, the Evesham signalman could send the current to the Moreton instrument, the token was withdrawn and the signalman walked with it from his signalbox, 25yd south of the station, along the platforms and handed it to the driver of the IC125. He then had to walk back to his signalbox in order to pull the down starting signal lever.

Meanwhile the guard of the departmental train had rejoined his driver, who remarked: 'You've left two on the main line.'

'Yes, that's OK.'

'You've got the token then?'

At that, the guard realised what he had done and tore off to the ground frame as fast as his legs would carry him.

The Moreton signalman walked along the platform, up the stairs of his box, went in the door and pulled the lever of the down starting signal.

As the signalman pulled the starting signal lever, the Honeybourne ground frame telephone rang. He completed the reversal of the lever and then walked to the 'phone.

At the far end of the station the semaphore arm dropped and the driver of the IC125 revved up and started to move.

The Moreton signalman answered the phone.

'Moreton'

'STOP EVERYTHING!' screamed the guard.

Without wasting a moment the signalman flung the down starting signal lever back into the frame.

As the IC125 moved towards the lowered signal, the Second Man got up to make fresh tea. He had first to empty the dregs from his can but, rather than do it from his own window, he stepped across to the driver's side window, both to empty his can and to watch the train as it left the station, as per the Rule Book. The cab passed the signal. The second man put his head out of the window, emptied his billy can and looked back. The signal arm was horizontal — at 'Danger'. He pulled his head back inside and said to his mate: 'The Bobby was a bit smart putting that board back.' The driver looked out and back. 'Yeah, OK. We'll stop.'

So a 100mph collision was avoided at Honeybourne in 1989. The Moreton signalman's actions had been admirably instant but his instant response would have been useless without a semaphore signal. If his down starting signal had been cleverly modernised, it would have been a colour-light and the second man, looking at the back of it, would have seen nothing wrong. He and his driver would have proceeded to their deaths, sipping tea on a beautiful sunny day.

# Purley:
## 4 March 1989

A narrow cul-de-sac called Glenn Avenue terminated at the foot of a 60ft-high, heavily-afforested railway embankment, 300yd north of Purley station, 13 miles by rail from London (Victoria) station. Glenn Avenue was a quiet road lined with quiet houses whose residents pursued their innocent occupations in undisturbed, suburban contemplation. At the embankment end of the cul-de-sac were the houses of Mr D. Lewis and Mr R. Taylor, the latter a retired police sergeant. At 1.40pm, Mr Lewis was working in his garden at the foot of the embankment, with his dog for company, and Mr Taylor was in his greenhouse, also at the embankment foot, enjoying that pleasant feeling of concentration one gets from lovingly administering water to plants. He emptied his watering can and left the greenhouse to go to the house for a refill. He had just reached the house when there was a terrific crashing noise. He whirled round and saw four large railway carriages sledging through the big trees down the embankment to land on top of his greenhouse. Coming down with them, flying through the air, were branches and shattered remains of the carriage bogies. One bogie embedded itself in Mr Lewis's garden, missing him and his house by a few feet.

Mr Lewis checked to see if his dog was unharmed and then ran indoors to report the emergency by 'phone and to call for the emergency services. He then went back out into his garden and found the driver of the fallen train staggering about by the wreckage. Inside the overturned coaches there were a number of passengers trapped. Mr Taylor also dashed indoors to call for help but when his 999 call received the 'engaged' tone he realised others were calling for help and went out to survey the scene, in order to decide what best he could do to help. He collected ladders from his garage and a saw and went to the carriages. By now neighbours were pouring onto the scene, some of them carrying blankets. Both Messrs Lewis and Taylor organised the arriving helpers. Mr Lewis used the blankets to cover the injured driver and Mr Taylor placed his ladder against the overturned carriages and got the younger helpers to go up them to open sky-facing doors and assist people out of the train. After about 15-20 minutes of intensive rescue work, Mr Taylor became aware of the sirens of emergency vehicles close by but not actually arriving. He realised that the crews did not know how to get to the emergency and dashed into Glenn Avenue and through an alleyway into Whytecliffe Road, where he found the Fire Brigade vainly trying to discover the way to the call. Mr Taylor showed them where to

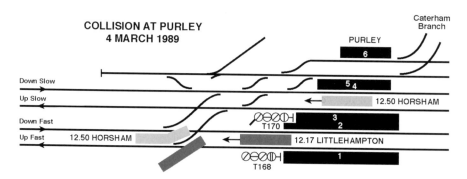

go but even then they could not get to the site because of parked cars in Glenn Avenue. Having got the emergency services to the scene, Mr Taylor allowed his house to be turned into a casualty clearing station and telephone liaison centre for the injured and the emergency services.

The train which came crashing down through the trees to shatter the peaceful suburban lunchtime was the 12.17pm Littlehampton-Victoria. It was driven by Mr R. Morgan, a man with 22 years' driving experience who had never been involved in any serious railway incident nor passed a signal at 'Danger'. He and the guard of the train, Mr A. Squires, had booked on that morning at 7.18am and worked an empty stock from Littlehampton to Brighton. They left the train at Lovers' Walk sidings and rode back passenger to Littlehampton. They got back at 9.50am and went outside to a café and had some breakfast together. Having finished breakfast, Mr Morgan bought a couple of sausage rolls for his lunch and he and Mr Squires went back to the depot. They sat around talking with whoever was about until noon when they made their way to the 2 x 4-car EMU of Class 421/2 (No 1280) forming the 12.17 for Victoria. They left on time. Everything was perfectly normal. Mr Morgan had no worries.

Signalman Owen was in charge of that part of the Three Bridges Panel which had controlled the Purley station area since 1984. The line was quadruple track with 'fast to slow' and 'slow to fast' double-line junctions. The signals were four-aspect colour-lights, each one equipped with AWS, and those signals relating to junctions were capable of being controlled manually through push buttons. The scheduled sequence of up trains between about 1.30pm and 1.39pm was a Gatwick Express on the up main, followed by the 12.50pm Horsham-Victoria from the

*Below:*
The crash site, looking south. *Brian Morrison*

*Above:*
The Littlehampton train in
Mr Taylor's back garden.
*Brian Morrison*

up slow platform, then crossed to the up fast, and the
12.17pm Littlehampton on the up fast. If the Horsham was
a little late and the Littlehampton was a little early, the
latter would be checked by signals as the former pulled out
of the up slow platform and crossed to the up fast. Should
these circumstances come about, there was no advantage in the signalman holding the Horsham
on the up slow to allow the Littlehampton to run through unchecked on the up fast, because not
only would that delay the Horsham still further, but they both stopped at East Croydon and
would arrive out of sequence — with the Littlehampton several minutes early. The
Littlehampton would then be held to 'wait time' and so cause even more delay to the Horsham
following along behind.

The signal on the up fast line at Purley protecting the junction from the up slow was T168.
With the junction set to allow the Horsham to run from up slow to up fast, signal T168 was
showing 'Danger', and so the others to the rear of it were showing, in order, a single yellow
(T178) and a double yellow (T182). Thus, a train approaching T168 had plenty of warning of
the need to stop. The Horsham train was a four-car EMU driven by Mr V. Brown. Standing at
the up slow platform, he saw a single yellow and the junction 'feathers' on the signal at the end
of the platform. The road was cleared for him to cross to the up fast. He started his train and
went over the snaking junctions at 25mph. Because the Horsham was crossing the down fast
on its way to the up fast, a Class 47 diesel, running 'light' on the down fast and driven by Mr
M. Brown, was held at signal T153, about 550yd north of the station. Driver M. Brown was
therefore looking south and could see the Littlehampton approaching from the south on the up
fast as the Horsham crossed over. He realised at once that it was running too fast to stop at

*Above:*
Signal T168, past which Mr Morgan drove at 'Danger'. Times have changed since 1989: the vegetation at the lineside is much denser and trains have got heavier and longer — longer in distance travelled as well as train length. On 19 May 2000 EWS No 66164 is hauling the 10.15am Bordesley-Brescia (Italy). The actual train was about half a mile long. *Author*

T168, that it would collide with the Horsham, and was actually getting out of his seat when, with three of the four Horsham coaches on the up fast and the last coach still on the crossover, the Littlehampton crashed into the side of the fourth coach. Before the wreckage had stopped, he was running to a signal-post telephone to advise the Three Bridges signalman that he had a major emergency on his hands at Purley North Junctions. As he was talking, a train on the down slow was brought to a stand by its driver. Mr M. Brown put detonators on the rails and saw that short-circuiting bars were placed to cut off traction current. He then went, with other railwaymen, to render assistance to the trapped passengers.

Driver Morgan of the Littlehampton train was completely at a loss to understand what had happened. He was able to recollect the signals at and approaching all the stations he called at, including Purley's T168, but he could not remember the aspects of the signals approaching T168 — T178 and T182. He remembered driving his train at about 70mph after leaving Gatwick, swanning along very happily, until, as he entered the southern end of the platform at Purley, he saw T168 at 'Danger'. He made an immediate emergency brake application as the thought ran through his mind that 'the signal should not be that colour'. Everything happened fast and became a blur. He realised he would not be able to stop in time and just hung on tight. His cab hit the side of the last coach which was, of course, coming across

*Above:*
Signal T170, which signalled the
12.50pm Horsham from up slow to up
fast. In the distance of this view, taken on
19 May 2000, the approaching train,
which is on the down fast, is just about
to pass over the junction from up slow to
up fast. Signal T168 can be seen on the
left, above the concrete fence. *Author*

from right to left at an angle to his own train,
at a closing speed of around 35mph. The
glancing blow deflected Mr Morgan's train to
the left. Six of the eight coaches were
derailed and those plunged down the
embankment, showering the peaceful
horticulturalists below with tree branches and
carriage bogies. When the train stopped

moving he slid out onto the ground from a gap in his cab and staggered about, mumbling, trying to think how the accident had happened. Even at the Inquiry he was at a loss to recall events clearly.

Five passengers were killed and 88 people, including three railway employees, were injured. Thirty-two were detained in hospital.

Signal T168 was obscured somewhat by the platform awnings but it was so positioned that, at 90mph, an approaching driver had it in view for the obligatory seven seconds before he passed it. More importantly, the warning signals preceding a red aspect at T168 — single yellow at T178 and double yellow at T182 — were amply visible. A driver passing T182 could see the aspect of T178 1,100yd ahead. Thus, Mr Morgan had a full braking distance to reduce speed and approach T168 slowly enough to see it at red for much longer than seven seconds, and to be well warned of the need to stop if required. Tragically for five people, and indeed for himself, Mr Morgan let his concentration slip for a short while. He must have acknowledged/cancelled his AWS warning at T182 and T178 without the importance of the warning registering in his mind. He was a conscientious driver. Every day he watched hundreds of signals and obeyed them, controlling his train accordingly. On this one occasion his concentration slipped and he made a terrible mistake. He bravely faced up to the error he had made and never tried to make any excuse for himself. He had worked on the railways for 40 years, carrying heavy responsibility, and had more commitment to the job than to hide behind lame excuses. How many of the newspaper editors, churning out their sensational headlines, could even lay claim to 40 years' service with one newspaper, let alone without making a mistake? Even if they did make a mistake, it would hardly be of any great import. They were paid ten times the salary of Driver Morgan, yet he was in a job of ten times — perhaps a thousand times — the importance of theirs.

Driver Morgan was charged with manslaughter and faced his trial on 3 September 1990, pleading Guilty. He was sentenced to 18 months' imprisonment with 12 months suspended. He was the first and only driver ever to go to prison for a working error. Mr Cooksey, the Deputy Chief Inspecting Officer, recommended that ATP be installed. There was less promptitude in this respect than in the pillorying of Driver Morgan.

*Above:*
After the crash a 'Garden of Remembrance' was established at Purley station. It seems to have been forgotten. The commemorative plaque is to the right of the bunch of irises. *Author*

# Bellgrove Junction:
## 6 March 1989

Bellgrove, station and junction for the Springburn branch, is a little over one mile east of Glasgow Queen Street Low Level station on the main line to Airdrie. At the time of the crash the suburban railway in that area was in the process of being modernised. The trains had been electrified on the 25kV AC overhead catenary system and a central signalling control centre was being built at Yoker, approximately 10 miles west of Bellgrove Junction. The vast layout had been simplified to enable the control centre to run it, and the colour-light signals, mostly four-aspect, which would eventually come under the control of Yoker, were being worked by conventional signalboxes. Each signal was backed-up with a conventional AWS magnet.

The line through High Street and Bellgrove had once been quadruple track with two double junctions at Bellgrove, one between the fast and slow lines and one from the slow onto the Springburn branch. On 20 April 1987, as a stage in the introduction of Yoker panel, two tracks were removed from the main line. The remaining two tracks, up and down main, passed on each side of an island platform at Bellgrove Junction station. At the east end of the platform the old, double-line junction was replaced with a modern single-lead junction as shown in the diagram. Within two years of its installation the head-on collision occurred.

Bellgrove Junction was operated by a signalman in a signalbox working to Absolute Block regulations, but operating the three- and four-aspect colour-light signals which would later be controlled from Yoker panel. The Bellgrove signalman had a busy time of it, handling 12 trains an hour: two trains in each direction on the Springburn branch and four each way on the main line. The signalman worked with bells and instruments to High Street box on the main line towards Glasgow, Parkhead North Junction towards Airdrie, and Sighthill Junction on the branch. Trains coming east, away from Glasgow, to Bellgrove were designated 'up', and those going west, towards Glasgow, were 'down' trains.

The track diagram issued with the Report on this accident inefficiently neglects to give any distances between signals and points, but I know from another source (Sheriff Mackay of Glasgow's Fatal Accident Inquiry 25.7.89.) that the up home signal was only 116yd from the fouling point of the junction. This distance ought to have been 200yd and because of the lack of the regulation 'overlap' (or 'clearing point', to use conventional Absolute Block terminology) between the signal and the junction it was protecting, the Bellgrove signalman was forbidden to give 'Line Clear' to the High Street signalman for an up train 'when the points were set from the Springburn branch to the down main'. Because the High Street signalman could not clear his starting signal, HS103, without a 'Line Clear' indication from Bellgrove, HS103 would remain at 'Danger' and so hold an up train at a safe distance from the junction if it was set for a train to come off the branch. What could, legitimately, happen is that the Bellgrove Junction signalman could 'give the road' to High Street for an up train destined for the branch and, therefore, the junction points would be set for the main line, with the down branch home signal, BL82 at Duke Street station, being locked at 'Danger'. When an up branch train stopped at Bellgrove Junction with the junction signal, BL86, at 'Danger' in front of it, the Bellgrove signalman could then set the road from the up main line to the branch and then clear signal BL82 for the down branch train to come onto the down main.

The signalman at Bellgrove Junction was Mr D. Graham, who had been a signalman for 31 years, with his last 12 years spent on 'relief' work. He was assisted by a lad telegraphist (or 'booking boy'), Mr Ackland, who had been working there for 15 months. On the day of the

**COLLISION AT BELLGROVE**
**6 MARCH 1989**

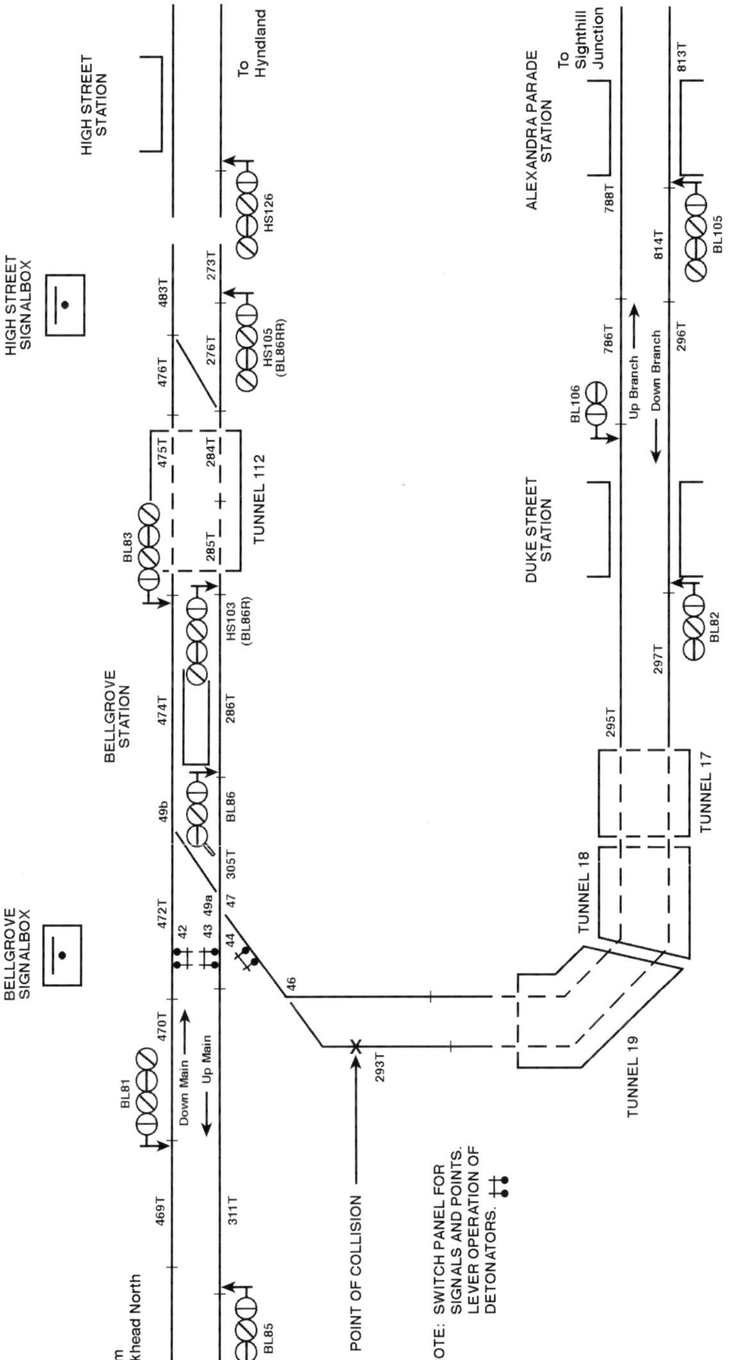

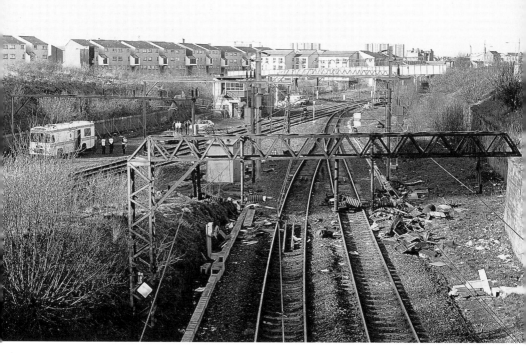

*Above:*
Bellgrove Junction, with the
branch line below the
camera. Bellgrove station is
just out of view on right. The
route is set for a train to
come from off the branch —
the left-hand track — and
enter upon the bi-directional
part of the up main line,
running against the flow of
traffic, to a crossover (out of
sight) which would take the
branch train to the down
main. The signalbox can be
seen centre left, amongst the
tangle of the overhead
catenary. *Tom Noble*

accident, he admitted that he had not recorded the time of every bell signal received and there were unexplained inaccuracies in some of the times he had recorded. The most remarkable of these inaccuracies was that Signalman Graham apparently gave 'Train out of Section' for the Springburn branch train at 12.45pm. This, I hope, was a 'booking' error because at 12.45pm the down branch train was still at Duke Street station, occupying the section, and Signalman Graham could not have seen its tail lamp. There was no written record of 'Is Line Clear?' having been 'asked' to High Street for the down branch train. Signalman Graham said he thought the boy 'might have overlooked this in the excitement'. But there was no excitement at 12.45pm, nothing but routine. The up train was still at High Street at 12.45pm. The signalmen at High Street and Sighthill Junction, on the Springburn branch, were not required to keep a train register. The result of all this is a lack of a record of the events leading up to the collision.

What is clear is that it was one of those 'coin-tossing' situations at a junction. The trains were timed closely at the junction, with the down branch train scheduled off the branch before the up branch train went onto it. But the down branch train was a minute or even two minutes late,

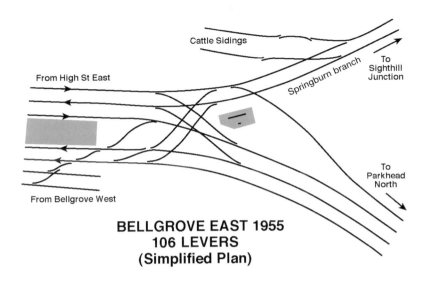

**BELLGROVE EAST 1955**
**106 LEVERS**
**(Simplified Plan)**

Cattle Sidings

From High St East

To
Sighthill
Junction

Springburn branch

To
Parkhead
North

From Bellgrove West

encroaching exactly into the 'path' of the up train. Had the junction been conventional double track, there would have been no problem; as it was, one or other of the trains was going to be delayed. Signalman Graham's problem was to decide which to stop for the least delay. The signalbox register for Bellgrove on the day of the accident showed that out of 15 up trains offered to Bellgrove from High Street, eight had been refused because of trains coming off the branch. Thus, seven ran unchecked into the platform and, conceivably, before the arrival of the other train. This shows that the Bellgrove Junction signalman was regularly faced with deciding which train to stop: the one coming off the down branch, or the one coming along the up main.

The trains involved in the collision were three-car electric multiple units of Class 303. These were in process of being refurbished and the up train, 2A02 12.20pm Milngavie-Springburn, had been so refurbished, while the down train, 2A01 12.39pm Springburn-Milngavie, was in its original condition. The driver of the up train, Mr McCafferty, told the Inquiry that he was brought nearly to a stand at HS103 before it changed to a single yellow. He said that this was normal working because the down train off the Springburn branch was usually given precedence over the junction and would normally be waiting at the opposite platform when his train ran in. As he approached Bellgrove station he saw the junction signal, BL86, was showing a red, but then saw it go directly to green with a 'feather' (junction indicator) for the branch. He stopped his train at the '3-car' marker. He was on the left of his cab and the signal was to the right, visible only if he actually turned his head to look at it. Driver McCafferty stated that, because the down train was not at the platform, he assumed that it was very late, or cancelled, and that is why he was signalled onto the branch. His train stood for a minute and, when he got two blips on the 'start' buzzer from the guard, he simply set off. He honestly admitted that he did not look at the signal before he moved off but assumed it was showing a green and feathers because, as he claimed, it had been showing that aspect when he last looked. The guard of the up train, Mr Bain, had not looked to see what the signal was showing before giving Mr McCafferty the buzzer signal to proceed.

The Rule Book Section H 5.1.3 states that, at unstaffed stations, the guard must, *where practicable*, ensure that the starting signal is cleared before giving the driver the signal to start. In 1979, British Rail officials had examined Bellgrove station with a view to providing, if necessary, a signal aspect repeater at some point along the platform so as to enable the guard to carry out the signal check. The officials concluded that it was practical for the guard to check the actual signal from the platform and then return to his carriage and no repeater was necessary. Mr Bain did not think he could have seen the signal from the platform owing to the curvature of the line so he did not look. He had complied with the Rule Book but the Rule was weak.

The signal was, of course, at red when Driver McCafferty moved off, because the route was set for the down branch train to come from the branch line to the down main, and damage to the points by Mr Mcafferty's train proves that this was so.

Whether BL86 had exhibited a green light when Mr McCafferty was at some distance from it is a difficult point. Signalman Graham was adamant that it had always shown red and Driver McCafferty was adamant that the signal had been showing green with the 'feather' when he last looked. Either scenario is possible. Signalman Graham could have set the route for the up branch and cleared BL86 and then, seeing the position of the down branch train, changed his mind and 'reversed the road'. He would first have replaced BL86 to 'Danger'. The interlocking would have held the points locked in position for 75sec before allowing them to be reset from the down branch to the down main. Because the Bellgrove train register was inaccurately recorded, it is impossible to know whether this is what happened or not. It is McCafferty's word against Graham's. But in the end it is the driver's responsibility to look at signals and Driver McCafferty did not look.

Mr Graham saw the up train move off and immediately pulled over his detonator lever to put detonators — explosive shots — on the line under its leading wheels, then ran to the window to wave in an attempt to attract the driver's attention. The shots were on the single-line section of the junction. They exploded and Guard Bain, at the rear end of the three-car set, heard them go off. So did Driver McCafferty, but he did not recognise the significance of the sound and a few seconds later crashed head-on into the down train. The closing speed was about 30mph. Driver McCafferty survived the impact, but the driver of the other train and one passenger were killed.

Had this been a conventional double junction or of the parallel single-lead type, the accident could not have happened. Driver McCafferty did wrong in passing the signal at 'Danger', but the dangerous situation into which he had passed was the result of cost-cutting policy, the responsibility of people far more highly placed than himself.

Eight reasons for installing single-lead junctions were submitted to the Inquiry by Mr Warburton, Director of Operations, BRB. They boil down to the simple fact that they are cheaper to construct and maintain than the conventional double-line junction, although how much cheaper was not stated. Mr Knox, Signalling & Safety Officer, ScotRail, stated that a single-lead junction was no more dangerous than a conventional double junction. I believe that the single-lead junction is more dangerous than the old-fashioned double junction and is also less efficient for traffic purposes. In both the conventional, double-line junction and the single-lead junction there is a risk that a train coming off the branch line and crossing the main line might be collided with if a train on the main line runs past the signal at 'Danger'. This happened at Purley only two days earlier. There is also a risk that a train passing over the junction on the main line might be cut through by a runaway train off the branch. The single-lead junction, however, introduces a third risk — the potential for a head-on collision. This is impossible in a conventional junction, so one might say that there is a 33% greater risk of accident in a single-lead junction when compared to a conventional junction.

The single-lead junction is less traffic-efficient than a conventional junction because it prevents a simultaneous movement of two trains between the main and branch lines and thereby causes delays to trains. The conventional double junction has less risks attached to it and facilitates traffic movements. But I was only ever a signalman and there are great experts in these matters who know better. Yet, in the period during which I gained my railway knowledge, the late 1950s, there were highly-placed persons who also perceived the additional risks and inefficiencies of the single-lead junction. In 1958, an Agreement was signed between British Railways and the Ministry of Transport so that no single-lead junction would be installed without the plan being submitted for approval to the Ministry. Clearly, in those coal-fired days, someone, somewhere was still old-fashioned enough to feel a little nervous about these monstrosities.

The installation of the single-lead junction at Bellgrove was done without the sanction of the Railway Inspectorate. The person responsible for submitting the proposal for a single-lead junction was Mr Knox. He did not, however, submit the plan for a single-lead junction to the Department of Transport because he did not think that the regulations applied as, he said, the arrangements at Bellgrove were purely temporary and not intended to last more than two years. This seems rather Jesuitical to me, since the objectionable junction was not temporary but part of the Yoker scheme intended to be in use for many years. What was temporary was its control from a manual signalbox and the signalling arrangements that went with it. Mr Knox was not paid to be a prophet and he could not know for how long the junction would remain manually controlled. Indeed, the manual signalboxes were not due to be abolished until September 1990 — 2½ years after the installation at Bellgrove. Mr Knox also stated that he did not apply for permission to install the single-lead junction at Bellgrove because he believed he was replacing 'like for like'; that there was no difference between the two kinds of junction. Mr Knox went so far as to assert that the original layout at Bellgrove was 'an extremely complicated series of double junctions [that were] fraught with danger'. But in the 70 years of their existence they had never caused an accident. Mr Knox was merely carrying out and — at the Inquiry — defending a policy made by others. The new junction at Bellgrove was the cheapest possible in money terms. The fact that it was also the most dangerous of the options available had therefore to be denied.

The best junction layout is the parallel single-lead junction. This combines the safety advantage possessed by the conventional double junction with the cheapness of construction and maintenance of the single-lead system. It requires slightly more space than the cheap and nasty version used at Bellgrove. There was ample space to install a parallel single-lead junction at Bellgrove, but it would have cost more and so was not adopted. The parallel single-lead junction is the only safe way cheaply to supersede the conventional double junction.

But the Chief Inspecting Officer of Railways, Mr Seymour, and the Principal Railway Employment Inspector, Mr A. Williams, accepted BR policy as laid down by Mr Warburton. 'The single-lead junction is easier and cheaper to maintain and therefore it is less prone to dangerous deterioration than the conventional junction.' The latter is a piece of tortuous pleading. One might well consult one's common sense and ask whether the gangers of old, finding a junction difficult to maintain, would have allowed it to deteriorate into a dangerous condition.

Mr Williams also asserted that: 'The single-lead junction is no different in principle from countless other situations where trains run in both directions over a single track.' But to say that is actually the same as saying: 'The single-lead junction is as dangerous as countless other situations where trains run in both directions over a single track.' The fact is that the adoption of this type of junction introduced the additional risk associated with single lines where no such risk had previously existed. Finally, Messrs Seymour and Williams agreed with Mr Warburton's statement that the safety of any railway, whatever the layout, must depend upon the principle that drivers stop their trains at signals. This is also true, yet it cannot be taken to its logical conclusion, which is that all you need for safety is an alert driver and a danger signal. If that were so we might as well go back to 'Time Interval' working. Drivers should indeed obey the signals, but strategic planners are not thereby absolved from the necessity of providing sensible layouts.

The report of the Railway Inspectorate stated that 'single-lead junctions are acceptable in principle on safety grounds', and went so far as to approve, in retrospect — since the Railway Inspectorate's permission had never been sought — the use of this type of junction at Bellgrove. The Report also stated: 'We do not believe that the limited benefits of a parallel [single-lead] junction would justify the realignment of Bellgrove Junction in that form.' It is worth remembering that the limited benefits referred to take the form of a guarantee of immunity from head-on collision.

The Report also recommended that 'British Railways should proceed as quickly as possible to the development and installation of an effective system of Automatic Train Protection'. This had been repeated so often as to take on the appearance of a mantra and was about as much use. I am left with the feeling that the Inspectorate is at pains to allow railway managers to make their operation cheaper. The Inspectors might say ambiguously that some hazard is 'noted', but they will not come down on the side of safety and say 'We disapprove of'. It is remarkable to what extent the Railway Inspectorate defended policy at Bellgrove when common sense suggested the opposite course. It is, in this respect, worth noting that the Sheriff of Glasgow, after conducting a Fatal Accident Inquiry into the accident, took a layman's view which was based purely on common sense. This was that at Bellgrove, British Rail had not taken the reasonable precaution of designing the railway system to avoid a dangerous situation.

*Above:*
With the route set for a train to come off the branch to join the down main line, there was nothing to stop an absent-minded driver from driving past the signal at Bellgrove station and going onto the branch, head-on towards the train signalled off it. Had the junction been of the conventional, double-line type, this could not have happened. *Tom Noble*

# Hyde Junction:
## 22 August 1990

One year and five months after Bellgrove another head-on collision took place, this time at Hyde North Junction, 6½ miles from Manchester, on the old GCR main line to Sheffield via the Woodhead Tunnel, a route now cut back to terminate at Glossop. However, this route was still referred to as the main line. The junction was of the single-lead variety and was controlled from a 'Panel' control console in Guide Bridge signalbox, about 1½ miles away. At Hyde North Junction a right-hand crossover — points 1008 — took trains to the down main, and points 1007 took them off the down main to the up branch. Points 1007 constituted a single track until, at points 1006, the down branch diverged and the branch line resumed its normal, double-track form. Points 1006 lay normally for the up branch line (see diagram). This 'branch' was actually the line out into the rest of the country, once Joint GCR/Midland Railway as far as Hayfield and then Midland to Sheffield via the Hope Valley.

On the morning in question, Guide Bridge signalbox was being operated by Signalman Blinston. At 9.45am he was dealing with three trains: a Manchester (Piccadilly) to Sheffield passenger train, 2E06, was approaching the junction on the up main line, a Glossop-Manchester was approaching on the down main line, and another passenger train, 2H57, was approaching Hyde North station and the junction on the down branch line. The 2E06 required to cross from up main to up branch and was held at the junction signal 862 for about a minute at 9.46-47am to allow the Glossop-Manchester to pass by. As the latter passed across the junction, the 2H57 arrived and stopped at the platform of Hyde North station, with signal 865 at 'Danger' protecting the main line in front of the driver. Ahead of him, the double line of the branch merged briefly into a single track before joining the down main line, and then the facing crossover to the up main.

The Glossop train was clear of the junction by 9.48am and Signalman Blinston set the road for the 2E06 from up main to up branch by reversing crossover points 1008 and 1007 and clearing signal 862. Mr Blinston then got on with other operations, but became aware that something was wrong at Hyde North when, at 9.51am, he noticed that the 'detection' indicator lights for points 1006 were flashing, telling him that the points were no longer properly closed and 'detected'. He also saw that the track circuit indication showing 2H57 standing at the down main platform at Hyde North was no longer illuminated. There were two trains but only one 'Track Occupied' indication showing on Guide Bridge panel. And the only length of track they could be occupying was a single line!

The 2H57 went against signal 865 and collided head-on at low speed with 2E06 which 'had the road'. This is proved by the fact that 2H57 'ran through' — or burst open — points 1006, because they were lying closed to the down branch, but set for the up branch. Out of 42 passengers, 28 were taken to hospital for minor injuries. There were no fatalities. Train 2E06 was a three-car DMU and 2H57 was a two-car set, both of Class 108, built at Derby in 1959/60. The driver of 2H57 was Mr Livingstone.

The Inspector's Report makes no reference at all to the dangers inherent in single-lead junctions, but investigates in some detail the quality of training Mr Livingstone had received and the quality of supervision which allowed him to drive trains.

Mr Livingstone was selected for driver training in November 1988. The BR training schedule applied to him had been brought into force the previous month. In order to cut costs and get more drivers through training and into work, the new training scheme was of shorter

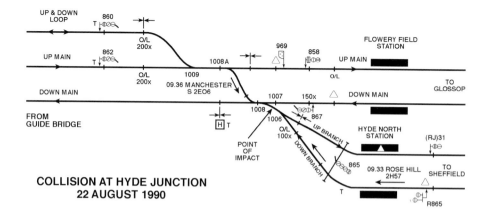

**COLLISION AT HYDE JUNCTION
22 AUGUST 1990**

duration than had previously been the case but the process by which people were selected for training was made, in the eyes of authority at any rate, more rigorous. In October 1988, five Train Crew Selection Centres were established around the country, and at these centres expert assessors applied psychological tests which had been developed in conjunction with the Netherlands Railways. This railway administration had had some 50 years of experience of these tests. As an ex-coal-fired railwayman I cannot help smiling at the naïvety of it all, but then I would certainly have failed the tests since my cynicism would have shown through. One must never be cynical of what the experts happen to believe in at any given point in history.

The aspirant to the post of Driver would spend a day at one of these centres to undergo these tests, which were designed to ensure that 'the person was capable of absorbing the information and knowledge required' (ie that he was alive), and that the person was possessed of 'certain key aptitudes which had been identified as important in the role of driver'. What kind of person had decided what were the key aptitudes for drivers is an interesting question. One of the desired aptitudes was 'speed of reaction', and the test was such as might be used for the would-be pilot of a jet fighter. People good at reacting very quickly and pressing buttons were the ones who would pass these tests, and this was said to show that they were suitable as train drivers. It might also show that those who passed were conversant with computer games and amusement arcades and those that failed were not. There was no test to gauge the intensity of a person's sense of responsibility or duty to his fellow creatures — no test to assess how seriously he would take his life-and-death responsibilities. He was tested as a species of machine, not as a human being. It was cheap, nasty and possibly irrelevant, but it was a quick fix and had a 'scientific' look about it. It must, of course, be said that most people going successfully through this process went on to become responsible drivers. Not because the tests had selected them, but rather because they were fully competent in spite of the tests. And it is also true that excellent aspirants to driver and signalman positions have been lost to the railway because they could not react as required to the experts' very clever psychological aptitude tests.

The name Train Crew Selection Centre was an example of double-speak because it had no responsibility for selection. On completion of the tests, the centre returned a report to the Train Crew Manager (TCM) who had put forward the applicant. The TCM read the report. He had never seen him in the selection process but was expected to decide whether the applicant was suitable for further training. The decision was solely his. If he was hard-up for drivers, he might be tempted to let a person into the system whom, in happier circumstances, he would not have accepted; in which case all the clever tests counted for nothing.

Mr Livingstone was accepted and sent to Crewe training centre. The latter dealt only with theory. There he spent five days absorbing 'the principles of route learning'. This was followed by four weeks learning about the vehicles he would be driving, how their controls worked, how to overcome certain basic failures. At the end of this he took his examination on what he had been taught. He failed this exam and was re-examined by a Manchester Area Traction Inspector and then by the Chief, Mr Cheetham. The latter passed Mr Livingstone, and at the Inquiry into the collision said that he put Mr Livingstone 'at about the middle of the range of drivers on that particular examination'. Mr Livingstone then returned to the Manchester depot from which he would be working for two weeks with a driving instructor, followed by four weeks at the controls under the eye of a 'minder'. There was no formal liaison between the local depot and the training school, no exchange of impressions. After six weeks out and about on trains, Mr Livingstone was returned to Crewe to begin a two-week course on the Rules and Regulations for train working. But, of course, two weeks means two working weeks, a total of 10 days, and the last of these Mr Livingstone spent in an examination on what he had been taught. So he had no more than nine days on the Rules. He was instructed by Mr Blaxill, whose impression was that Mr Livingstone 'gave the appearance of not concentrating and perhaps was a little lax in his ways. When questioned, the answers were forthcoming, although perhaps a little bit slowly, which', he recognised, 'could be the man's thinking time, rather than that he did not know the answer'.

One is bound to ask why, if Mr Livingstone had rather poor concentration and was slow in responding to questions, the answers to which he knew, this was not pin-pointed by the very clever aptitude tests of Netherlands Railways. Furthermore, these not terribly good results were not communicated to the TCM at Mr Livingstone's depot.

After passing his Rules exam, Mr Livingstone had another two weeks under a driving instructor pending the final exam on his ability to drive. The principal criterion was 'safely, not expertly'. So it would appear that, after 15 or 16 weeks, he was handed the onerous responsibility of driving a train full of passengers. Once upon a time he would have spent 15 or 16 years learning his craft.

Mr Livingstone, it would appear from the foregoing, began driving on his own responsibility in March 1989.

Mr Livingstone stated to the Inquiry, through his lawyer, that, as he ran into Hyde North station, signal 865 was at 'Danger' in front of him. While he was standing at the station he never took his eyes off the signal and, after about 1-1½ min, the signal changed to single yellow. A few seconds later he got the 'Proceed' bell from his guard. He stated that he then selected second gear to start and moved away. He was running at 20mph as he approached points 1006. His statement made no mention of whether he noticed that these points were set wrongly for his train, but he said that, as he approached the points, he saw 2E06 coming towards him. Mr Livingstone made a full brake application then got up and opened the door from his cab to the passenger area with the intention of shouting a warning, when the collision occurred. This was the second time he had passed a signal at 'Danger' that month. On the first occasion he had been given a full examination on the Rules and a practical exam on the type of traction he was driving by the Chief Traction Inspector, Mr Cheetham. Mr Cheetham told the Inquiry that Mr Livingstone had answered his questions 'reasonably well', which sounds as if he had reservations. But there was no 'feed-back' between instructors and inspectors, or even between inspectors. Everything was piecemeal and the whole picture was never realised.

The signalling system was in perfect working order and it is not possible that Mr Livingstone could have been given a 'Proceed' aspect by signal 865 because points 1006 were not reversed for his train to pass over them. He was asked whether the yellow aspect had remained steadily at yellow and he replied: 'I did not see it for very long. I got the bell almost immediately it changed to yellow. I did not look at it after getting the bell because I am fairly new. I was watching my gear selection because there were a number of occasions while I was training when I put it into second gear instead of first.' In spite of looking carefully to make sure he got it into first instead of second gear, he still put it into second, and yet, according to the first part of his statement, he selected second gear deliberately.

Mr Livingstone claimed that he saw a yellow aspect in 865. This would have happened if the signalman had cleared the route for 2H57 to proceed and then changed his mind and restored the signal to 'Danger'. But had he done this there would have been a two-minute delay, as the locking would have held the routes before allowing a conflicting route to be set up. Had Mr Livingstone seen the yellow and almost at once got the bell to proceed, he would still have had the points 1006 correctly set for the passage of his train. But they were smashed by his train. Clearly they had always been set for the up branch and he had passed the signal 865 at 'Danger'. The train register at Guide Bridge also showed that 2E06 was not delayed beyond the time it took to get the Glossop train across the junction.

The Inspector criticised the lack of ATP and did not totally blame the driver. The Inspecting Officer wrote: 'Having concluded that the accident was caused by a failure of the driver to obey a signal, I am satisfied that he had no deliberate intention of doing so. I have formed the opinion that his lapse stemmed from his basic lack of ability as a driver.' What use psychometric tests? The Inspecting Officer's summing up made no reference to the actions of the guard of the train, Mr Rayworth. Paragraph 17 of the Report states that he saw the repeater for signal 865 at 'Danger' and in paragraph 19 he admitted that he did not observe the actual aspect of signal 865 before giving 'Right Away'. This would be an infringement of Section H 5.1.3 unless, of course, it was not 'practicable' for him to have observed it even from the platform. It is surprising that the Report does not make this clear, one way or another.'

Had the long-recommended ATP or TPWS been installed at 865 the accident would not have happened. Had the junction not been of that most objectionable single-lead variety it would not have happened. Had Driver Livingstone been better trained, better looked after and not rushed so hastily into the job when it seems likely that he was not ready for it, then, perhaps, it would not have happened. That other people went through the same training and did not fail is irrelevant. The system was a scientific sausage-machine, clearly not taking account of the needs of individuals. Ultimately, cost-cutting ends up costing more.

# Newton:
## 21 July 1991

Eleven months after Hyde North came another collision on a recently-singled, ex-double-line junction, this time at Newton Junction, about 6½ miles southeast of Glasgow, where the West Coast main line (WCML) connects with the Glasgow suburban network. The hitherto complex — but accident-free — layout at Newton had been rationalised by signalling experts so as to be as cheap to install and to maintain and to increase speed on the West Coast main line. It is indeed Orwellian that the introduction of such a layout should have been described as 'rational'. But there is much that is 'double-speak' on the modern railway, as railway sense is overtaken by commercial considerations.

The Newton layout contained some bizarre features which gave as many opportunities as possible for erring drivers to engage in unprotected head-on collisions. Those who had to work over it found the heightened risks of collision which had been introduced worrying. They did not like the absence of catch-point or sand-drag protection, and found the design of the layout not only amateurish but also disturbing. It had, of course, been approved by the Railway Inspectorate.

The collision at Newton was different from the other two single-lead junction mishaps inasmuch as the train was being operated on the 'Driver Only' principle, with no guard to give a misleading 'Proceed' signal to the driver. The driver involved was no 'strapper' (beginner), but a man with 43 years' unblemished service and whose skill, competence and physical fitness were held in the highest regard. Driver McEwan was described as 'a quiet man' and 'a gentleman' who was always smartly turned out for work and dedicated to safety. He was driving train 2P55, the 9.55pm Newton to Glasgow. The other driver was Mr Scott, working the 2J66 8.55pm Balloch to Motherwell. He had started on BR as a traction trainee in 1983, became a driver's assistant in that year and became a relief driver in 1988.

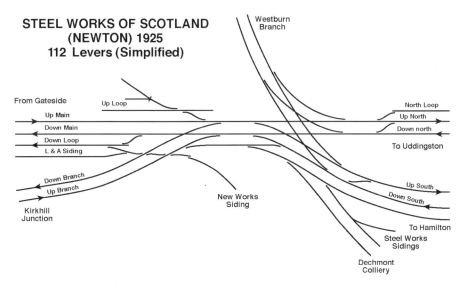

STEEL WORKS OF SCOTLAND
(NEWTON) 1925
112 Levers (Simplified)

It was about 9.45pm on the night of 21 July and a flurry of four movements was scheduled in the next 10 minutes in and out of Newton's up and down platforms and over the single-line connection. Timed first was 2J65, a Motherwell-Balloch which needed to use the down platform, then 2J66, the 8.55pm Balloch-Motherwell train driven by Mr Scott, which would use the up platform. Finally, Mr McEwan's train would run from the 'turn back' siding to the down platform to form 2P55, the 9.55pm Newton-Glasgow. But 2J65 was running 10min late, Mr Scott on 2J66 was running 2min late, while Driver McEwan's train was 'waiting time' in the 'turn back' siding. So the panel signaller decided, quite correctly, to bring Mr McEwan's train, 2P55, out of the siding to the down platform, as 2J65 was still a fair way off. He held 2P55 at signal M145 to wait while 2J66 came over the north connecting line into the up platform. Then, 2P55 could then leave for Glasgow on time, leaving the platform clear for the late-running 2J65. It was a good bit of signalling improvisation, and the sort of thing a signaller has to do regularly.

If all trains had been running to time, Driver McEwan would have sat with his train in the siding for six or seven minutes, but because the Motherwell-Balloch was so late he had only just gone into the siding and 'changed ends' when he got 'two white lights' in signal M163 with the indicator for the down platform. Mr McEwan drew out over points 35 and crossover 26 and came to a stand in the down platform, with signal M145 at 'Danger' in front of him. The signalman then set the route for 2J66 from the up main (WCML), across the north connecting line to the Newton station up platform, and onwards towards Motherwell. Mr McEwan's train stood at the platform for about 4min. Mr McEwan, a steady and highly-experienced railwayman, was one who found the new layout potentially more dangerous than the old. He had voiced something of his misgivings only that day to the Ticket Examiner on his train, Mrs Hanlon. Mrs Hanlon had an assistant with her that day, Mr McKinnon, but neither was involved in safety duties, only with tickets. They were busy with financial matters as the train stood at the platform for about 4min — much longer than usual, because of the out-of-course timetable — and then moved smoothly away. The train was working under Driver Only Operation conditions, and Mr McEwan did not need a signal from either Hanlon or McKinnon to start his train. Soon after leaving the platform, Hanlon and McKinnon felt a heavy braking, and about 20sec later there came a noise like an explosion and the train shuddered to a halt. The 9.55pm Newton-Glasgow had collided head-on with the 8.55pm Balloch-Motherwell. Both drivers were killed and also two passengers: Mr Kenneth Meechan and Miss Tracey Donachie. Twenty-two passengers were injured, but only four were kept in hospital overnight.

The new signalling system at Newton had had a lot of 'teething troubles'. Thirty-four faults were reported in three months and doubtless others were seen by drivers and not reported. The place must have been something of a nightmare for the drivers whose lives depended on the correct functioning of the Solid State Interlocking. Three of these incidents were potentially lethal. On 25 June, points 22 moved of their own accord due to a cable fault; on 9 September, points 19 and 20 both moved in error, and the following day points 19 and 37 moved of their own accord. Three 'faults' reported by drivers regarding incorrect signal aspects were found to have been signalmen's errors and the other 30 were signal aspect errors due to faulty equipment. On 29 July a train was standing in the up platform with signal M156 showing red. The aspect then changed to green and back to single yellow. The fault was in the 'module' working signal M166, next ahead of M156, on the south connecting line. The accident report does not state if this was a 'wrong-side' failure — ie that the signal had changed aspects of its own accord, due to the faulty module — or whether the signalman had cleared the signal and then the faulty module caused the aspects to change in an incorrect sequence. This 'module' was the cause of nine 'right-side' signal aspect errors between 28 July and 8 September. On 8 September, the faulty module of M166 caused M156 to make a rapid change of aspects as follows: yellow (Y), double yellow (YY), green (G), red (R), Y, YY, G, R, then Y. While this was taking place, the route indicators (feathers) were flashing, so it was quite a spectacular sight. When these stupid events take place on a regular basis on a brand-new installation, the morale of railwaymen is undermined with contempt for the system. However, it should be noted that signal M145 and its associated points were never reported for a fault, which is not to say that they could not have had one. Whether or not Driver McEwan got a 'Proceed' aspect from signal M145 we shall never know. The points were definitely set for the Balloch-Motherwell train to enter the station, the train was entering and so, one supposes, Driver Scott had the signals to admit him — and the track circuits were occupied. Under these circumstances it does not seem at all possible that the interlocking could have allowed M145 to show a 'Proceed' aspect. So the mystery remains: why did a highly experienced, conscientious driver like McEwan pass a signal at 'Danger', especially when he had earlier the same evening told Mrs Hanlon of the dire potential for collision which had been created by the 'experts' with the new layout?

The situation at Newton consisted of several single-lead junctions concentrated into a small area — an affront to any ordinary railwayman's common sense but, clearly, not to the intelligence of highly-trained signal engineers, nor to the Railway Inspectorate/Health & Safety Executive. However, after Newton and the public outcry about the increased risks at these junctions, the Health & Safety Executive had no choice but to place a moratorium on the installation of such layouts. Having done this, it then requested its Major Hazards Assessment Group (MHAG) to perform a comparative assessment of the relative risks of the conventional junction and the single-lead. British Rail commissioned a private company to do the same, and also taken into consideration was a risk assessment submitted to the Newton Inquiry by Dr I. Murphy, Lecturer in Mathematics at Glasgow University. The result of these three separate studies was to reach the same conclusion as all ordinary railwaymen — that there was a greater risk of a collision in single-lead junctions than in double-line junctions! One wonders why the HSE had not reached these conclusions after Bellgrove, instead of continuing to support the insupportable.

The final confirmation of the risks of the particularly-bizarre layout at Newton came on 30 January 1994, when it was returned to

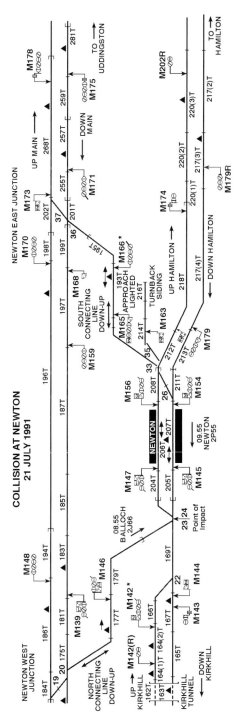

double track with a single crossover — between the down and the up Kirkhill lines — leading to the junction with the north connecting line. There was still a risk of head-on collision, should an up Kirkhill train overrun signal M142 when a down train was using the crossover as a junction, but the number of risks had been reduced by this revised rationalisation of the layout.

It was very fortunate that the junction from the Bristol line to the Plymouth line at Reading was not 'rationalised' when MAS was installed in 1964. One day in April 1994 an IC125 left Paddington, scheduled to run non-stop through Reading in the direction of Bristol. The driver was unaware that a certain proportion of the brakes on his train had been isolated in Old Oak Common depot by fitters carrying out maintenance. There is the main train pipe charged with compressed air and from this, supply pipes branch out to each brake calliper at the wheels. To avoid draining the air from the entire system before dismantling the callipers, the branch pipes can be isolated from the main pipe by turning a cock. The fitters forgot to reopen the cocks after they had completed their work. The ferry driver, taking the train slowly along the carriage lines to Paddington, did not notice the lack of brake power. The driver for the journey carried out the brake continuity test with his guard, but this only shows that the main pipe is continuous from end to end of the train and cannot reveal the fact that the branch air pipes to each brake are isolated. The train set off with only a certain percentage of its brakes operative. It was running out of Sonning Cutting at 125mph when the driver saw his first double yellow of the journey. He braked, and not a lot happened. The single yellow was looming up and the driver had dumped his air, but this had no effect on the brake callipers that were isolated from the system. The train was decelerating, but not with full brake power and so went by the junction signal at 'Danger', just as a train from the Plymouth direction was coming off the junction. Because the junction was conventional, the facing points in the down main were set for the diverging route, and so the runaway was diverted harmlessly round the curve onto the 'branch'.

# Severn Tunnel:
## 7 December 1991

The Severn Tunnel was built by the Great Western Railway. The shareholders approved an expenditure of £750,000 in 1871. The Company obtained its Act for an eight-mile-long railway from Pilning to Portskewett on 27 June 1872. After fantastic difficulties, hardships and bravery, the first goods train — conveying Aberdare coal — passed through the tunnel on 9 January 1886, and the first passenger train on 1 December. The tunnel was — and still is — 7,668yd long and cost the company £1,806,248 to build. It was signalled as a block section. There was a signalbox at each end, with a signalman, to ensure that no train entered the tunnel until it was known to be clear. This was proved by the signalman at the other end of the tunnel seeing the tail lamp of the train, proving that the train was complete and clear of the tunnel. He would then send 2-1 on the bell to his colleague at the other end, unpeg (release) the block instrument from 'Train On Line' and, when required, peg (send) the 'Line Clear' indication which unlocked the signal lever operating the tunnel entrance signal. This system, given conscientious men, worked for 83 years without ever a mistake being made. But there was a disadvantage: the block section of the tunnel was very long, relative to the number of trains that had to pass through it. It took 15min for a coal train, for instance, to go through. This reduced the line capacity and caused a bottleneck, but at least the line was very safe, and the Great Western Railway considered safety more important than capacity. In November 1941, with wartime increasing the number of goods trains using the tunnel, an attempt was made to increase its capacity by installing an Intermediate Block Section (IBS) within the tunnel. This approximately halved the length of block section and thus, in theory at any rate, doubled the number of trains that could pass through the tunnel. The intermediate stop and distant signals in each direction were controlled from the signalbox in their rear, and track circuits were now required for safe operation. Goods train drivers did not like the arrangement because, ideally, goods trains needed a clear run through the tunnel in order to manage the change of gradient, and probably the IBS track circuits failed fairly often in the wet conditions: a track circuit failure would lock the signals at 'Danger' and time would be lost as safety checks were carried out to ensure that the problem was no more than a track circuit failure. The intermediate signals and their track circuits were removed in 1947.

On 6 July 1969 the Tunnel East and West signalboxes were abolished and the tunnel was placed under the control of Newport Panel. Track circuits were then installed throughout the tunnel. The tunnel still formed a single block section and only one train could be within it on the down line and one train on the up line. The tunnel had to be clear on either line before another train could enter on that line. Inevitably, there were occasions when the track circuits were short-circuited by water on the sleepers — as many as 18 such incidents in a year. The wiring having been done correctly, all these failures were on the side of safety. The tunnel entrance signal was held at 'Danger' and trains were delayed while their drivers went to the signal-post telephone to receive their instructions, or were hand-signalled through.

The civil engineering maintenance regime in the tunnel had been thorough in the days of the Great Western Railway. Even in the 1930s and 1940s, when the company was hard pressed to make a profit, the tunnel was kept in first-class order by meticulous maintenance. This regime required a lot of men — long-service men — trained in the job and very knowledgeable of their duties, which, whilst hard, were simple enough to understand. The GWR-style regime, the ethos of manpower and safety regardless of cost, was continued by

British Railways into the 1970s. Every Sunday, from November to March, the tunnel was closed and trains were diverted. London-South Wales trains had a circuitous journey via Kemble and Gloucester. Until 1964, Plymouth-Crewe trains had a more exotic itinerary. They went over the Midland from Bristol Temple Meads to the Standish or Tuffley Junction where they re-joined the Western to go through Gloucester (General), turning north at Grange Court to run over the Ross-on-Wye line to Hereford. All this involved extra time, and the extra cost of maintaining branch lines was still, years after the demise of the GWR, considered acceptable in the interests of safety. Cost-cutting coupled with increased speed was not acceptable.

Meanwhile the gangs were out in force, re-laying track and re-pointing the tunnel's brickwork. There was a special wagon, of 6ft gauge, for running on the two inside rails of each road. From its superstructure the centre of the tunnel arch could be repaired.

There was no serious accident in the tunnel from 9 January 1886 until 7 December 1991. This lack of trouble was not so much due to expensive or special equipment as to the presence on the track of very highly-skilled, long-service men who had commitment to a lifetime's railway employment. They had been there long enough to have the job 'at their fingertips'. They handled magnificently the ordinary equipment with which they were issued.

Only two 'incidents' were of a serious enough nature to come to public notice, the second of these occurring in 1961. But there were, occasionally, broken couplings, although never in 90 years of loose-coupled trains through the tunnel did a broken coupling create anything more than a minor loss of time. A typical but infrequent incident occurred at 10am on 5 July 1947, when a 51-wagon coal train hauled by ex-ROD 2-8-0 No 3028 and piloted by GWR 2-6-2T No 4137 suffered a broken coupling, four wagons back from the engine. The rear of the train had passed beyond the trap point outside the east end of the tunnel and, had the uncoupled wagons run back, they would have been derailed over this, preventing them from running down into the tunnel. A gang of 10 permanent-way men, from the Pilning, Patchway and Severn Beach permanent-way gangs, were working on the line and saw the breakaway. They ran immediately to the wagons and pinned down their handbrakes whilst yelling to the guard to apply his handbrake. The drivers saw what was happening and the two sections stopped 150yd apart. The train was re-coupled and went on its way. The Ganger was awarded a 'gratuity' of one guinea and the Sub-ganger and men half a guinea each by the company.

It was extremely rare ('unheard-of', say those who were there in the 1950s and 1960s) to have a broken rail in the tunnel. This was due to the excellent practice of British Railways — following GWR practice — of renewing the track so regularly that the rails very rarely, if ever, broke. Track was never more than six years old in the tunnel and, on being recovered, was re-laid on other parts of the railway. Clearly there was a great deal of direct and indirect expense involved in keeping the tunnel in good order.

Track circuits, although safe, were unreliable in the harsh environment of the tunnel, and something else was needed. Local men could have been re-introduced as signalmen at each end of the tunnel, thus avoiding all delays and improving safety. Instead, axle counters, made in Germany by Alcatel SEL AG of Stuttgart, were installed. An axle counter is a device consisting of two 'heads', one attached to each running rail and connected to an electronic junction box about a metre and a half away. Two different frequencies are fed to the heads from the junction box. As the wheels pass the heads, each axle causes a phase reversal which is detected and transmitted to the evaluator in the relay room at Severn Tunnel Junction. The latter 'counts' the axles into the tunnel and another set of detectors 'counts' the axles leaving the tunnel. If the two numbers tally, the device then releases the signal at the tunnel entrance.

If the voltage to the heads goes out of tolerance — which can occur with a change in humidity and temperature — or if any other non-standard event occurs within the system, it fails safe and puts the signal in the rear to 'Danger'. The men responsible for the maintenance and repair of these delicate and complex machines had been given a one-day training course, and thereafter had learned on the job through years of practical experience. But this was rather better than the usual procedure on the modernising railway. When multiple-aspect signalling was first introduced on Western Region, the steam-age Signal & Telegraph Linemen went straight into the route-relay-interlocking rooms without any re-training at all. It says a great deal for their intelligence and expertise that they made the change unassisted.

Mr Schofield, S&T Engineer, Regional Railways South Wales & West, told the HMRI Inquiry that he had a total of about 200 technical staff and was 'pretty well staffed up', but of course not all of the 200 technicians Mr Schofield commanded worked at Severn Tunnel Junction. Indeed, only a handful of the 200 technicians were even authorised to enter the tunnel. He said that 80-90% of faults were repaired by the 'first-line' faulting team. Sixty per cent of failures were repaired by this team in an hour, and 80% within two hours. Faults requiring a more detailed knowledge were referred to the second-line faulting service, and a third line was provided by the Maintenance Support Engineer, who also had a System Engineer specialising in electronic systems.

Mr Schofield stated that he found no difficulty in recruiting well-educated people to train as technicians but, of course, he could only recruit to the number his employers permitted. Mr Schofield was being very loyal to his employers, who had, in fact, pared his staff to the barest minimum that would suffice, or even fewer, given the complex nature of the equipment. In the days of mechanical signalling, each one of his 200 technicians could have dealt with any electrical fault that arose in any signalbox, but in 1991 the man responsible for the supervision of technicians working on the axle counters, Mr John Daniel, Signalling Maintenance Supervisor, Newport District, had only a 'very limited' knowledge of axle counters. Indeed, so few technicians were qualified to deal with faults in the axle counters that Mr Schofield was short of qualified staff on Friday 6 December because one man was on leave and one on a course.

Mr Schofield gave evidence as to the reliability of the axle counters. He said that they had been attended to by technicians 18 times in 1991 prior to the accident, usually following civil engineering work affecting the counting heads, but on three occasions the voltage drifted out of tolerance, and once a head had become cracked. An analysis prepared by consultants for British Rail showed that in 1991 the combined total of recorded failures of the up and down axle counters was 64 — one every 5.7 days, on average — and, of these, 36, or 56%, were unexplained. All of these failures were on the safe side. If the magnetic field degenerates or disappears, the device becomes 'dead' and the signal it controls stays at — or goes to — 'Danger'. The failure rate was higher than for track circuits, and one wonders why a railway which was always so strong and reliable should have to be fitted with such pathetic equipment.

The rear-end collision which took place within the tunnel on Saturday 7 December 1991 was the culmination of a shambles of equipment failures, shortage of staff, misunderstandings and breaches of the Rules. The time it took to discover and repair the fault had a direct bearing on the accident occurring, and was due to cost-cutting, a shortage of staff and a lack of training of those who were available.

First came the failure of the cable carrying electric currents to the TDM. Modern signalling is full to overflowing with acronyms whose decoded state is often impressively 'modern'. TDM stands for multi-station Time Division Multiplex. This failure took place at 9.15am on Thursday 5 December. It was put right after an hour but failed again at 1.42pm and the available technical staff were unable to repair it, so a request for reinforcements from Western Region S&T was made and the work postponed until Sunday 8 December, when an extra man could attend. This was the third time that year that the TDM had failed, but that was an improvement on 1990. The TDM carries a large number of signalling messages between Newport Panel and the various relay rooms where the route-relay interlocking is housed. When this cable failed in the tunnel area, the Newport Panel signalman was projected back in time. His panel — so far as the Severn Tunnel area was concerned — was a blank, with no track circuit indications to show the position of trains, nor the aspect of signals. He therefore followed the correct procedure and switched into 'Through Route' working. This put the tunnel signalling in fully-automatic mode, locking all the points in the vicinity of the tunnel for straight running, allowing only the route for the up and down mains to be in use, and leaving the signals at the east and west portals of the tunnel to be operated by the axle counters. The Through Route mode also rendered inoperative the emergency signals in the tunnel, that on the down line being just over one mile from the eastern portal.

Principal Technical Officer David Croke worked on tracing the TDM fault with help from Mr Sperring of the Tunnel Engineering Faulting & Maintenance team. Mr Sperring worked without any detailed knowledge of what was being done, carrying out actions at the request of Mr Croke — removing and replacing printed circuit boards, for instance. Mr Sperring was on duty from 6.30am to 6pm that day. On the following morning he was on duty again, carrying out routine maintenance and also rectifying a fault on the telephone at Caldicot Crossing. He returned to Severn Tunnel Junction relay room for his midday meal and, at 1.15pm, he received a call from the Sudbrook Pumping Station reporting a fault on its local railway telephone circuit. Mr Sperring associated this with the fault he had just repaired at Caldicot. He went to the main distribution frame, removed the links in the telephone circuit and tested the voltage with a meter. He got a reading of 60V and concluded that someone was trying to use the phone. Instead of waiting until the person had got off the line, and then pursuing the fault, he gave up the tracing and replaced the links. Mr Sperring was certain he had removed and replaced these links correctly, but was prepared to admit the possibility of his having removed the wrong links. The links had no identifying marks. He then left the relay room at about 1.45pm. He was not a qualified telephone engineer and it seems as if he had removed the links in the axle counter circuit. This would have had the effect of putting N164 to 'Danger'.

At 2.10pm, the signalman in charge of the blanked-out Severn Tunnel section of Newport Panel received a call from the driver of a Portsmouth-Cardiff service reporting that his train was standing at N164 at 'Danger'. The signalman then arranged for standby signalman Terry Wood to go through the tunnel to N164 and act as a handsignalman. Terry Wood took his handlamp and two point clamps with him, got on a light engine and travelled through the tunnel on the up line, making sure that the down line was clear as he passed through. When he got to the east end he attempted to clip all the facing points as required by the Rules, but had not brought enough point clips.

The Rule Book does not make it obligatory to position a handsignalman at a defective colour-light signal. This is because there is always a telephone on the signal post by which means the train driver can contact the panel signalman. But having a handsignalman is a better way of doing things. He can save several minutes' delay to each train, since a driver does not then have to wait for two minutes, as stipulated by the Rule Book, before climbing down, walking to the signal-post telephone, receiving instructions and then walking back to his train. The handsignalman already has the instructions and can quickly convey them to the driver. Having a handsignalman is also a safer procedure because there is a man at the foot of the signal post with a detonator on the rail and displaying a red flag. The handsignalman is there to stop the train and 'tell the driver the tale'. When he has done so, he removes the detonator from the rail and displays a yellow 'Caution' handsignal for the train to proceed.

The late-turn Newport Panel signalman also arranged for another man to go to the west or Welsh end of the tunnel, to signal N170. There he was to act as 'tail-lamp man', to report by signal-post telephone when the train had come out of the tunnel complete with tail lamp, so that the man at N164 could be authorised to allow another train to pass that signal at 'Danger'. Terry Wood stood in the freezing cold and damp at N164 until 8pm, when he was relieved by Signalman David Hardwick; the latter stayed at this grimmest of posts until 6.30am the following morning, when he expected to be relieved by Terry Wood.

At a few minutes before 6am on Saturday 7 December, Signalman Ken Morgan returned to Newport Signalling Centre to take up his early turn on the Severn Tunnel end of the panel. The man he was relieving told him the current situation, unchanged since he had left duty 16 hours earlier. Mr Morgan had been a signalman since 1954, and so knew the reliability of the old system. He had been in Newport Panel box since 1981, so maybe, after 10 years, he had become reconciled to signal failures that could not be repaired for days on end.

No sooner had he taken over the panel than the tail-lamp man at N170 phoned in to say that he had done his night shift and was off home. There was no-one to take his place so Mr Morgan phoned the crossing keeper at Bishton, a mile or so west of Severn Tunnel Junction station, and asked him to give 'tail lamp' on each down train that passed him, until such time as a man could be found for N170.

Mr Morgan then phoned the Bristol Panel Supervisor and asked him if he had anyone who could act as a tail-lamp man; he was offered the services of a trainee signalman, Mark Elliot, who was competent to tell whether a train was complete or not as it passed him. Mr Morgan accepted the offer and it was agreed. But Mr Elliot had to go from Bristol, over the Severn Bridge, to the Welsh side of the River Severn and then walk back to the signal near the west tunnel mouth. On reflection, Signalman Morgan thought it would be better to divert Elliot to N164 on the Bristol side of the river, and to send Terry Wood, coming from Newport, to N170 on the Newport side of the river. Mr Morgan was unable to advise Terry Wood of the change of plan but he 'phoned Bristol Panel again and asked for Mark Elliot to be redirected. The Panel Supervisor did this, but it did not occur to him that, on the Bristol side of the tunnel, Mr Elliot would be acting as 'handsignalman' — liaising with the panel signalman

and handsignalling trains into the tunnel. Because he still thought Mr Elliot was required only as a tail-lamp man, he allowed him to go out without flags or detonators. Mr Elliot asked no questions, but thought all would be revealed when he got to the site.

On arrival at Severn Tunnel East, Mark Elliot introduced himself to the handsignalman, David Hardwick, as 'Mark Elliot, trainee signalman from Bristol'. Mr Hardwick expected to be relieved by Mr Wood, a qualified signalman, but he, Hardwick, had endured a long, miserable night at N164 and was understandably keen to get away. So, having told Mark Elliot what he was required to do, he went gladly home, taking his red and yellow flags and his detonators with him.

Not long after the departure of Mr Hardwick, Terry Wood turned up at N164 to find he had had a long journey for nothing. He spoke on the signal-post telephone to Ken Morgan, who told him to go back over the Severn Bridge and take up position as tail-lamp man at N170. He took his flags and detonators with him. Mr Elliot had set out from Bristol believing he would be acting as tail-lamp man, but now found himself in a position for which he was neither trained nor equipped. Had he been properly trained, he would have taken the signalling flags and detonators from one or other of the signalmen. Nonetheless, he applied himself enthusiastically to the job and contacted Mr Morgan in Newport Panel.

As it was a raw, cold morning, Mr Morgan told Mark Elliot not to stand at the foot of the signal, as the Rule Book required, but to shelter in a hut near N164; he would phone him when a train was near and give him the necessary instructions. Mr Morgan had called Mr Elliot out as a tail-lamp man but was now using him as a handsignalman, and never thought of asking him if he was properly equipped to do the job. However, irregularities apart, Mark Elliot did the job well and it went smoothly until about 9.5am. Then, Driver R. Forder, with the 6.10am Portsmouth to Cardiff, brought his train to a stand at N164. There was no handsignalman at the foot of the signal post, but a person in civilian clothes, without signalling flags but wearing a high-visibility vest, emerged from a lineside hut and approached him. Driver Forder watched as he came across the tracks to his cab and listened as he informed him that the tunnel axle counter was out of order, but that the tunnel was clear, and that the train could pass N164 at 'Danger' and continue through the tunnel cautiously, ready to stop short of any obstruction.

Driver Forder did not like the ill-preparedness of Mark Elliot. If he was the handsignalman for N164, why was he not standing at the foot of the signal, and where was his red flag? In spite of such misgivings, Driver Forder obeyed the instructions of this unorthodox handsignalman and, without having received a yellow flag signal to proceed past a red light, departed into the stygian depths of the tunnel. When he got to signal N170 at about 9.17am, he stopped and phoned Ken Morgan at Newport to complain that the handsignalman at N164 was not properly equipped. Mr Morgan contacted his opposite number in Bristol Panel and asked if the requisite flags could be sent to Mark Elliot at N164. When the Bristol signalman told his Panel Supervisor that Mark Elliot was handsignalman at N164 and was in need of flags, the Supervisor immediately contacted Ken Morgan and told him to withdraw Mark Elliot from duty because he was not qualified to be a handsignalman. Mr Morgan phoned Mr Elliot at 9.30am and told him to leave the job and go back to Bristol. That left N164 to its own devices.

The 8am Paddington-Swansea, 1B08, stopped at N164; the driver got down, took instructions over the SPT and departed into the tunnel at 9.39am, clearing N170 at 9.49pm. The next train to approach N164 was the 8.30am Paddington-Cardiff, 1B10. It stopped, and at 10.22am its driver was authorised, by telephone, to pass N164 at 'Danger' and to proceed with caution through the tunnel, obeying all other signals. At that stage, the signal technicians were working on the axle counter fault in the Severn Tunnel Junction relay room.

When the axle counters failed on Friday 6 December, Mr Trevor Cantle, Signalling Maintenance Manager, Newport, was called out. Taking with him Martin Perry, Senior Technician, Newport, he went to Severn Tunnel Junction relay room. Mr Cantle saw that the down line axle counter was showing an 'in-count' of 350 axles. He obtained the signalman's permission to press the reset button, but the machine did not reset. Further investigation revealed that there was no current present, but he could not ascertain the point of disconnection. The missing links were not noticed in the course of this investigation. Mr Cantle contacted Mr Button, Maintenance Support Engineer, who advised that certain voltage tests should be undertaken. As a result of these tests, Mr Cantle felt that a lineside amplifier was the problem. A spare would have to be brought to the site from Cardiff, which could not be done until the following day, and more expert staff would have to be gathered together. He then told the signalman that the down line axle counter would be out of order until 2pm on Saturday and that, in the meantime, signal N164 should be hand-signalled.

Sometime before 9am on Saturday, Mr Stephen Andrews, Principal Technical Officer, Cardiff, arrived at the relay room at Severn Tunnel Junction with a spare lineside amplifier.

Mr Andrews was an expert on axle counters and was a member of the fault-tracing team. As a result of Mr Cantle's arrangements from the previous day, by 9am a team of eight people had congregated in the relay room: Mr Andrews, Mr Waters, Mr Reed, Mr Bunce, David Croke, two lookout men and Mr Daniel, the Signal Maintenance Supervisor. Mr Daniel regarded himself as being in charge as Supervisor, but left Mr Croke and Mr Andrews to sort out the problem with the axle counter because he, Mr Daniel, knew very little about them.

Just after 9am, as they were about to start making their tests, the up line axle counter failed. Mr Daniel later recalled that he thought Mr Waters rang the signalman to ask if it was in order to reset the machine and that, on receipt of the 'all clear', the machine was reset and the signalman advised. The signalman, however, had no recollection of being consulted on this, and the Log Books of events kept in the relay room and in the panel did not record the transactions. The failure of the down line axle counter was not recorded in the relay room's log.

The two experts, Messrs Andrews and Croke, along with Mr Daniel, began their investigation of the down line axle counter. Mr Andrews began by removing the WDH fuse in order to isolate the machine from the interlocking system. The machine could still be worked by its rail-mounted detector heads, but it could not affect the aspect of signal N164, which would remain at 'Danger' until the WDH fuse was restored. Mr Andrews placed the fuse on top of the axle counter evaluator. He and Mr Daniel made voltage readings and concluded that the fault was on the lineside. They and the lookout men went off to the location boxes at the Welsh end of the tunnel, leaving the vital fuse lying on top of the evaluator. As Mr Cantle had discovered the day before, there was no voltage at the lineside location so they went back to the relay room.

Mr Croke said that on returning to the relay room he went directly to the evaluator, took the fuse from where it was lying on top of the machine and put it in his pocket. Mr Andrews went to the back of the evaluator to check the voltage output. He did not look to see that the fuse was where he had left it on top of the evaluator. No-one other than Mr Croke admitted to seeing the fuse when they returned, but perhaps Mr Croke was first into the room and had immediately picked it up. From the evaluator, Mr Croke went to re-test the lighting protectors while Mr Daniel went to the telecommunications main distribution frame, from where he called out the news that some links were missing. Mr Andrews and Mr Croke went to see this because it was a very unusual occurrence and possibly the cause of the fault. Mr Croke confirmed that the links were missing from the axle counter leads and used two spare fuse links as temporary replacements, sending Mr Waters to go and find some permanent links.

With the links replaced, the axle counter equipment was restored to working order and required only the push of the reset button to bring it into action. If the WDH fuse was in circuit at that moment then, with the pressing of the reset button, the machine would have been reconnected to the interlocking, which would turn N164 to green.

However, Mr Daniel, Mr Andrews and Mr Croke were adamant that the WDH fuse had been removed and placed on top of the evaluator from the outset. In addition to this evidence, there is a remarkable piece of evidence from Mr Phil Fortey, who was in charge of British Rail's Technical Investigation Centre at Reading. He was called upon to test the axle counter detectors, the evaluator, all relevant electrical wiring and the signal head of N164. He reminded the Inquiry that it had heard evidence that (a) the detector heads were cracked and thus more susceptible than usual to changes in temperature, and that (b), soon after 1pm on the Saturday in question, the voltage indicator for the detector heads mounted on the evaluator was illuminated, meaning that the heads were inoperative due to lack of voltage; also that (c) at 3pm that afternoon the heads were within tolerance but at 10.30am the following day they were again out of tolerance as indicated by the illumination of the warning light. Mr Fortey put forward his hypothesis based on the foregoing and on the records of Bristol Weather Centre, 9⅝ miles from the tunnel. The temperature at 10.30am on Saturday was about the same as it was at 10.30am on Sunday and thus, if the heads were out of tolerance on Sunday morning, they could also have been out of tolerance and inoperative on Saturday. In that case N164 could not have been showing a green light when the Portsmouth train passed it, even if the axle counter evaluator had been restored to working order and connected to the interlocking.

What a coal-fired railwayman such as myself finds particularly remarkable about Mr Fortey's explanation is that the railway's signalling now depends on such cracked technology as this, that can fail due to a temperature change.

With the links replaced, Mr Croke and Mr Andrews went back to the evaluator. It is important to remember that, with the WDH fuse removed, the evaluator could only work within its own system, but was isolated from the signal interlocking. Only if the fuse was in place would the machine be connected to the interlocking and have its designed effect upon the signals.

Mr Andrews started to replace the back cover while Mr Croke pressed the 'T1' button to clear out the erroneous '81' count stored in the machine. As soon as the '81' was cleared a count of '8' came in. Mr Croke mentioned to Mr Andrews that there was a train passing through the tunnel. The latter said: 'Well, that's handy, we'll watch him.' As he spoke he walked round to the front of the instrument and observed the '8' count.

As they waited for the count-out from the Welsh end, the train seemed to be taking rather a long time and then Mr Waters came in to report that the tunnel tell-tale wire was 'down'.

The tell-tale wire had — and still has — two functions: to put the signals at each end of the tunnel to 'Danger' and to operate a visible and audible alarm in the panel. Thus a train emergency would be protected and the signalman warned. The wire must be flimsy enough to be broken easily by hand, but this modern wire was so flimsy that it could be broken by the slipstream of a passing train and had already been broken accidentally 49 times during 1991!

My friend, Bernard Price, was Tunnel Inspector for 18 months from 1966. His father was the Tunnel Inspector before the war and Bernard's brother also had working experience of the tunnel. Bernard knew the signalmen at the East and West end who had worked the tunnel for years, had spoken with them and had first-hand experience of his own. He is happy to be quoted as saying that, if the tell-tale wire was ever to be broken accidentally, it would be the talk of the railway for ever more. The wire only ever broke because a worker had deliberately broken it in an emergency, and that was a rare event. To what depths had the management of the tunnel sunk when the wire could break so easily, so often, and be shrugged off as a routine nuisance?

Until the tell-tale wire was repaired, the signals remained at 'Danger' and this caused lengthy delays. In the event of the tell-tale alarm being given, the signalman was to hold trains outside the tunnel until he knew it was clear or was required to send in the rescue train. Just how quickly matters could be adjusted in mechanical-signalling days is illustrated by the following.

On 24 December 1947, a coal train of 55 wagons entered the west end of the tunnel at 1.50pm. It was hauled by ex-ROD 2-8-0 No 3047, piloted by 2-6-2T No 3167. At 2.1pm the tell-tale bell sounded in Severn Tunnel East box. The engines and 36 wagons emerged from the tunnel at 2.3pm and were allowed to proceed into the loop at Pilning. At 2.8pm the guard telephoned Tunnel West box from No 3 'phone to report his portion of the train complete,

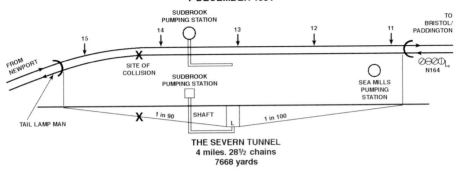

**COLLISION IN SEVERN TUNNEL**
**7 DECEMBER 1991**

THE SEVERN TUNNEL
4 miles. 28½ chains
7668 yards

stationary, on the rails and not foul of the down line. A light engine with the Severn Tunnel Junction Inspector on the footplate entered the tunnel at 2.21pm. This propelled the broken-away rear part through the tunnel and emerged at 2.55pm. The two parts were re-joined in the Pilning Loop.

The tell-tale wire was repaired at 2.40pm.

Returning now to the accident in the tunnel in 1991, Mr Croke telephoned Mr Cantle to tell him that the axle counter would be fully restored to working order by 2pm. While he was speaking to Mr Cantle, Mr Daniel came in and took the 'phone from him to inform Mr Cantle that there had been a collision in the tunnel. Messrs Croke, Andrews and Daniel went to the mess room in a state of shock to discuss whether anything they might have done could have led to the collision.

It was at this point that Mr Croke produced the vital fuse from his pocket and showed it to the others.

The crash took place at about 10.35am. The 1F08 7am Portsmouth Harbour-Cardiff had collided with the rear of the 1B10 8.30am Paddington-Cardiff.

Driver Carpenter, of Fratton, driving 1F08, attended the Inquiry with the intention of giving evidence but was advised by his lawyer not to do so. Mr Carpenter was still suffering the effects of his injuries — severe concussion — although he offered no medical evidence to the Inquiry as to his medical condition. The Inquiry reported, therefore, what Mr Carpenter had told the earlier internal Inquiry: that he approached N164 at red at walking pace; that after he had passed over the AWS magnet, 200yd from the signal, the aspect changed from red to green and he had accelerated up to 'not far short of line speed'; that when he saw the tail lamps of the IC125 ahead he made an emergency application of the brake but was unable to avoid a collision.

Mr Brian Nicholl, the conductor guard of 1F08, stated that he had ridden 'countless times' in trains driven by Mr Carpenter and had total confidence in him. On the day of the accident Mr Nicholl had noticed nothing untoward about his driving. The train approached N164 at walking pace as if it was going to stop. He looked out of his window and saw the goods line signal at 'Danger' but could not see N164, which is central above the running track. Then the engines revved up and the train accelerated past the signal. Mr Nicholl assumed that N164 had gone from red to green.

Mr Carroll, Quality Manager at BR InterCity HQ, was riding in the train as a passenger with his family. He described the journey from Bristol as being 'rather punctuated by a series of slowings and accelerations'. It was as if the train was following a slower train in front. Mr Carroll thought the train actually stopped, momentarily, at N164 before accelerating into the tunnel.

The signal head of N164 had a maladjustment of the internal 'hot strips'. This device, when properly aligned, focuses the aspect not only forwards but also downwards, so that the driver can still see the red light even when his cab is standing below the signal. In the case of N164, its red light disappeared when the cab of a Sprinter was 5yd from it. But Mr Carpenter said he saw the signal go to green when he was 50-100yd away from it. It is not a matter of the driver thinking that the disappearance of the red meant the green had come on.

The tunnel is straight for three miles from the Bristol end. The line descends at 1 in 100 for nearly two miles, is then level for 264yd before climbing at 1 in 90 for another half mile. Then comes a gentle curve to the left, 1¾ miles from the Welsh end. It was just around this corner, out of sight of Mr Carpenter, that 1B10 was negotiating the rising gradient at 20mph. The Portsmouth Sprinter was running at something between 60 and 65mph, entered the curve and there, 200-250yd ahead, were the tail lights of the IC125. Mr Carpenter braked as hard as he could and collided with the rear of the IC125 a few seconds later. The Sprinter's speed at impact was estimated at 55mph. This was calculated from the extent of damage caused. To have been able to reduce from 60-65mph to around 55mph in a few seconds proved that Mr Carpenter's reactions were instantaneous and, therefore, that he was alert and concentrating.

Because the IC125 was moving ahead at 20mph the actual speed of impact was 35mph. This blow was enough to send a shock wave through the IC125 so that the front accelerated sufficiently sharply to break the coupling with the rear power car. This, of course, fractured the brake pipes and brought all the vehicles to a stand.

Mr Robertson, driver of the IC125, thought his train had become derailed. He got down, broke the tell-tale and went to the telephone, where he made contact with Ken Morgan within two minutes of the impact and no later than 10.37am. Having made his report and given his position — Telephone 29 — he walked back along his train and met the senior conductor coming forward. He reported that the rear power car was detached and standing 30ft to the rear of the rest of the train, and that they had been rammed by a Sprinter whose driver was bleeding badly.

Mr Robertson attempted to get into the cab of the Sprinter. The door was jammed and Mr Robertson suggested that one of the group trying to open it go and call the Emergency Services. Shortly afterwards, they got the door open. Mr Robertson then returned to his own cab, advised his passengers of the reason for the delay and that the Emergency Services were on their way. Later on, he was told to take his train out of the tunnel at 5mph, which he did. He was not hurt at all but felt very shaken-up and, after reporting to the British Transport Police, he was relieved by another driver and taken home by car to Bristol.

A passenger in the IC125, Mr Andrew Morgan, a lecturer in surgery at the Westminster & Charing Cross Medical School, was travelling with two nurses. They got down onto the track and walked towards the Sprinter. It was bitterly cold in the tunnel and the air was full 'moaning, groaning and crying' from those in the Portsmouth train. Mr Morgan described Driver Carpenter as being 'heavily concussed', with a 2in gash over his right eyebrow. Mr Carpenter's level of consciousness was diminishing, and it was clear to Mr Morgan that he had a serious head injury.

Ken Morgan was not surprised when, at 10.35am, the tell-tale alarm went off, because 1B10 had been in the tunnel for so long. He said that Driver Robertson told him he was calling from '14 miles 28 chains'; when Signalman Morgan asked for the number of the 'phone, the driver said he thought it was '29'. Immediately after finishing this conversation, another call came into his telephone concentrator. This was from the guard of the Sprinter, 1F08, reporting a serious collision, with many injured, and asking for the Emergency Services. Mr Morgan called out to the rest of the men in the panel to send for the Emergency Services as he was still speaking to the guard.

Standing next to Mr Morgan was Philip Hill, a Technician Officer for the panel. He heard Mr Morgan say that the collision was at 14 miles 28 chains — that is, a mile in from the Newport end of the tunnel. Mr Hill then telephoned the relay room to tell the technicians not to mend the tell-tale because 'it might be a genuine alarm'. Ten minutes later he set off for Sudbrook because he was a member of the Tunnel Rescue Team.

If Mr Morgan had been working in Severn Tunnel East or West signalbox he would have been alone and would have conveyed the necessary information just received from the guard to the Controller. There is no doubt that Mr Morgan knew where the crash was, but, as is the way in panel boxes, he just called out to the room at large, expecting someone else to take it up and do what was required. Although by no means ideal, it is the panel box way of doing things. Someone in the panel obligingly contacted the Swindon Controller, Mr House, at 10.36am to say that the tunnel tell-tale wire had been cut at 10.35am, that there had been a collision in the tunnel and that the Emergency Services were required. If we are to believe what is stated in the HMRI Report, Mr House was not given the location of the crash and he did not think to ask where it was. Mr House then passed the message on to his Manager, Mr Cheeseman. The latter told the Inquiry that he understood from Mr House that the crash was 'at the Bristol end'. It is very clear that far too many people were involved with this message, and it was to rumble on incorrectly through several more carriers after this.

It took 14 minutes for the news of the crash to reach Mr Isaac, Shift Supervisor at Sudbrook. He stated that he was contacted at 10.50am by a Newport Panel signalman with the message that the incident was located at '14 miles, 28 chains — 50yd from the Bristol end'. Mr Isaac ordered the Emergency Train into the tunnel and then wrote the miles and chains location on the Control Room blackboard. He still did not notice the contradiction within the message he had been given.

The Bristol end of the tunnel was at Milepost 11, while Sudbrook was 13 miles 55 chains on the Welsh bank of the river. The accident was, therefore, even further towards Wales than Sudbrook. The Emergency Train had always been kept at Severn Tunnel Junction locomotive depot. In 1987 the depot was closed and the Emergency Train re-located at Sudbrook, two miles away.

The Emergency train left Sudbrook at 11.3am. It consisted of a carriage with accommodation for stretcher cases, two open four-wheel wagons for the rescue team, a four-wheel van carrying rescue and fire-fighting equipment, and a 5,000-gallon water tanker. It was hauled by diesel shunting locomotive No 97806. It had to make a reversal from the Sudbrook Siding to the Sudbrook branch and then cover about 2 miles to Severn Tunnel Junction, at a maximum speed of 20mph, before reversing again to travel about a mile to the mouth of the tunnel.

Mr Isaac returned to his office to contact by 'phone those rescue team members whose pagers were not working. He said that, while he was doing this, an officer of the Gwent Fire Brigade came into his office to whom he gave the location of the accident. He spoke to no other Fire Officer until Divisional Officer Jarvis arrived, 'quite a while after 11am', to take control. It is a remarkable feature of this story that Divisional Officer Jarvis did not find out where the accident was located until 11.44am, and he discovered this not from Mr Isaac but from the Avon Fire Brigade Control.

But a member of the Fire Brigade, Station Officer Jenkins, stated that he got to Sudbrook at 10.56am and met Mr Isaac and Leading Firefighter Allmark walking across the yard. At that stage, according to Mr Jenkins, Mr Isaac did not know the location of the accident. Mr Jenkins said that they all went back to the Control Room, where Mr Isaac made a telephone call and then told Jenkins that it was '50yd inside the tunnel, Avon end'. Leading Firefighter Allmark radioed this information to Fire Brigade Control. The message was logged as received at 11.8am.

While he was in the Control Room, Mr Jenkins did not see the correct mileage written on a large board boldly marked 'Incident'. He said that, had he done so, he would have known that this mileage was incompatible with the location he had been given. He and Mr Allmark then went to the lift at No 3 shaft and saw some of the railway rescue team members loading their emergency trolley. Messrs Jenkins and Allmark descended into the tunnel by No 1 shaft lift and set out to walk towards the Avon end.

As a member of the rescue team, Mr Sperring had a pager, but it was not working. The failure of the pager did not matter because he was called in, on his day off, to repair the tell-tale wire. He went to the relay room, where he was told of the crash, and then went at once to the Sudbrook Pumping Station Rescue Centre. He said he arrived here at 11.10am and was told by the Team Captain to find out all the details he could about the accident. The shift Supervisor, Mr Isaac, had known for 20min, but the Rescue Centre at Sudbrook was on the opposite side of the site to the main Control Room where Supervisor Isaac was located, and there was no communication between them. Mr Sperring stated that he phoned the panel and that Signalman Morgan told him the accident was at 14 miles 28 chains, which Mr Sperring knew was about a mile from the Welsh end of the tunnel. He wrote the mileage in chalk on the Rescue Centre Incident Board. But there was no-one but him to read it. The rescue team had already gone down the Sudbrook shaft with the components of the motorised rescue trolley and some rescue equipment. Having ascertained the location, Mr Sperring followed them into the tunnel and found the rescue trolley assembled and loaded with equipment. It was on the down line, facing east to Bristol.

The collision was, to be precise, at 14 miles and 7 chains — 704yd to the west of where they were standing, and hidden by the gentle curve in the tunnel. Mr Sperring told the Inquiry that he 'mentioned' to a fireman who was present that the incident was at the Welsh end but, because they were standing close to the ventilation fans, conditions were noisy and 'he was not sure if he had been heard'. Then another team of fireman arrived out of the Sudbrook shaft lift and said they were going to walk towards the Bristol end. Mr Sperring believed he was working under the control of the Fire Service, thought it must have better information and so could not argue. So he got aboard the motorised trolley and travelled with it away from the crash site.

The diesel shunter, meanwhile, was grinding its way slowly backwards to Severn Tunnel Junction, arriving there at 11.34am, having taken 31min for 2 miles (a speed of 4mph) — if, in fact, the train left when it was reported to have left.

Messrs Jenkins and Allmark had walked eastwards in the tunnel for 20min when they met a team from the Avon Brigade. The latter, coming from the Bristol end, had found nothing. At about 11.40am the motorised trolley from Sudbrook caught up with them. It may be safely assumed that they were all very puzzled at not having come across the incident, and that this was the main subject of conversation. The firemen boarded the trolley and continued to drive towards the Bristol end, knowing there was nothing there to find, while carrying on the trolley a man who knew where the incident was but was saying nothing! On the way, Mr Jenkins stopped the trolley and used an emergency telephone to speak to a signalman in the panel. Mr Jenkins asked to be connected with the Sudbrook Control Room. He was left 'hanging', and after several minutes put the phone down and moved on. It never occurred to him to ask the signalman. Twice more he tried, but in these instances the telephones were defective. A DMU, hastily summoned from Bristol as an emergency train, now reached them, running down the up line, and it was then that the rescue team learned where the collision lay.

The emergency train from Sudbrook experienced a great deal of delay. Having arrived at Severn Tunnel Junction at 11.34am, the driver of No 97806 insisted on having a third railwayman in the cab with him. The Rules required him to be accompanied by 'a competent person'. He had someone with him on the engine, but perhaps the driver did not consider this person as competent. A third person was located and breathing apparatus found for him, and only after all this delay did someone think of obtaining the written permission which it was necessary to have before entering the tunnel against a 'Danger' signal. The requisite form was signed and delivered to the Driver at 12.11am.

The diesel shunter, travelling up the up line, headed into the tunnel, while the DMU from Bristol was coming down the up line — it is remarkable that there was not another collision. As it was, the two trains may have arrived alongside the crash at about the same time. A passenger, Miss Miranda Green, made notes as the incident took place and she stated that the train arrived from Gwent at 12.30am, but Mr Carroll, the Inter-City Quality Manager already mentioned, said it came from the English side. Probably both trains arrived at about the same time.

Whilst awaiting rescue, and indeed throughout their ordeal, the passengers remained very patient and even cheerful. For the first five minutes they sat in darkness until someone got the lights going again. The train grew bitterly cold and after 45 minutes of this they were offered cold drinks! After an hour, the air in the train was becoming unpleasantly stale and stuffy, although warmer, and hot drinks were being offered. Those passengers with injuries suffered most because they were in shock and grew cold from that cause. On the Portsmouth train, apart from the driver with severe concussion, there was a passenger who had a broken leg and was shocked from loss of blood. Four more had spinal injuries, two or three had broken arms and about 75 had facial injuries: broken jaws, noses, cheekbones and lacerations. Hot drinks and warm clothing were brought to the Sprinter from the IC125 by the crews of both trains, and by one of the passengers, Mr Keyese of Frome.

Two hours after the crash the rescue trains came alongside. A controlled evacuation then took place. First, those who could walk were taken off the Sprinter and put on board the IC125. They were followed by 17 stretcher cases. This took two hours, and when it was accomplished the IC125 moved off very cautiously, minus its rear power car, at 2.30pm, taking an hour to cover the 2½ miles to Severn Tunnel Junction. Here there were minibuses waiting to take the two trainloads of passengers to Caldicot Leisure Centre for tea and sandwiches. Passengers were, of course, very concerned to contact relatives and found one telephone amongst them all, although one passenger did volunteer the use of a mobile phone, and later an office phone, being used by the police, was made available. At 5pm Miss Green boarded a road coach to take her to Cardiff.

It took two hours to reach the crash victims and two more hours to get them out of the tunnel. In 1961 a fire on a diesel locomotive was the second of the two noteworthy incidents in the tunnel which the HMRI Report into the 1991 crash had noted. In this case, the train was reached and passengers evacuated in 40min from the time the tell-tale was cut. Of course, none of the passengers in the 1961 incident was injured and all were able to move unaided, but even so it does make me wonder what had happened to degrade the railway to that extent after 30 years of modernisation.

We shall never know for certain what caused the first ever collision in the Severn Tunnel. Could experienced technicians have forgotten to remove the vital WDH fuse from the circuit before they started work? That seems very unlikely, but it is not impossible. However, the axle counter heads were 440yd beyond N164, towards the tunnel. The '8' count is said to have arrived immediately the axle counter evaluator was reset. If this is what happened, it proves that the train had passed N164 before the resetting of the evaluator and thus while the signal was still at 'Danger'. It is a matter of timing and what you want to believe. If the '8' count came into the evaluator 20sec after the resetting, then the proof that the signal was passed at 'Danger' is destroyed. But two men said it was 'immediate'. There is also the evidence of Phil Fortey, who pointed out that the axle counter heads were cracked and, given the low temperature, could not have been working, so the signal would have been at 'danger', wherever the WDH fuse was.

Could a driver slow down almost to a stand at a red light and then drive past it? That seems impossible, and yet we know that at Newton, Hyde and Bellgrove, a driver of an already-stationary train, facing a red light, had moved away from the platform to pass the signal at 'Danger'. And this was to happen again at Cowden.

# Cowden:
## 15 October 1994

Cowden is a wayside station on the line from a junction with the Victoria-Brighton main line at South Croydon, through Oxted to Uckfield. The line had once been double track, an alternative route from London to Brighton and Eastbourne via Lewes. In February 1969, the route south of Uckfield was closed, converting a double-track secondary main line into a country branch. It soon became clear that its branch-line status was taken seriously by British Rail, which proceeded to arrange its maintenance so as to give it the authentic ambience of a country branch line through beautiful countryside. By 1985, the ambience was so authentic that a number of permanent speed restrictions were introduced at the most neglected places in the track. British Rail saw that the line would have either to be repaired or closed. The organisation was short of money and so the decision was taken to reduce maintenance costs on the worst-affected areas by reducing three sections of the double-track route to single-line. One of these was the Hever-Ashurst section, which included Mark Beech tunnel, 400yd to the south of which stood Cowden station.

These savings were effected between 1989 and 1990 when the three bottlenecks of single track were introduced. The whole line from Oxted was re-signalled with two-aspect colour-light signalling driven by Solid State Interlocking housed in a control centre at Oxted. Automatic Warning System magnets were provided at all signals. The carrying capacity of the line was reduced by the single-line sections, thus increasing its irrelevance to modern needs. No-one (and that includes the Railway Inspectorate) wanted to see that safety had been compromised by working the single lines without the precautions that, to the mind of an old-fashioned railwayman, should be installed on single tracks when local signalmen and tablet instruments have not been provided to maintain order. The electric train tablet system was patented in 1874 and versions of it are still in use today on Railtrack. There are two cases of it failing to prevent collisions, both of which were due to human error, but two errors in 136 years of hourly operation seems like a record modern systems might envy.

The Uckfield branch single line was signalled according to standard modern practice, and indeed the two-aspect signals were spaced so far apart as to provide plenty of braking distance between the distant and stop signal. The interlocking of the points and their signals was operated by Solid State Interlocking (SSI), and there were no fewer than three interlocking microprocessors, each one of which, in triple sequence, checked the logic of the electric command before allowing the electric current to go out into the wires to the points and signals. Another microprocessor acted as a diagnostic module to monitor the activities of the other three. Data Link Modules (DLMs) connected the signalbox processors with the Data Highway. The DLMs were also used at lineside locations to connect the Trackside Functional Modules (TFMs). These TFMs were nothing more or less than 'double-redundant microprocessors'. It is all highly-technical jargon, but the brilliant cleverness of Solid State Interlocking came to nought because the whole thing was wide open far enough to drive through with the proverbial coach and horses. There was logic in plenty but there was nothing to prevent a driver being illogical and making unauthorised entry into the single-track section. That antique device, the trap point and sand-drag, would have been infallible, but this was not part of Standard Signalling Practice. It was too expensive. The omission was the equivalent of installing the finest Chubb lock on your front door — and then leaving the door open.

At the time of the head-on collision at Cowden, responsibility for the line had just passed into the hands of Railtrack plc, but the existing conditions were those created under British Rail.

The 8.4am Oxted to Uckfield, the down train, 2E24, was formed of two three-car Class 205 DEMUs. It was driven by Mr Rees who was accompanied by Guard Boyd. The 8am Uckfield to Oxted, the up train, 2E27, another 2x3-car Class 205 formation, was driven by Driver Barton, accompanied by Guard Brett-Andrews. The weather conditions were patchy fog, some of it quite thick. The intention of the signalman at Oxted was to 'cross' the two trains in Ashurst station and he had set the route accordingly. The up train was scheduled to arrive first and it did, at about 8.22am. The route at that moment was set for the down train to enter Ashurst. The down train would leave single track and regain double line at Blackham Junction, about one mile north of Ashurst. Points 532 at Blackham Junction lay for the down line. The up line signal, OD58, nearly ½ mile beyond the north end of Ashurst station but south of the merging junction into the single line, was at red — 'Danger'. The signalling and the track AWS was in working order, with the exception of the one signal, OD58, which allowed or forbade access to the single line from Ashurst station. But the trouble was that, even if OD58 had been in perfect order, it did not possess the power to prevent unauthorised access to the single line by Driver Barton's train.

*Below:*
*The peaceful scene at Cowden station, looking towards the accident site — but in August 1954, when the track was still double and ran through to Lewes.*
*R. C. Riley*

Signal OD58 was described by witnesses as giving a 'reasonably good' light. A comparison between the intensity of the light from the bulb in OD58 and the light given by a similar signal lamp taken at random from the laboratory shelf showed that the OD58 bulb produced 86.5% less light than the comparison. If that level of intensity gave a 'reasonable' light, then British Rail or Railtrack could have saved more money by using as standard, bulbs with 50% lower wattage than previously, and still have had a 'good' light. The weak light emitted by the bulb was then obstructed by 'significant deposits of tungsten' on the inside of its glass, because the bulb was near the end of its life. This light was further obstructed because the interior surface of the red glass lens through which this miserable light had to pass was coated with the excrement of flies which had entered the signal head. Besides this, there was contamination from an unauthorised aerosol spray which the signal technician had used to waterproof electrical contacts within the head. 'A more than ordinarily powerful cleanser was required to clean the back of the lens'. To refer to the light emitted by such a signal as 'reasonable' seems to be stretching the meaning of words just a little. And the morning was one of patchy fog.

Although the track system was, more or less, in order, the errant train's equipment was not. There was a large question as to whether the errant 8am Uckfield to Oxted train's AWS was working. After the crash the train's AWS was examined and found to be in order, except for the isolating switch. This was located outside the front of the unit, below the headstock. The electric contacts of this switch were discovered to be 'contaminated'. This is a word of broad meaning. Were they perhaps coated in varnish or badly corroded? At any rate, the contacts were so dirty that they would not pass current, certainly not sufficient current to operate the AWS. An intermittent 'right-side' failure of the AWS would have been the initial response of the system to this fault and, if left unresolved, a total failure of the AWS on the 'right side' would have resulted. In either case, the driver would have found his brakes automatically applied and he would not have been able to release them except by operating the AWS isolating switch. He would then have been driving the train without AWS protection. Following the total destruction of the front ends of the units in the collision, it was impossible to say if the isolating lever had been turned but, given the known condition of those contacts, the AWS would, of necessity, have been isolated in order to have moved the train off the Selhurst depot.

It seems to me that dirt on electric contacts does not build up — to the extent of disabling their function — overnight. It seems feasible that the isolation of the AWS, due to dirty contacts, was a continuing fault dating back some weeks. The Inquiry did not produce the evidence of the defect-reporting papers or the repair cards. Driver Barton should have known that the AWS was isolated, either because he had to isolate it himself to release the brakes on the train or because he saw, when checking round the unit before he took it out, that the AWS had already been isolated. If the AWS had been isolated previously and he did not check it, he

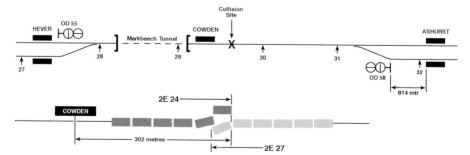

**COLLISION AT COWDEN  15 OCTOBER 1994**

*Above:*
With the line singled, but
without the foolproof single-
line controls of yesteryear,
the crash, a little way south
of Cowden, occurred. What
a shame and a waste.
*Brian Morrison*

would not have known it was switched off until he was actually driving the train on the passenger lines, because British Rail had carelessly forgotten to provide any test magnets on the 'outgoing road' from the Selhurst depot. Once Driver Barton realised that he had no AWS he was bound by the Rule Book to stop and report it. Appendix 8, paragraph 6.1 of British Rail's Rule Book states: 'A traction unit must not enter service if the AWS is isolated in any driving cab', and 6.3 lays down: 'If it is necessary to isolate the AWS (that is, during a journey) the driver must inform the signalman at the first convenient opportunity. The train must be taken out of service at the first suitable location without causing delay or cancellation'. In fact, then, the unit could remain in service for as long as BR management desired, the onus of safety being placed on the driver. It would be nice to read of a rule obliging all British Rail traction depots to be supplied with test magnets on the outgoing road.

Driver Barton made no report regarding a lack of AWS, although he had ample opportunity to do so, and, on the strength of this fact alone, the Inquiry reached the conclusion that the AWS was working. The Report stated that 'it was not in Driver Barton's character to have been that reckless [as to omit to report the AWS failure]'. This conclusion, underlining Driver Barton's good character, conveniently let BR off the charge of bad maintenance, because there was no doubt that the AWS contacts were unserviceable. There was also negligence in failing to provide AWS test magnets inside Selhurst depot. But the lack of a report from the driver,

who could have ignored the Rule Book, is weak, negative evidence against the very positive evidence of the dirty contacts which would have required the disabling of the AWS.

So away went Driver Barton down to Uckfield, and then back as the 8.0am, 2E27. He stopped perfectly at Ashurst station. Eight hundred yards ahead of him, in the mist, was the 'reasonable' red light of OD58. He set off from Ashurst and passed over the AWS magnet for the signal after travelling 700yd. If he had no AWS, as seems possible, he would have received no siren. If he did get a warning, he cancelled it and drove on. Having 'proved' that the AWS was working, 'on the strength of his good character', the Report now emphasises that for Driver Barton 'to have driven on without registering the aspect of the signal is not only inexcusable and blameworthy but totally irresponsible'. Is this the same man who would not be so reckless as to omit to make a telephone call?

Riding in the cab with Driver Barton was the train guard, Brett-Andrews. Mr Brett-Andrews had passed his guard's rules examination first time. He very much enjoyed working on the railway and in particular on the Uckfield line, so much so that when he was on main-line duties he occasionally changed turns with the rostered Uckfield guard. Traction Inspector Bushell, who supervised Driver Barton, had never driven over the Uckfield branch since it had been singled, although he knew it well enough from its double-track days. Train Crew Supervisor Tyron hardly knew Guard Brett-Andrews because he, Tyron, had only been at Selhurst for seven months. Trains Inspector Ward had ridden with Guard Brett-Andrews. He knew him as a very cheerful, friendly, talkative person who had ambitions to become a driver. There were three occasions when, whilst on duty as a guard, he, Brett-Andrews, had been caught riding with the driver and was admonished first by Mr Ward and then with increasing severity by more senior figures. But that had not stopped him doing it. If there was any place away from the eyes of authority where he and an amenable driver could change places, this rather neglected rural branch line was it. And he was with Driver Barton on that fatal morning — for which his punishment was death. Whether Brett-Andrews was driving is a matter of conjecture, but it is also irrelevant; Driver Barton was still responsible.

The line north from Ashurst has some relatively long 'straights' connected by left-hand and right-hand curves, but a mile from Cowden the gradient steepens to 1 in 100 and the line develops into a closely-connected series of left- and right-hand curves. Owing to the curvature at the Cowden end, the trains' drivers were hidden from each other until, at close range, they sprang into each other's vision from around the bend. It was any driver's worst nightmare come true. The two trains met at about 8.27am, 335yd south of Cowden. Each train weighed 122 tonnes and this weight now collided head-on at a closing speed unspecified in the Report. The down train had just left Cowden on a 1 in 100 falling gradient. The up train was climbing this gradient and, perhaps, braking for the station. The closing speed on impact might have been 55-60mph.

The guard of the down train, Mr Boyd, felt the emergency brake application made by Driver Rees, and almost immediately after the first bite of the brake came the terrible 'crunch' of the collision — except that Guard Boyd did not realise there had been a collision but thought his train had struck an obstruction on the line and become derailed. He got down onto the track and walked forward to what he thought was the front of his train and found the driving cab empty. What he was looking at was the rear cab of the up train. Thinking that Driver Rees had gone forward to protect the derailment he put down more detonators and a red flag and then walked back to his own train and reassured his passengers. He then walked back to Cowden station to report the incident where he met a colleague, Mr Hodges. There was a telephone at the station but neither man knew the number of Oxted panel, so they phoned the Oxted Supervisor and got the number of the panel. Contacting the signalman, Mr Boyd discovered that his train had been involved in a head-on collision. He was taken to hospital suffering from shock.

Driver Rees, Driver Barton and Guard Brett-Andrews were killed, together with Mr and Mrs Pointer, who were in the leading coach of the up train.

The Report made 22 recommendations including — as ever, since the Hidden Report on Clapham in 1988 — that ATP or some form of it should be installed, and that 'every signalling or re-signalling scheme which does not incorporate ATP should be accompanied by a risk assessment of the measures selected for the mitigation ['reduction' might be a better word] of SPADs — ie signals passed at danger'. But if the ATP or TPWS equipment is to be no better maintained than was the AWS gear on 2E27 it might be no more effective.

Was it not 'totally irresponsible' to omit AWS test magnets at the depot? Was it irresponsible to allow the AWS system to become so badly corroded that electric contacts were unreliable? When were the signals last inspected by a person other than their own technician? Was it irresponsible to install a single-line layout without foolproof guarantees of safety?

# Ais Gill:
## 31 January 1995

Ais Gill is a remote, moorland location at the summit of the railway from Leeds to Carlisle, known as the Settle & Carlisle line. At 1,169ft above sea level, it is a wild and lonely spot, but it is probably the best known location on any railway in Britain! It has been an unlucky place. At 5.48am on the morning of Christmas Eve 1910, there was the tragedy of the down Scottish express which collided with a pair of light engines near the south end of Shotlock Hill tunnel, a mile south of Ais Gill. The light engines had been standing on the down main at Hawes Junction, forgotten by the signalman, and had left northwards when he cleared his signals for the express. When the express ran into the engines the gas-lit, wooden carriages caught fire and six of the eight were burned to ashes, taking 12 passengers with them. The second disaster occurred at 3.4am on 24 September 1913 near Ais Gill's up distant signal. The ultimate cause of this could be said to have been the poor-quality coal supplied by the Midland Railway to its depot at Durran Hill, Carlisle. An up express train, the 1.39am Carlisle, had run out of steam and had stopped to recover pressure near Ais Gill up distant signal. The signals at the box in rear, Mallerstang, were at 'Danger' but the following express train, the 1.49am Carlisle, was also in trouble with steam pressure. The driver was preoccupied with his fireman's problems and did not see Mallerstang's up distant signal at 'Danger'. The Mallerstang signalman, seeing the train getting close and not going very fast, thought that the driver, obeying the up distant, had reduced speed, ready to stop. So the signalman lowered his home signal, expecting the train to run gently on and come to a stand at his starting signal. The driver chose that moment to look out and saw the home signal 'off' and returned to the problem of the fire, thus missing the frantic waves and shouts of the signalman and passing the Mallerstang starting signal at 'Danger'. Meanwhile, the guard of the stationary train had gone forward to his driver to ask the reason for the stoppage, and was told that they were short of steam, but that they would not be stopped for long. The guard thought, therefore, that to walk a mile to the rear of his train to put down protecting detonators, and then to walk the mile back again, would take him longer than it would take the footplatemen to raise steam, and that he would be delaying the train. So he did not go back. He had been put off doing his clear duty by the driver's remark and by a desire not to delay the train any further. So the second train, running away past Mallerstang's signals at 'Danger', crashed into the back of the first. The gas-lit coaches caught fire and 16 people died.

The railway over the fells from Settle to Carlisle has always been among the most difficult to keep in good order and the toughest to work on. It is battered by the worst winter weather, snow, rain and storm-force winds, and has traditionally been maintained in particularly good condition because of this. The wooden sleepers used on the line were of a high quality not found elsewhere in Britain, except perhaps in the Severn Tunnel, and a small army of permanent-way men was employed to keep the drains and culverts clear, in the hope of carrying away the torrential rains. Ninety inches a year is not unknown on the higher parts of the line, turning lineside ditches into torrents, and under-line brooks into raging rivers. Melt-water from snows had the same effect. In February 1933 the line was closed completely for almost a week due to blizzards and again, during the eight weeks of February and March 1947, the line was buried in snow. Landslides were an ever-present menace which could only be guarded against by the constant vigilance of scores of experienced permanent-way men.

They knew the sites of likely danger and would be especially vigilant in times of heavy rain, but even they were not always able to spot impending trouble.

On 19 January 1918 at 3.40pm, the 8.50am St Pancras-Glasgow St Enoch 'Scotch Express' was running downhill towards Carlisle between Little Salkeld and Lazonby. Heavy snow lying on the ground had been melting for days, and now the waterlogged cutting-side was heavy and quivering to fall. The driver saw the line ahead quite clear, but the next moment the bankside slid out across his path. The train was running at 55mph and, being heavy, ploughed through the mud for some way, but the mud grew deeper and finally derailed the engine and 11 coaches. Seven passengers were killed. The site had been passed twice by a member of the permanent-way gang in the half hour prior to the crash and he had seen nothing to arouse his suspicions. On other occasions, drivers have seen a landslide in time to stop.

The weather on the Settle & Carlisle line had been bad in January 1995, and on 31 January continuous torrential rain had fallen all day. An additional inspection of the line had been undertaken earlier in the day but, of course, the land was not then as waterlogged as it later became, and no sign of a landslip was apparent. The heavy rain began to create a flood between Settle Junction and Ribblehead station. The water became so deep as to damage the electric motors on the power bogies of trains. And so, at 5pm, the line was closed. Heading south from Carlisle at that time was the 4.26pm to Leeds (reporting number 2H88), a Class 156 two-car DMU. York Control, which had responsibility for the route, contacted the Kirkby Stephen signalman at 5.18pm and asked him to go to the 4.26pm Leeds when it arrived and find out if there were any passengers for south of Ribblehead and, if so, how many. On arrival at Kirkby Stephen at 5.23pm, the train was held while these details were obtained, the driver and guard being informed that they would be terminating at Ribblehead and returning to Carlisle. The train left Kirkby Stephen at 5.51pm to enter the 18-mile-long block section to Blea Moor. This was semaphore-signalled and double-track, so there was no track circuiting except in the vicinity of the signalboxes.

At Blea Moor signalbox the double track becomes single across Ribblehead Viaduct. The train trundled across the howling void, high above Batty Moss, and arrived at Ribblehead station. The strange thing is that not all the passengers de-trained here. Presumably Control had asked for passenger destinations so as to organise a bus for the rest of the journey southwards, but not all of the passengers availed themselves of the offer, and some chose to return to Carlisle. Perhaps Kirkby Stephen station had no waiting room, so the passengers opted to stay on the train rather than wait at Kirkby for its return.

The driver of 2H88 changed ends at Ribblehead station and, using his National Radio Network (NRN) link, asked for and received permission from the Blea Moor signalman to return over the single track. At Blea Moor signalbox the train was turned onto the down main and set off for Carlisle at 6.34pm.

Meanwhile, the 5.45pm Leeds, train 2H92, was running on the up main line between Ormside and Crosby Garrett. This train arrived at Kirkby Stephen at 6.47pm and the 'Train Entering Section' signal was sent by the Kirkby Stephen signalman to Blea Moor at 6.49pm. Most curiously, Control had not asked for details of passengers, and neither the driver and guard, nor the passengers, knew that they would be unable to proceed beyond Ribblehead station and would be returning to Carlisle.

Meanwhile, 2H88 was clipping northwards along the down main through the darkness in torrential rain at about 55-60mph. It passed over the summit of the line at the site of Ais Gill signalbox and was about 1½ miles north of there when the lightweight train ran into a landslip which was covering the rails. The front car was thrown to the right, derailed, and came to rest blocking the up main line. Even if Ais Gill and Mallerstang boxes had been in existence, their signalmen could not have saved the situation because the landslip would have been out of sight of both boxes.

As soon as both the cars of 2H88 had left the track, the lights in the passenger saloons went out. The driver had suffered a broken ankle, and was immobile and in considerable pain. Although he later had no recollection of it, he immediately pressed the 'E' button of his NRN radio and made an emergency call. The train was running on a route within the area of York control but the NRN Emergency system was designed to broadcast the message to Crewe Control. The Controller there received it at 6.48pm. At 6.49pm, 2H92 left Kirkby Stephen on the up main — a line which was blocked 5¼ miles away.

The Crewe controller told the Inquiry that reception was not perfect but he understood from the driver of 2H88 that he had hit a landslide and was fouling both lines between Kirkby Stephen and Blea Moor. The driver had asked the Controller to protect both lines and the Controller replied: 'We'll arrange all that, Driver.'

The passengers in 2H88 were of the opinion that their Conductor, Mr Wilson, had gone to see the driver as soon as the train stopped. It seems possible, therefore, that Mr Wilson heard the radio conversation with Crewe and the reassuring reply from the Crewe controller. The Rule Book required Mr Wilson to go outside and protect his train. He should have picked up three detonators and gone as fast as he could along the up line towards Kirkby Stephen, before clipping them, 10yd apart, to the up line rail, ¾ mile or so from his train. Should an up train come along, it would then explode the three detonators and the driver would at once bring his train to a stand. Detonator placement represents an excellent piece of old-fashioned railway work. But the night was utterly vile, pitch dark, freezing cold and raining cats and dogs. The Crewe Controller had just said that he would attend to the protection of the train, so Mr Wilson went back into the train to reassure passengers and assist them in moving to the rear car which was less damaged. He was a Conductor on the modern commercial railway and was possibly conditioned by today's culture to think more of customer care and ticket examination than operating imperatives, otherwise he would have been off along the line as fast as he could go.

The Crewe Controller had no right to say that he would protect the train. It was impossible for him to protect it. He had no training in the use of the NRN to deal with emergency calls and was unaware of the facilities which existed on the NRN for him to make group calls to all trains in an area. He had no telephone connection to any of the signalboxes on the Settle & Carlisle line, nor did he have any direct line to York Control. The Crewe Controller went to the directory, looked up the number and got through to York Control at 6.54pm. At just about that moment, or within the next minute, the crash took place.

Someone had switched off the headlights of 2H88 and switched on the twin red tail lamps in their place, facing north and oncoming trains. The driver had no recollection of doing this, but then he had no recollection of making the emergency call, but this sensible precaution was most likely carried out by him. The driver of 2H92 saw the lights dimly through his streaming windscreen, at first thought they were on the other line, and then braked, but it was too late to avoid the collision. He was too badly injured to take any further action, but his Conductor contacted Settle Junction to report the accident with its precise location. A passenger in 2H88 got down onto the track and found Mr Wilson lying against a wheel of his train, badly injured. It seemed as if he was standing in the doorway at the time of impact and was thrown out.

The Deputy Chief Controller at York, after hearing of the derailment of 2H88 and the need for the Emergency Services, advised his staff and then called Cumbria Police at 6.57pm to co-ordinate the Emergency Services, but he did not know exactly where the derailment was and so could not direct the ambulances. At 6.58pm, the Deputy Chief Controller contacted the Kirkby Stephen signalman. From him he learned that 2H92 had left nine minutes earlier, but still did not know the site of the derailment. He found out shortly after 7pm from the Settle Junction signalman — who had been advised by the guard of 2H92 — the precise mileage location of the accident, enabling a grid reference to be given to the police.

The Report is garbled as to the sequence of events around the time of the crash. Paragraphs 20, 22 and 29 are mutually contradictory. Paragraph 20 states that the guard of 2H92 gave the exact location of the crash to Settle Junction, but does not say when this information was passed. The message would have been received about 7.1pm, giving the Conductor time to get his shocked wits together, get down from his train and search in the dark for a milepost.

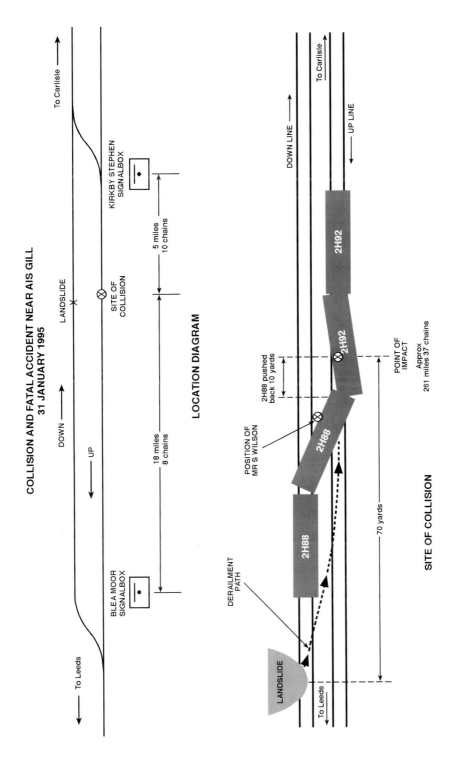

# COLLISION AND FATAL ACCIDENT NEAR AIS GILL
# 31 JANUARY 1995

DOWN →

LANDSLIDE

← UP

To Carlisle →

KIRKBY STEPHEN
SIGNALBOX

⊗ SITE OF
COLLISION

5 miles
10 chains

18 miles
8 chains

BLEA MOOR
SIGNALBOX

← To Leeds

## LOCATION DIAGRAM

DOWN LINE →

To Carlisle →

UP LINE →

2H92

2H92

2H88 pushed
back 10 yards

POSITION OF
MR S WILSON

⊗ 2H88

⊗ POINT OF
IMPACT

Approx
261 miles 37 chains

70 yards

DERAILMENT
PATH

2H88

LANDSLIDE

To Leeds

## SITE OF COLLISION

131

Paragraph 22 states that the Settle Junction signalman was made aware of the derailment at 'about 7pm', when the telephone in his signalbox rang and a voice said — not terribly informatively, according to paragraph 22, because the caller did not identify his train nor give the location of the crash — 'This is the Conductor on the Carlisle train. We're derailed.' This must have been Mr Wilson, the Conductor of 2H88. But it could not have been at 7pm; it was more likely to have been at 6.55pm. Paragraph 22 continues by stating that, having heard this much, the signalman handed the telephone to a Railtrack Supervisor who was with him, whilst he, the signalman, advised Blea Moor of the derailment. Paragraph 29 of the Report continues by stating that the Supervisor took the 'phone from the signalman and heard a voice say: 'Collision — injuries — need help.' If this description of events were true, we would be justified in supposing that the man the signalman spoke to and the man the Supervisor spoke to were one and the same. But that is impossible. The man who had reported a 'derailment' was lying, fatally injured, on the track, seconds after the 'collision' took place.

But back to the course of events as described by paragraph 29. Having heard this very uninformative message, the Supervisor told the caller who was, apparently, the Conductor of a train, to protect the opposite line. Then he, the Supervisor, rang York Control to report what had happened.

But paragraph 22 states that the Supervisor, having taken the phone from the signalman and heard what was said, 'left to find the accident site before a second call from the derailed train, when the conductor gave the mileage of the accident site'. This garbled sequence of events contained in paragraphs 22 and 29 is not borne out by the chronology given in Appendix 1 of the Report.

It seems to me to be typically modern that a report on a fatal accident cannot be written coherently. Humans can invent the most fantastically-clever electronic gizmos but find it impossible to use them with the same clarity of thought as the pen-wielding railway accident inspectors of 25 years ago. And maybe that is what is going wrong with the railway: humans are placing their natural intelligence in a position subservient to the machine intelligence they have created. It is possible that Mr Wilson believed more in the power of the radio than of his own two legs to save the situation. Had he carried out protection he would have saved his own life, he might have prevented the collision and he would certainly have reduced the force of the impact in which the two drivers and 24 passengers had to be taken to hospital to be treated for injuries

On 13 May 1995, Railtrack issued a reminder to all train crew members, emphasising the urgency of carrying out detonator protection of trains 'even when NRN radio has been used'. The men had to be reminded that electronics are not the all-embracing super gismos modern people might consider them to be. This circular was re-issued in 1997. In 1998, Railtrack employed a firm of consultants to investigate the advantages and disadvantages of guards having the role of 'train protector'. The conclusion was that they should no longer have that role, and in October 1999 a new rule was issued by Railtrack making drivers responsible for train protection, but that if the driver is incapacitated then the guard must do the job. It seems to me to be a waste of time to change the rule, since the guard might have to carry out the protection work anyhow. And if the guard's vital role as the protector of his train is to be diminished in favour of his focus on commercial duties, will that not make the guard an even less well-motivated protector, should the need arise? At Ais Gill, where the conductor was the person required by the Rules to carry out protection, his mental attitude (so it seems to me) had already been corrupted by the commercial ethos and the faith in, or reliance on, electronic aids. Is there some kind of superstition evolving?

But it is as well to remember that, in 1913, the 'Golden Age' of railway operating, a guard of what today we would call 'the old school', free of any 'customer care' or other commercial-jargon considerations, free of any feeling of reliance on electronics, was also seduced from his duty to protect his train by the comment of the driver, 'We shan't be long.'

# Watford:
## 8 August 1996

The West Coast main line from Euston runs in an northwesterly direction through Watford Junction and towards Rugby. In the vicinity of Watford the route is a quadruple track, laid out, from west to east as: down fast; up fast; down slow; up slow. On the slow lines the maximum permitted speed is 90mph. At the London end of Watford Junction station are four 'single-lead' crossovers connecting the down slow to the down fast and the up slow to the up fast. This is Watford South Junction. A train being crossed from up slow to up fast must cross the down slow. In fact, it is more than a crossing movement because these are 'single-lead' crossovers, and there is a moment when an up slow to up fast train is running head-on to the down slow line. To protect such a movement across the junction from trains approaching on the down slow line, a four-aspect colour-light signal, WJ759, was placed 162yd to the south of the crossover. This distance should have been a minimum of 200yd. When WJ759 displayed a red aspect the two signals to the rear — WJ755, 927yd away, and WJ751, 1,410yd to the rear of WJ755 — displayed a single and a double yellow respectively. A driver passing WJ751 at double yellow at 90mph had 2,337yd in which to stop at WJ759.

On Thursday 8 August 1996, at 5.18pm, the 5.4pm Euston to Milton Keynes passenger train left Harrow & Wealdstone on the down slow line. It consisted of a four-car Class 321 EMU, carrying about 195 passengers. It was driven by a man with 29 years' driving experience. Since 1988 he had, on five occasions, passed a signal at 'Danger', three of which were due to his misjudgement during poor adhesion conditions on the rails, and had once been caught in a radar speed trap. He had achieved high marks in all the rules exams, had been assessed on the job not long before the crash and was considered to be a good driver. From 1933, when a national disciplinary code for all railwaymen was established, drivers' offences were judged, and punishments awarded, in the light of their past record. Whether the LMS or GWR or even BR in earlier days would have tolerated a driver who had five times misjudged conditions and thereby passed a signal at 'Danger' is a debatable point.

As the 5.4pm Euston sped northwards, an empty train (ECS) consisting of a Class 321 EMU, the 4.50pm Bletchley, was north of Watford, heading south on the up slow line. It was following a freight train and had lost 2min as a result. The empty train was required to work the 6.10pm from Euston to Milton Keynes. The signalman at Watford Panel decided he would turn the ECS onto the up fast line to get it past the freight. Between 5.19pm and 5.20pm he restored to 'Danger' the slow and fast line signals protecting the South junction so that he could set the route from up slow to up fast for the empty train. He was perfectly entitled to do this. The 5.4pm Euston was more than three miles away from WJ759 and WJ751 was still out of sight of the driver. He would not see it 'step down' from green to double yellow.

The down passenger train passed Carpenders Park station at 80mph and approached WJ751 at 5.22pm, braking for the 60mph permanent speed restriction (PSR) through the length of Bushey station. Signal WJ751 was showing double yellow. The driver cancelled the AWS warning he received, continued to brake and passed through Bushey station at 64mph. At the north end of the platform, he passed the '80' sign and began to accelerate. At that moment the up ECS was entering Watford Junction station at 60mph, braking to take the crossover to the up fast.

The 5.4pm Euston headed north, under power, swinging round the long, left-hand bend. In the course of this turn, the beam from the green light of the down fast line signal, WJ753, would have crossed his vision before he saw his own signal, WJ755, at single yellow. This signal was focused perfectly into his cab and the driver would have had it in view for at least 12sec. This ought not to have confused an experienced driver since the signal was well across to his left. The driver cancelled his AWS warning automatically and continued under power until WJ759 came into view around the long bend. It was at 'Danger'. It was 403yd way, 9sec running time. He braked hard but was unable to stop. He passed the signal at 'Danger' at 45mph, braking hard, and came to a stand 222yd beyond it, fouling the crossover trailing from down slow to up fast.

He was now head-on to the ECS, which was at that moment coming through the up slow to down slow crossover at 50mph. The ECS driver had no chance of stopping and the collision took place. The driver of the passenger train saved his life by diving to his right across the cab to avoid the impact. The driver of the empty train also survived. The passenger train was driven backwards 25yd with its brakes hard on by the terrible blow which was so severe that a female passenger sitting at the rear of the front coach was thrown through the plate glass window onto the track and died of her injuries. She was the only fatality.

The driver of the passenger train stated that he could not recall seeing the double yellow or single yellow signals, or hearing the AWS warning siren. But he must have heard it in order to cancel the warning and thus prevent the brakes from being automatically applied. He was committed for trial on a charge of manslaughter but was found Not Guilty by the jury.

No-one else was put on trial nor in any way publicly called to account for their actions so that seems like the end of a fairly straightforward explanation of a tragic accident. But there was a lot more to it than that.

The track and signalling layout at Watford was first modernised in 1965, and a scheme to re-signal the layout was drafted in October 1988. This design was altered four times before the revised signalling layout was brought into use in May and June 1993. The Re-Signalling Notice for the Watford Junction scheme, issued by BR to everyone concerned, made no mention of a reduced safety overlap between WJ759 and the junction crossover, nor did it explain the purpose of the 60mph PSR at Bushey. Drivers believed the latter had been imposed through the platforms because of 'condition of track'. The new signalling was brought into use without prior inspection by the HMRI. There was an Act of Parliament which required that railway 'new works' be inspected and approved by Her Majesty's Railway Inspectorate on behalf of the Minister of Transport, but, because re-signalling work has to be brought in by stages to avoid too much delay to traffic, it was accepted practice for HMRI to make an inspection of the completed scheme. Thus, all of the changes would have been implemented prior to formal approval being given.

In October 1993 the Director of the organisation then running that part of the railway system, InterCity West Coast (ICWC), notified HMRI that the Watford Junction signalling scheme had been commissioned, and included a Certificate of Compliance. The vital letter and Certificate were not received at HMRI! I am surprised that ICWC could not afford to send it 'recorded delivery'. Five months later, someone at ICWC must have realised that they had not had a response from HMRI and the letter and Certificate of Compliance were resubmitted.

'Certificate of Compliance' seems, on the face of it, to have been a slightly odd title, because it certified that part of the installation did *not* comply with standard signalling practice, the points at Watford South Junction lying within the usual safety overlap of 200yd ahead of the protecting signal.

But the people who make the rules can put in as many loopholes as they like. Under Standard Signalling Principles (SSP), the 200yd exclusive safety zone ahead of a signal could be reduced in length in special circumstances, ie 'when it is considered essential to avoid restrictions to traffic movements the overlap may be reduced in length. The length of overlap shall be based on the maximum attainable speed of the train, with no signal restrictions, at a distance 440yd on the approach to the signal'. In order to retain the short overlap and to comply with SSP, a 60mph permanent speed restriction (PSR) was imposed on the down slow line through Bushey station.

The thinking behind siting the PSR at Bushey appears to have been that, with WJ759 at 'Danger', a driver would see a double yellow at WJ751, brake from 90mph to 60mph for the 487yd-long Bushey PSR and then, with a single yellow ahead, would not be tempted to accelerate again. This was all very rational and carefully thought out, but the 60mph PSR terminated 1,506yd away from WJ759. That left plenty of distance for a modern EMU to accelerate back up towards 90mph. The driver of the 5.4pm Euston obeyed the 60mph PSR at Bushey, but ignored the yellow warnings. If the commencement of the 60mph PSR had been placed at WJ755, extending ahead of that signal for 487yd, so that the red WJ759 was well in sight as the train left the restricted area, the accident, given the way this driver was driving, would not have taken place.

If this situation — ie a junction lying within the safety overlap of a signal — had existed in a semaphore-signalled layout, the Regulations would have required that the signalman would either have not allowed the train to approach when the route was set across the crossovers — it would have been held back at Bushey — or he would have accepted it from Bushey under the Warning Acceptance. Then, the signalman at Bushey would have brought the train almost to a stand and warned the driver of the situation ahead.

To replicate this old-fashioned — but eminently safe — method of railway working, the colour-light signalling system would have been best designed so that, when Watford South Junction was set for a crossing movement, signal WJ755 would have been at 'Danger'. This would have been the perfect solution because it would have dispensed with a speed restriction which was in existence to 'protect' a crossing movement which only happened a few times a day. For almost all the 24 hours of a day, the 60mph PSR was a waste of time.

There was a feeling that, had drivers been told the reason for the speed restriction at Bushey (it was a vital part of the signalling system after all), they would have had a proper understanding of the circumstances at the junction, and that might have made them take more notice of that section of line.

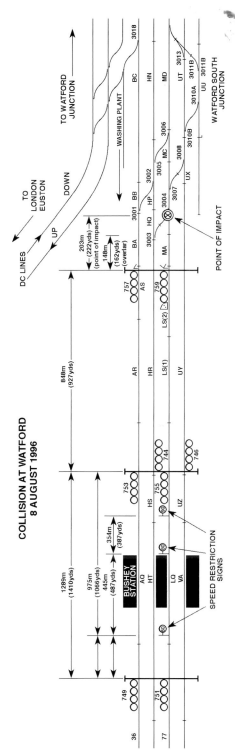

COLLISION AT WATFORD
8 AUGUST 1996

135

*Above:*
The wreck of the 5.4pm Euston lying in front of the rebuilt town of Watford, which bears a striking resemblance to Babylon. The leading end of the train is projecting over the edge of the embankment, and a careful look will reveal the angled crushing inflicted on its cab by the empty stock train, coming in from the right in this view. *Ken Brunt*

The Certificate of Compliance also stated that arrangements were in hand to provide a full overlap distance of 200yd between WJ759 and the junction. The ICWC people had noted the non-standard length of the overlap ahead of WJ759 and recommended it be lengthened in December 1992. In October 1993, BR had included the short overlap in its Certificate of Compliance; in the 2½-year period which elapsed between the Certificate finally reaching HMRI and the crash taking place, HMRI had not inspected and approved the layout, nor had Railtrack (which by now had taken over infrastructure responsibility from BR) regularised the situation regarding the safety overlap. Of this, the Report by HMRI into the crash stated: 'It was only after the scheme had been commissioned in 1993 that HMRI learned of the reduced overlap protecting an overrun past WJ759 and the imposition of a 60mph PSR as a means of complying with SSP 20. It was not stated where the marker board for the start of the 60mph PSR had been placed. Subsequent investigations revealed that it had been placed in an inappropriate location and not strictly in accordance with the SSP'.

There were at least three instances of drivers passing WJ759 at 'Danger' in 1995. And yet, in spite of the lack of a proper safety overlap between WJ759 and the junction points, in spite of the danger of a head-on collision in case of an overrun, in spite of overhanging vegetation which to some small extent obscured the view, and most of all in spite of Railtrack's own rules (Group Standard 3252) in respect of multiple SPAD incidents, no Signal Sighting Committee was convened to see what could be done to improve matters.

The 5.4pm Euston was operated by North London Railways (NLR) Train Operating Company (TOC) and the driver was its employee. When NLR TOC was formed out of Network SouthEast, a Driver Performance Profile (DPP) system was introduced to keep records and indicate those drivers who were 'incident prone'. This was an obligatory part of

the NLR 'safety case', necessary for its licence to operate. In September 1994, Railtrack issued Railway Group Standard GO/RT 3252 'Safety requirements for train drivers', and NLR altered its 'guidance notes' accordingly. In December 1994, the British Railways Board (BRB) issued a more detailed Code of Practice regarding the monitoring of drivers. The BRB Code was more stringent than NLR's, so it was not adopted by NLR because that organisation thought it had done enough by satisfying Railtrack's requirements.

Before any would-be TOC can obtain a licence it must submit its safety case to Railtrack which can then accept or reject it. Part of the NLR safety case stated that: 'The Production Director will ensure that train crews perform to the required level of safety'. Elsewhere it was stated that: 'The Driver Manager is responsible for the safe management of drivers. Employees will be trained and continually assessed in accordance with the relevant Railway Group Standard'. Not only was there no explanation given as to how these desirable ends would be achieved, but there was no-one designated in the NLR organisation, at that time, to put into place such specific systems (paragraph 159 of the Report). Nevertheless, this vague, non-specific safety case was accepted by Railtrack in September 1995. It was not until July 1996 that NLR appointed a Production Standards Manager.

The Inspecting Officer made 21 recommendations in his report. In paragraph 192 he had stated that the accident would have been avoided if ATP had been fitted, but noted that this had been considered too expensive a project to continue beyond the experimental schemes. Recommendation 16 said: 'Railtrack to evaluate the full cost of this accident and other recent accidents that could have been prevented by ATP and review whether this affects the cost benefit assessment that determined its train protection strategy'.

Recommendation 4 stated: 'Railtrack to identify all locations with reduced overlaps, carry out risk assessments at each one and take appropriate action to mitigate any hazards that may be present'. Recommendation 5 took this further: 'Railtrack to adopt a track layout assessment method in order to identify the risk of collision at specific locations resulting from a signal being passed at danger, taking into account the pattern of the train service and passenger loading. Railtrack should then prioritise those junctions that may require redesign or the adoption of additional safety measures'. Recommendation 13 urged: 'Railtrack to review all current resignalling works inherited from BRB to ensure that the designs are safe and comply with the appropriate Group and Signalling Standards'. Excellent, except that those standards were the ones which allowed a metaphorical coach and horses to be driven through the junction at Watford.

# Worle Junction:
## 28 November 1996

This story is one where there were no ill-effects. It is instructive, however, with a touch of farce, and illustrative, again, of the operating difficulties inherent in the fragmented nature of the railway and also of the shortcomings of the NRN radio system. NRN is a useful tool but, as was seen at Ais Gill, and now here, it has its limitations.

At approximately 4.40pm on 28 November 1996, the Cross Country train service, 4.7pm Exeter St Davids to Leeds IC125, reporting number 1E39, was approaching Worle Junction, coasting at about 70mph. The train was driven by Mr Evans sitting in the cab of power car No 43093. Mr Evans had a situation on his hands. He had routinely tried his brake, like a good man, and had discovered that the train's normal braking system had failed. This was because the air valves were controlled by electricity rather than by the simple mechanical opening of an aperture as would have been the case on a steam engine. There were rare failures of the brake on steam-hauled trains but these were due to blockages in the train pipe, not the failure of the brake valve. So, he had shut off power and was coasting thoughtfully along towards Bristol, coolly considering what to do. He could always bring his train to a stand by letting go of the deadman's pedal, or he could dump the air from the train pipe with the emergency brake — the brake handle position beyond 'full service'.

His thinking was good and went more or less along these lines. He had had a clear road all the way from Taunton, the signals ahead were green, he was more or less in his correct path so he should be all right to run unchecked as far as Yatton, about 4½ miles further on. He decided he would coast on and bring his train to a stand at the facing points, up main to up loop, at Yatton. Then he could contact the signalman and be placed in the loop to clear the main line, if that was what was required, or, with Bristol Panel warned, continue to Bristol. Good initiative, good railway thinking. So, having decided on this straightforward course of action, he decided to tell his Control using the NRN radio link.

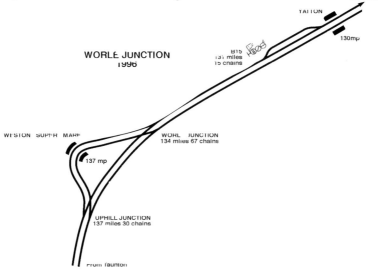

Cross Country train control was in Birmingham. The Controller who answered we shall call 'Bill'. Driver Evans told him that he had no brake application *unless he went beyond 'full service'*, and that he was coasting at about 70mph. The Controller asked if he had told Bristol Panel and the driver replied: 'No, I will tell them next...', and then the message was cut off by some freak of the NRN. He had said nothing about 'running away' because, of course, he was not.

The Controller did not understand the practicalities of what the driver had said or he would have realised that the driver did indeed have a brake. It is a pity that the NRN radio cut out, otherwise the Controller would have been told by the Driver what he was going to do. Mr Evans was very much on top of the situation. The Controller, however, went into a nose dive and telephoned something called Customer Service Centre, Swindon, which was in fact the Railtrack Control Office. The following *emergency message*, was sent from Birmingham.

A person at Swindon (S), whom we shall call 'Fred', answered the phone:

'Swindon.'
Birmingham (B). 'Hello there.'
S. 'Hello there.'
B. 'Cross Country Trains, Birmingham, here.'
S. 'Hi!'
B. 'Fred?'
S. 'Yeah.'
B. 'It's Bill here.'
S. 'Hello there.'
B. 'I've just received an emergency call from 1E39.'
S. 'Yeah.'
B. 'Currently going at about 80 to 90 miles per hour.'
S. 'Yeah.'
B. 'Brake in full service.'
S. 'Right.'
B. 'Nothing happening.'
S. 'Oh shit!'
B. 'All right?'
S. 'All right, mate.'
B. 'I've told him to tell the signalman right away.'(!)
S. 'If he can. All right then.'
B. 'OK?'
S. 'Ta.'

Fred at Swindon put the phone down and turned to the office at large: '1E39. Driver's got it in full service and can't stop. 1E39. Telling Bristol Panel now.'

At 5.5pm Swindon Customer Services Centre contacted Bristol Panel Supervisor John Turton. Mr Turton (JT) answered the phone:

JT. 'Bristol Panel.'
S. 'John, 1E39, driver says he's running away. He's got the brake in full service and can't stop.'
JT. '1E39 is running away and can't stop. Got the brake in full service...so...yeah, OK. He's approaching Yatton. There's nothing ahead.'
S. 'Nothing ahead, good.'
JT. 'We've got plenty of breathing space, we'll set the route through Temple Meads.'
S. 'Good idea.'
JT. 'Where shall we send him? Where he knows the route?'
S. 'Which is the fastest connection?' (ie highest permitted speed over points)

JT. 'Yeah.'

S. 'No point through any short connections.' (ie sharp turns)

JT. 'We'll have to find a route through Temple Meads, the fastest route. There's a bit of a halt there.' (with a nice touch of dry wit)

S. 'All right. I'll come back to you if I hear any more.'

JT. 'Thanks Fred.'

S. 'All right.'

Mr Turton then informed Steve Fell, the panel signalman working the Taunton end of the console. Mr Fell checked to see that there was no traffic or blockage ahead of 1E39 on his section and then spoke to the man on the next part of the console to organise the passage of the station. They agreed to run the train through Platform 7 and then up the Filton Incline. As they completed their planning at 5.7pm, the signal-post telephone light for B15, the signal at Yatton Loop, started flashing. Mr Fell answered it and found the driver of 1E39 cool and collected and quite in charge of the situation. He told Mr Fell that he had used his emergency brake to stop and that he was in a position either to go into the Loop or come through to Bristol. Mr Fell told him to come on in to Temple Meads at reduced speed, that he would be routed into Platform 5 and the signal at the far end would be cleared in case the train 'overshot'.

So it was well organised in the conventional way, with good railway work from ordinary railwaymen using their initiative and a perfectly ordinary telephone. The NRN and the Control in this instance had been no more than a farce, and in fact superfluous: as ever the driver and signalman sorted it out between them.

Train 1E39 arrived at Bristol Temple Meads at 5.22pm where it terminated and was taken empty to St Philips Marsh depot.

Driver Evans' reward for his cool thinking was to be criticised for not pressing the 'E' button on his NRN. He said that if he had done this he would have got through to Railtrack's Swindon Control and he thought he ought to contact his own controller. Asked if the latter had offered any assistance or helpful advice, Mr Evans could only reply 'No.' And since he had sorted the whole thing out on his own, it seems churlish to criticise him for anything.

Power car No 43093 was detached from train set XC58 on 28 November and sent to Laira for inspection. The fault was found to be in the 36-way jumper connection in the nose of the vehicle which, by causing a false feed, had energised certain electrical circuits which disabled the electrical controls of the brake system. Old-hand locomen, used to the utterly-reliable method of applying brakes and using nothing more than a sliding plate uncovering a hole, had long before questioned the safety of electric relays in brake systems. But, of course, they were scorned as 'dinosaurs' or 'worriers' by their Instructors and told: 'Don't worry, it can't go wrong.' There are plenty of men out there who could vouch for that one.

Power car No 43093 had had brake trouble for some time. On 16 September, the parking brake was left applied during a high-speed journey which resulted in large 'flats' on the wheels. On 5 October brake power fluctuated. On 14 November, when it was attached to set XC76 forming train 1S71, the brakes suddenly went hard on in Dainton Tunnel. On 24 November, attached to set XC65 forming train 1V66, the brakes failed to operate on the approach to Bristol Parkway and the driver stopped by using the emergency position. The power car was taken to St Philips Marsh, where the brake controller was found to be defective and was changed. On 26 November, attached to set XC73 forming train 1V38, the brake failed until the emergency brake was used on the approach to Birmingham New Street, and a new compressor was fitted.

Then there was the failure with which this story is concerned, and for which the vehicle was sent to Laira. The engineers there seem to have cobbled it together again because it was out on the road on 30 November / 1 December when it suffered another brake-related problem and was transferred to Craigentinny for further investigation.

# Southall:
## 19 September 1997

On Thursday 18 September 1997, the 6.02pm Paddington to Oxford left on time. The service was operated by an InterCity 125 unit belonging to Great Western Trains. The IC125 was driven by Mr Taylor with power car No 43163 leading and No 43173 trailing. The whole train was identified as 'Set PM24'. The controls were in working order and the AWS was functioning correctly, but the buzzer communication system between the guard and the driver was buzzing continuously in No 43173 and would not buzz at all in No 43163. This meant that the guard could not give 'Right Away' to the driver in the routine way. When the train got to Oxford it unloaded and moved northwards, out of the station and clear of the crossover giving access to the up platform. Driver Taylor walked to the 'London end' power car, No 43173, and took the train across the roads into the up platform. The up platform departure signal was at 'Danger' and, as the train passed over the AWS magnet for that signal, Driver Taylor got the warning siren and a brake application. He carried out the cancelling procedure but this failed to have the desired effect and the train was brought to a stand by the AWS brake application. It was stuck half in, half out of the platform, blocking the layout. To release the brake, Driver Taylor went into the engine room and operated the AWS isolating switch. Having done that, he returned to the cab to release the brake. At that point the Station Supervisor came to the cab door to see what was wrong. Mr Taylor told him what had happened, or at least as much as he thought he needed to know, and asked him to request Oxford Panel for permission to move up to the starting signal. But Driver Taylor did not inform the signalman that he had isolated the AWS — something he was bound by the Rules to report.

The Oxford panelman, Signalman Parker, having no knowledge of the true state of affairs, did not feel the incident worthy of comment, did not make a note of the occurrence on his occurrence sheet and did not tell Control. As far as he knew, there was nothing to tell. Driver Taylor made an entry in the defects book: AWS ISOLATED, UNABLE TO CANCEL. He then drove the train back to Paddington and took it onto Old Oak Common depot where he forgot to fill in a Defect Report or an Incident Report. Thus, the fitters at Old Oak depot did not know there was an AWS fault on the train.

As early as 1995, Great Western Trains (GWT) had shown signs of slipping back from the high standards of safety required. One of these 'slips' occurred at Maidenhead in September of that year, when the fuel tank fell off a power car of a down IC125, due to the failure of the securing nuts, resulting in a serious fire. Readers might recall this event, when passengers leapt from the burning train and one was killed by an up IC125 travelling at full speed. Fourteen months later, an investigation was conducted into this incident, and the report was published in January 1997. While the investigation was pending, an audit of GWT safety 'found significant areas of non-compliance' with its safety case. Between June and November 1996 there were nine incidents of component failure on GWT IC125 trains, which amounted to a failure by GWT to comply with its obligations under the safety case by which it was granted its licence. GWT then commissioned a special audit by an independent auditor, David Parkes. His report was published in January 1997. In it he was highly critical of some areas of fleet maintenance and of maintenance staff performance monitoring. David Parkes' audit also questioned 'whether there were adequate human resources [why not call them people?] to undertake key safety work'. As a result of this criticism, GWT agreed to provide additional resources, proposed corrective actions and commissioned Halcrow Transmark to assist in

## PLAN OF CRASH SITE

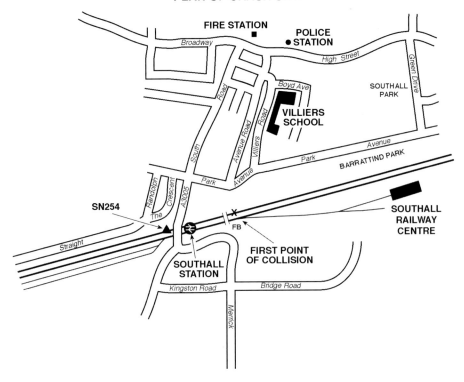

updating maintenance policy 'to ensure compliance with the Safety Case and Group Standards'.

As a result of all this high-powered investigation into manning and administration, GWT management believed by mid-1997 that it would have 'plenty of spare capacity' if it could abolish the demarcation of trades amongst its fitters at Old Oak Common and get every man to do any job. The workforce supported the proposed changes in working practices, and in September 1997 a 33% *reduction* was effected in the number of men per technical team. This was the response to a question regarding the adequacy of manning levels: reduced numbers, increased workload, greater pressure to finish a job and a motivation to do no more than was necessary to get any particular job done. Before this change in working practices was adopted it was subjected to a risk assessment, the conclusion of which was that the performance of the reorganised staff would require careful monitoring.

If the fitters were to be multi-skilled, they would require re-training and examination, and records would be needed of who was trained to do what. But, having reduced the size of the workforce, which is easy, the much more difficult task of re-training was not systematically carried out, and only inadequate records of re-training were kept. Indeed, the Shift Supervisors had to go out and help their men rather than do administrative work.

Two of the fitters on duty on the night of 18/19 September, Mr Thomas and Mr McKenzie, did not know that the AWS test should be carried out as part of the 'A' examination. Had the monitoring advised by the risk assessment been carried out properly, shortcomings in training would have been revealed. But there were insufficient people to look after the trains, and so 'monitoring' was not what it ought to have been. The Maintenance Supervisor, Mr Francis, had physically to assist his teams of fitters in order to get the maintenance work done, and thus paperwork and records were left untouched.

When Driver Taylor left his IC125 train, numbered PM24 for maintenance purposes, at Old Oak depot, the fitters had no idea — and nor could they have had — that it had a fault with the AWS on its 'London end' power car (No 43173) and that this had been isolated, ie switched off. When the team had nearly completed the maintenance routine on set PM24, Mr Thomas went into the cab of power car No 43173 and, looking in the Defect Book, saw the note about the fault with — and isolation of — the AWS. He called for the assistance of Mr McKenzie to carry out a test of the AWS.

The test required for this fault involved one man going under the train with a magnet to simulate the action of the track magnet for a restricted aspect. Three times the south pole of the magnet was applied to the receiver on the train, and each time the AWS horn sounded and was successfully cancelled by the reset button. What they did not look at were the contacts within the reset button cover. Why should they? The button worked correctly three times in a row. But the contacts of the reset button were contaminated with a substance described in the Uff Report only as 'polish'. I imagine this was 'Brasso', but the Report does not specify and, since there is no brass to polish in the cab of an IC125, I am left wondering what sort of polish it was and what it was doing there. But there was enough of this substance on the electrical contacts to produce an 'intermittent failure'. There was at Old Oak depot a 'test box' for use in replicating other faults to which the AWS was liable, but to go through the test routines with this equipment would have taken half an hour and they did not use it, presumably because they were too pushed for time. Even if they had used it, it would not have shown up the particular fault on power car No 43173. The fitters were confident that the AWS was working properly, so they returned the AWS isolating switch back to the 'running' position and put the train back into service.

They did not wire and seal the isolating switch because they did not think the requisite lead seals were present at Old Oak Common, one of the largest maintenance depots on the erstwhile Western Region. Plastic seals were kept in the engine room of the power car, but these were not used. No record was made of the work that had been carried out, not even on the counterfoil of the driver's Defect Book in which the fault had been noted. Furthermore, that Defect Book was full, but a new one was not put into the cab. The Shift Supervisor was busy working on another train, helping his fitters get through their full schedule of work, and so set PM24 was allowed to enter service with the AWS isolation switch unsealed, which was a breach of the Rules. An outsider, knowing no more than what is written in the Uff Report, is led to the conclusion that this situation was fairly routine — a hectic scramble to keep up with scheduled maintenance.

Set PM24 was taken over by Driver Tunnock at 4.40am on 19 September. He checked all round the set, but did not notice the absence of a seal on the AWS isolating handle in power car No 43173. He did a brake test, with a shunter as his assistant, and took the train away to Paddington. He passed the AWS test ramp leaving the depot and received the correct warning horn, which he cancelled. He passed other restricted aspects on the way up and the AWS worked correctly every time. At 6am he got into Platform 3, where he shut down the engines and walked along the platform to the 'country' end, got into No 43163 and put in his key to bring the systems to life. It was then he found that the driver/guard communication buzzer was not working. He shut down at that end and walked back to the 'London end' power car, No 43173, put in his key, turned it and got a horn from the AWS which the reset button would not silence. In order to release the brakes he had to operate the AWS isolating switch in the engine room of No 43173.

Driver Tunnock went at once to the GWT Operations Supervisor at Paddington, Mr Barnfield, and reported that the AWS reset button would not function on No 43173 and asked for the station fitter. But the fitter could not be found. The Uff Report states that: 'Mr Barnfield then rang what he thought was Swindon Control and handed the phone to Driver Tunnock'. Tunnock spoke to a male voice which identified itself as 'Swindon Control'. This could have been either the GWT or Railtrack Controller, but supposedly GWT. Both organisations had Controllers, sitting in the same room, at Swindon. Driver Tunnock told this person that the

AWS reset button on No 43173 did not work, and that he had isolated the AWS in that end in order that the brakes of the train could be released. The train would, therefore, come back from Swansea without AWS unless the fitters at that station could attend to the job. Mr Barnfield testified to hearing Driver Tunnock have this conversation.

There were three men on duty in GWT Swindon Control on the night shift from 10pm on 18 September until 7am on 19 September. All three denied having this conversation with Driver Tunnock. Evidence was even introduced which attempted to establish that no telephone call was made to Swindon Control at the relevant time, but other records showed two calls coming into the Control Office, at 6.12am and 6.31am. Unfortunately, the origin of the calls was not recorded, but there was proof that a call was made at the relevant time. The Uff Report believes that the call was made at about 6.30am and the message was lost in the change-over to a new shift of Controllers at 7am.

Driver Tunnock took the train to Swansea, and the AWS worked perfectly in No 43163. On arrival at Swansea there were no fitters to meet him and he went at once to a telephone to contact GWT Swindon Control. The call went to the 'phone of Fleet Maintenance Controller

John Harris. He was not at his desk and the call was answered by Mrs Sandra Hallett. She was a former train hostess who, after four weeks' training, had become 'Information Controller'. She had been in this post for three weeks. Her training must have been for some other work than taking safety-critical messages from train drivers for, after seven weeks in the office, she was not yet familiar with 'railway jargon' and acronyms. She did not know what the letters AWS stood for and was generally unaware of the importance of the message she had received. She recalled at the Inquiry only that a driver at Swansea had called regarding 'isolating something'. She said that she had written a note of the message and had given it to Service Controller Philip Maylon or John Harris. Both men denied all knowledge of this message and Mrs Hallett said that the piece of paper on which she wrote was thrown away at the end of the shift. Subsequently she stated that no papers were thrown away at the end of the shift and so it appears that she had not made a note of Driver Tunnock's message.

After his brief conversation with Mrs Hallett, Driver Tunnock did not feel confident and went to the Station Services Manager, William Palmer, for assistance. Mr Palmer called Landore depot to ask for some fitters, and two men were sent out. But they were under the impression that the fault they had been called out for was the driver/guard buzzer which was sounding continuously. So somehow the existence of this minor fault had managed to work its way into the consciousness of Control, but not the major fault. The fitters arrived at 10.15am and the train was due away at 10.32am. They had no time to repair the faulty so they isolated the circuit.

An easy and eminently practical way out of the problem would have been to have turned the train through 180° by sending it around the Landore triangular junction, so that power car No 43163, with functioning AWS, was at the London end. The Uff Report, paragraph 6.24, deals with this possibility in a curiously contradictory way. The first part of the paragraph states that 'It is now accepted by GWT that the train could have been turned by use of a 'triangle' at Swansea'. The latter part of the same paragraph states that: 'GWT further accepted, however, that the train would not have been reversed in this manner, even if Control had known of the AWS isolation. The failure to turn the train was therefore due to the absence of an appropriate procedure [for negotiating such unscheduled manoeuvres]'. When the signalman and the train crew worked for the same firm it was a simple matter to ask for an additional movement to be made. Fragmenting the system divided the operating of trains between self-interested firms which required payment for everything they did for anyone else. But essential railway work still has to be done and the same quick interface between groups has to be maintained to replicate, as far as possible, the ideal system where all operating staff are working under one rule. Ever since the railway was fragmented, a procedure known as 'Very Short Term Planning' (VSTP) has been in place to deal with unplanned train movements. A request form for a special train movement is filled in and faxed from the TOC to Railtrack and back again, approved. The TOC would, of course, have to pay for the extra movement. In the nine months prior to the Southall crash, failures of the AWS on GWT were occurring at the rate of 10 a week and isolations of the AWS at two a week, and yet 'there was no record of GWT ever making a request to 'turn' a train'. The conclusion drawn from this by Professor Uff is that train 1A47 was not turned and was allowed to run with AWS isolated because (a) there was no method of getting it turned at short notice and (b) running without AWS was accepted practice on GWT. Experienced railwaymen have personal experience of turning IC125 trains on triangular junctions, owing to faults such as a defective speedometer at one end, a broken windscreen wiper or even a broken windscreen.

It seems to me that the true situation was that train 1A47 might have been turned, if only Control had taken seriously the message given to them at Paddington. In the case of a broken windscreen or windscreen wipers, drivers were absolutely compelled to have their train turned, and indeed, in a motor-car-driving world, everyone can understand the dangers inherent in these defects, but a defective AWS was different, something that could be lived with. GWT management had issued to its Controllers no definite instructions on this score,

*Left:*
The crash scene from above and to the south of the line. The IC125 was running on the up main, as were several of the ARC stone wagons. Coach 'G', bent into a 'U' shape, can be seen at centre left, with the ARC stone wagon crushing it. Coach 'F', the buffet car, ran past 'G' and crashed end-on into the ARC wagon, making a 'T' shape with the one behind it.
*Ken Brunt*

and so, prior to Southall, trains were frequently allowed to run without AWS because of a lack of firm direction.

The growth of importance of the AWS because of extremely high speed and close-spaced signals had not been appreciated by management, nor indeed by all of the men. In 1997 it was unlikely that an experienced driver would have refused to work a train which lacked AWS. Traditionally, the AWS was regarded by drivers as an aid to driving rather than an essential part of the safety equipment, but then, traditionally, drivers were not faced with a signal every 20sec. In a multiple-aspect-signalled, 125mph railway, the AWS had become of far greater importance than it had been in steam and semaphore days. If management realised this, it did not show it by any change in (or addition to) its Rule Book or working practices. While various authorities were agonising over the cost of ATP or TPWS, a good stop-gap measure would have been to increase the importance and status of AWS in the minds of drivers and controllers — but that would also have led to delays and even increased expense as men 'failed' trains because the AWS was not working.

If Control had not lost Driver Tunnock's message, would the faulty train have been taken out of service? The Rule, dating from 1993, on what to do with trains on which the AWS was faulty runs as follows: 6.3 'If it is necessary to isolate the AWS the driver must inform the signalman at the first convenient opportunity. The train must be taken out of service at the first suitable location without causing delay or cancellation'. So the Rule contradicted itself. The Rule is not so much a 'loophole' as a 'barn door' wide open. The main thing was to keep the trains in service and not think too deeply about the risks. The signalman to whom the fault should have been reported worked for Railtrack, while the faulty train was hired from a leasing company by GWT. At whose convenience was the train to be withdrawn from service? Who was to make the decision to withdraw it? The so-called Rule is silent.

The train, 1A47, left Swansea at 10.32am — on time, without incurring a fine for loss of time, but without a functioning AWS system in the leading power car, No 43173. At Cardiff, Driver Tunnock, still anxious about the dangers of driving without AWS, left written on a large piece of paper 'AWS ISOLATED. REPAIR BOOK FULL'. This he left in a prominent position on the dashboard and was relieved by Driver Harrison, who was rostered to take the train to Paddington.

Driver Harrison felt very confident of his abilities as a driver. He was a long-serving, experienced railwayman and felt quite safe without the assistance of the AWS. He had his Driver's Safety Device (DSD), which he had to keep depressed with a foot and which, about once a minute, he had to release and depress again if the train's brakes were not to be automatically applied. So relaxed was he that he had both feet up on the driver's console as he allowed the train to coast very slowly into Bristol Parkway station. Several witnesses testified

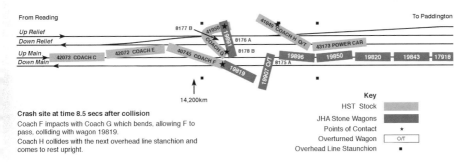

**Crash site at time 8.5 secs after collision**
Coach F impacts with Coach G which bends, allowing F to pass, colliding with wagon 19819. Coach H collides with the next overhead line stanchion and comes to rest upright.

147

to the truth of this. There was also technical evidence that, if the DSD were allowed to rise and not be reset, the train would creep forward at walking speed, which is how the train ran into Bristol Parkway station. Driver Harrison drove the train safely to Swindon station where he brought it to a stand. Witnesses on the platform stated that he came in with one foot up on the console.

From Bristol Parkway, the train was running on track equipped with ATP. As we know, the AWS was isolated on No 43173 but the ATP gear was installed and in working order. Unfortunately, Driver Harrison did not feel competent to use it and had switched it off. He had been through a basic training course in the use of ATP but had never driven, unsupervised, with the ATP switched on and had not had a refresher course since September 1995. The GWT Rule Book did not require drivers to maintain their competence by attending refresher courses, which seems to make the original course a waste of time. Neither did GWT's rostering of drivers put ATP-competent men on those services which were ATP-designated. Service 1A47 was an ATP-designated service. This installation of ATP, from Bristol Parkway (and North Somerset Junction out of Temple Meads) to Paddington was a 'pilot scheme', an experiment started by the British Railways Board and continued jointly by Railtrack and GWT. These two organisations had no legal obligation to undertake this experiment, and, as can be seen from the state of Driver Harrison's training, ATP was not taken with full seriousness by GWT.

At Swindon, Driver Harrison was joined in the cab by Mr Mayo, a Railtrack employee whose job it was to travel in driving cabs and observe the sighting of signals. Mr Mayo commented on the note on the console but Mr Harrison dismissed the comment with a non-committal shrug of his shoulders. Driver Harrison took the train out of Swindon and raced through the Vale of White Horse at 125mph in a normal and confident way, according to the evidence of Mr Mayo. The latter then left the train at Reading, for which he must be eternally grateful.

Train 1A47 powered away from Reading on the up main and roared through Slough at 125mph at about 1.10½pm. It passed the building housing the Integrated Electronic Control Centre where Signaller Forde was sitting before his computer screen, watching the progress of 1A47 and the other trains in the area. The timetable scheduled 25 trains per hour over the main and relief lines in the vicinity of Slough and Southall. In addition to these were empty coaching stock movements and unscheduled freight trains running under the VSTP arrangement.

Because of the speed and frequency of the trains, they were, for the most part, controlled by an Automatic Route Setting (ARS) computer, including the switching of trains from one track to another, but for some switching movements a signalman had to intervene. One such movement was that of transferring the 9.58am Allington freight train from the down relief line to Southall Yard, the latter being outside the area controlled by the computer. This was a scheduled movement, one of 12 such movements daily. The Allington was an EWS-owned train, reporting number 6V17, consisting of a Class 59 diesel-electric, No 59101, driven by Alan Bricker, and 20 empty, eight-wheel road-stone wagons. It was booked to cross to the Yard at 12.31pm and was, on this day, running about 45min late.

There was, in the aftermath of the crash, some outrage from an ignorant media over the fact that a freight train was turned across the line 'in front of' a High Speed Train. When the freight train was ready to leave Acton Yard, Signaller Forde had two choices. He could turn it across to the down main for the 3¾ miles to Southall Yard or he could bring it out onto the down relief line (DRL). The terminology of 'down main' and 'down relief' dates back to GWR days and is equivalent to 'down fast' and 'down slow' on other railways. Signaller Forde brought 6V17 out of Acton Yard on the down relief line. The latter course avoided a relatively lengthy occupation of the down main line. Such an occupation of the down main would also have involved bringing the train to a virtual standstill at junction signal SN249, which gave access to Southall Yard. This signal had a 'timed out' delay before it cleared to a 'Proceed' aspect to ensure that the train went into the Yard at a low speed. By bringing 6V17 on the DRL to Southall East Junction, Signaller Forde gave himself more time to assess the situation

*Above:*
No 59201 with the 7A19
Allington-Brentford on
23 June 2000. It is on the
Southall 'ladder', in the same
position as train 6V17 on
19 September 1997 when hit
by the 10.32am Swansea
IC125. *Ken Brunt*

regarding the freight and passenger trains, and also the additional option of placing the train in the Hanwell Loop if need arose. This loop cannot be accessed from the down main. The down main line for the 3¾ miles from Acton to Southall was thus kept clear for express trains. Next behind 6V17 on the DRL was a passenger train for Bedwyn, and there were other trains on the DRL behind that. More trains were approaching on the down and up main lines; in all there were no fewer than 10 trains within 10 miles of Southall East Junction. When trains are travelling at 90-125mph, the signaller has to take into consideration, when making regulating decisions, trains which are 10 miles away.

Signaller Forde had to get 6V17 off the DRL or it would bring to a stand those trains behind it and yet, when crossing over the up main and down main lines to the Yard, it would cause some small delay to main-line trains because there were so many of them. There was never a 'good' time to make the movement; the trick was to find the best moment to send the train across so as to cause the least delay. That is the nature of railway work, and that is why there are highly-developed safety systems to interlock the points and the signals and keep the trains apart. A moment's thought will show that, if a signaller had to take into account the possibility of a driver ignoring the signals, no train would ever leave a station.

Signaller Forde looked at his VDU screen and assessed not only the position of trains but also his own position, the state of play. He had to judge the position of trains from the indicated track circuit lights on his VDU screen. If a track circuit indication is equal to 1,500 or 1,700yd on the ground, this method of knowing a train's whereabouts is only accurate to within 1,500yd or so — and distance is time on a railway. Signaller Forde had to think quickly.

At about 1.11pm, Forde saw that he had as good a chance as he was ever likely to get. Train 6V17 was showing on the track circuit next in rear of the 'berth' track for SN243, which was the signal that would route it across the up main and down main to Southall Yard. The up Swansea, 1A47, was six miles away from Southall East Junction — a fraction under 3min at 125mph. It was the best opportunity he was going to get. If he did not get 6V17 across now, he would be creating greater delays on the down relief behind the freight.

Signaller Forde telephoned the Shunter in Southall Yard and got his permission for the train to enter his domain. The Shunter pressed the acceptance plunger which unlocked the route to the Yard, taking it out of the control of the ARS computer. Signaller Forde could then manually set the route from down relief to Southall Yard at about 1.12pm. The Swansea was then 5¼ miles away. On the up main, signal SN254, 450yd to the rear of the crossover, was at 'Danger', protecting the crossing movement. SN270, 1,675yd to the rear of SN254, was at single yellow and SN280, 1,145yd to the rear of that — just to the west of Hayes & Harlington station — was showing double yellow. Driver Harrison was still approaching signals to the west of that, all at green. When signals SN254, 270 and 280 were proved, electronically, to be protecting the junction, the junction points were turned. It was now about 1.12pm. Train 6V17 was closer to SN243. It had only to occupy the 'berth' track circuit in the last 200yd to the rear of the signal and the aspect would then clear for the chosen route across all roads.

Signaller Forde watched his VDU screen as anxiously as steam-age signalmen watched for the first cloud of steam from the chimney of a goods train engine for which they had 'pulled off' to run it out of a loop, between one express train and the next. To his dismay, the SN243 berth track did not become occupied as soon as he had expected. There may well have been a good reason, but from where he was sitting, from the time he called the route to the time 6V17 passed SN243 was a long wait — almost two minutes. Train 6V17 passed SN243 at 1.13.50. The series of crossovers was spread over half a mile, from SN243 to getting inside the loop, clear of all main-line track circuits, and thus releasing the junction to be returned for main-line running. Train 6V17 went over the serpentine route at about 25mph and therefore required 1¼ minutes to get the tail of its long train into the loop. When 6V17 passed SN243, at Milepost 8½, the Swansea was passing Milepost 10¼ at Hayes & Harlington station and closing the 1¾-mile gap between it and the up main points at Southall East Junction at 125mph. There was a little less than a minute to go.

Signaller Forde's decision to cross 6V17 was based on his experience of the usual time required by an empty train to cross the road. It is possible that the train was further away from SN243 than he thought when he made his move. The track circuit indications are not a precise guide to a train's position. Signaller Forde had expected that the crossing movement would cause 1A47 to slow somewhat, to be 'checked', but as he watched the track circuit indications on his VDU screen and saw no apparent movement on the freight, he realised that the delay to the express would amount to a dead stand.

So far as safety was concerned, this did not matter. The signal protecting the junction was at 'Danger' and the double yellow warning signal was 1.6 miles to its rear, on the western side of Hayes & Harlington station. Unfortunately, as Driver Harrison's train roared through Hayes & Harlington, he was tidying up his belongings and putting things into his bag, ready to get off the train as soon as it arrived at Paddington. With no AWS siren to warn him, he missed the double yellow and the single yellow aspects on SN280 and SN270.

Watching the progress of 1A47 as a series of lights on the track diagram displayed on his VDU screen, Signaller Forde could judge that 1A47 had not slowed down after passing SN280 and he soon realised that it was a runaway and that a collision with 6V17 was inevitable. Moments later, hitherto-unoccupied tracks showed 'occupied' and Mr Forde realised that the track circuit indications on his VDU screen were the result of metal vehicles falling across the rails. He could have pressed an emergency button to set all signals in the area to 'Danger' but instead he decided to do the job more rapidly and also more precisely by manually operating only those signals relevant to the collision to 'Danger'. The modern equivalent of 'throwing all the boards to Danger' was to use the tracker ball and click on the signals' symbols.

Larry Harrison believed in himself and his abilities as a driver. He was indeed one of GWT's best men. He had an excellent record as a driver and in GWT's league table of drivers likely to pass signals at 'Danger', he was placed in the 'least likely to' category. He had twice passed a signal at 'Danger', but that was at slow speed and back in the 1970s. He had also once started a train without the guard's permission.

A kind of folklore grew up around 'Driver Harrison's bag'. This was a sports-type holdall. It was alleged that he used his bag, weighted with cans of soft drinks, his 'Bardic' lamp and a vacuum flask, as well as railway books and papers, to hold down the 'dead man's pedal' and thus save himself the trouble. In fact, the bag was not heavy enough to have held it down to the satisfaction of the safety system, and in any case he would still have had to lift it off the pedal every minute when the vigilance warbler sounded.

Driver Harrison was travelling at 125mph. He was, therefore, well aware of the need to keep a sharp look-out for the signals. He saw the green light in SN298. The double yellow of SN280 was 1,200yd ahead, obscured at first by the buildings of Hayes & Harlington station, but visible when the cab of No 43173 was 430yd from it. From that point the

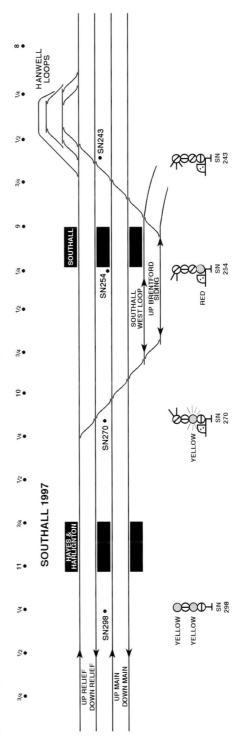

151

double yellow was in sight for 6.7sec. Driver Harrison had become engrossed in packing his bag as he 'whizzed through Hayes & Harlington'. This lack of attention lasted long enough for him to miss both the warning signals, ie for 16.3sec.

The fact that Driver Harrison had to keep his eyes on the road without looking away even for 20sec is an indication of the level of concentration demanded of any driver. Of course, he ought to have looked where he was going, but he should have been assisted in his task by good management decisions, and, clearly, some reassessment of AWS status was long overdue. This is particularly true in view of the fact that neither Railtrack nor GWT was over-enthusiastic about progressing the far better — but much more costly — ATP system.

There was some misalignment of signals SN280 and SN270, but both were showing an ample light and the drivers of the preceding three trains, when questioned, agreed that they had had no difficulty seeing the aspects.

Driver Harrison became aware of the red signal — SN254, at Southall station, covering the East Junction — immediately after he had blindly passed SN270 showing a single yellow warning light. He then saw, about ¼ mile ahead, SN254 at 'Danger' and, beyond that, the Class 59 diesel locomotive 'at a funny angle' to the up main. At a point approximately 90yd beyond SN270 he braked as forcefully as the system allowed, but realised that he was going too fast to stop at the red.

Driver Bricker, on No 59101, was bringing his train across the crossovers at 20-25mph. He saw 1A47 coming towards him and for a second he was not worried. Then he realised the speed at which it was travelling and knew there was going to be a collision. He tried to accelerate but it was too late to draw the train entirely clear. He and the locomotive with the first four or five wagons had reached the safety of the down main, but the rest were either on the crossover between the down and the up main or were still running along the up main — in the down direction.

At about 1.15pm, the front of power car No 43173 grazed an empty hopper wagon. The wagon was on the up to down main crossover. It was at an angle to the IC125 so the blow was a glancing one, but the closing speed was between 80 and 90mph and the shockwave went back through the IC125 to the guard's compartment at the rear where Senior Conductor Abdul Khanghauri was thrown about with great force and stunned.

The power car was derailed and deflected to the left, coming to a stand on its wheels, at an angle, in the ballast. The following coach, 'H', went with it but became detached, turning on its side and skidding through the ballast until it smashed into one of the stanchions supporting the overhead catenary. The empty hoppers coming along the up main at perhaps 20mph were

SKETCH OF SIGNALS AND DISTANCES ON UP MAIN LINE APPROACHING SOUTHALL struck by the coaches of the IC125 travelling in the opposite direction at perhaps 65mph. Hopper wagon No 19890 was toppled over by coach 'G', bringing it head-on against wagon No 19891. The effect of the tremendous impact was to derail coach 'G', while swinging the wagon around, broadside to the tracks, and lifting it several feet off the rails. The wagon hit a catenary stanchion on the opposite side of the track and fell on top of the London end of coach 'G' which had been deflected to the opposite side of the track. Coach 'G' was pinned to the ground as coach 'F' drove forwards against one of its corners, bending it into a severe 'U' shape. Coach 'F' carried on past coach 'G', hit wagon No 19891 head-on and stopped, derailed, approximately upright but slewed across the up main and down relief lines. Coaches 'E' and 'C' were derailed but upright. Coaches 'B' and 'A' remained on the rails. There was no coach 'D' in the train. Out of 214 people on the IC125, including crew, seven passengers were killed and 150 injured. Driver Harrison was also injured.

Driver Harrison escaped death because he ran back into the engine room, but he was still exceedingly lucky. He must have been tremendously shocked but he crawled out of the wreckage taking with him a red flag and his 'job diagram' in order to report correctly the circumstances to Slough Control Centre. The first signal-post telephone he tried was not working but the next, on SN251, connected him to the IECC, where there was a certain amount of shocked and noisy conversation taking place. The conversation, automatically tape-recorded, was remarkably civilised, given the terrible shock Driver Harrison had suffered, and went as follows:

Signaller Forde. (S) 'Hello there. 316 received.'
Driver Harrison. (H) 'This is the driver of the, the HST requesting into the, er……'
S. 'Driver, can you hold on a minute there please? Keep quiet guys, I've got a driver on the phone. Right, can you repeat all that please?'
H. 'Er, yeah. I'm, I'm ringing from SN251 at the moment, that's the first signal, er, telephone I could get to.'
S. 'What train were you driving?'
H. 'The HST.'
S. 'You were driving the HST?'
H. 'Yeah. I've got the headcode. Hang on. I've got to go in my pocket. Hang on. Hang on. That's One Alpha Forty-Seven.'
S. 'One Alpha Forty-Seven, right. And you're at a stand and you're ringing in from SN251. Driver, are you OK?'
H. 'I'm OK. Yeah. I was just putting my stuff away in the bag, the A, the A, the, the AWS has been isolated because some, some brake problem, I believe, so I had no AWS, so I put my stuff away in the bag and the next thing I knew I was coming up against a red, up, such coming through, through…'
S. 'Through Southall station?'
H. 'Through Southall, yeah.'
S. 'Right, I see. Driver, can you bear with us one moment? [Signaller Forde then called to his Shift Supervisor (SS).] That's the driver of the train — have a word with him.'
(The Supervisor, a man of few words, was unsure what to say.)
SS. 'Hello driver.'
H. 'Hello there.'
SS. 'Hello mate. Are you the driver of One A Forty-Seven?'
H. 'One Alpha Forty-Seven, yes.'
SS. 'Right……er.'
H. 'AWS is isolated.'
SS. 'Right.'
H. 'And I was just putting my stuff away in the bag, like I would normally do, you see?'
SS. 'Right.'
H. 'And er, all of a sudden I was whizzing through Hayes with a red at Southall.'

SS. 'Right.'

H. 'I see the slow train crossing over then.'

SS. 'Right.'

H. 'I went back into the engine room.'

SS. 'Uh-huh.'

H. 'And this is the first time I've been able, I've, I've put…' (his voice became inaudible)

SS. 'Is your train off the track driver?'

H. 'Er…Yes, it's blocking all lines.'

SS. 'It's blocking all lines.'

H. 'Yes, I need the electricity turned off.'

SS. 'OK. All the electricity has been switched off but as I say you can approach it but don't touch the electrics.'

H. 'There's a police officer that would like to have a word with you, mate.'

P.C. 'Hello to you. I'm a police officer from Southall.'

SS. 'Yes mate.'

P.C. 'Are you aware what's happened, are you?'

SS. 'We are aware what's happened. We don't know the full details, we just know there's been a collision, that's all.'

P.C. 'Right. We've got, um, as he said, it's fully blocked. We've got a train on its side.'

SS. 'Right.'

P.C. 'We've got several fatalities.'

SS. 'Oh Christ!'

P.C. 'A few walking wounded. We've got all the emergency services responding but we need everything turned off and that coming through on this line.'

SS. 'Yeah, yeah. I'll tell you this, Officer, we have switched off the power.'

P.C. 'Right.'

SS. 'At Southall.'

P.C 'Yep.'

SS. 'Now it's safe to approach but do not touch the wires.'

P.C. 'OK. I can.'

SS. 'Until you get… If you're around that area, make sure no-one touches the wires.'

P.C. 'No one touches the wires.'

SS. 'Until someone from the electricity part of it is there.'

P.C. 'OK.'

SS. 'They will test it and give you the authority to make sure.'

P.C. 'Right. OK.'

SS. 'OK.'

P.C. 'You know there's a train approaching from the east that stopped about 200yd away?'

SS. 'Yeah, yeah. We've got all trains at a stand. No trains will be moving.'

P.C. 'OK. Magic.'

SS. 'OK.'

P.C. 'OK.'

SS. 'Cheers.'

P.C. 'Right-e-ho. Cheers.'

The Uff Report has two lists of causes of the crash. Paragraph 7.15 states that 'The accident at Southall would not have happened had ATP been operational in power car No 43173. A cause of the accident was, therefore, GWT's failure to roster ATP-competent drivers for train 1A47'. Paragraph 7.16 states: 'In the absence of ATP, the AWS system became critical… The absence of AWS was a contributory factor to the failure of Driver Harrison to respond to signals SN280 or SN270'. Paragraph 7.17 opens with the statement: 'Responsibility for the non-functioning of the AWS on 1A47 rests firmly with GWT'.

Paragraph 7.19 gives the 'primary cause' of the crash as 'Driver Harrison's unexplained failure to respond to two warning signals', and then goes on to list the other causes of the accident 'which rank equally in their potency'. These were:

> • The failure of GWT's maintenance system to identify and repair the previously-reported AWS fault in power car No 43173.
> • The failure of GWT to react to the isolation of the AWS on power car No 43173 by turning the train or removing it from service.
> • The failure of Railtrack to put in place clear rules to prevent any normal running of an IC125 service with AWS isolated.

The fifth reason concerns the ATP but is written in an incomprehensible manner and I have not included it.

There is a sixth cause missing from this list. Southall East Junction was one of those iniquitous 'single-lead' affairs. If the junction had been laid out in the conventional manner, as it had been in the days of the *real* Great Western and indeed in BR(W) days, Larry Harrison's passing of SN254 at 'Danger' would have been far less serious and even harmless, depending upon the speed for which the junction crossovers were laid out. The trains would not have been led head-on into one another. There might have been a derailment of the HST but the damaging effects would have been minimal.

Driver Larry Harrison was arrested by the police on suspicion of manslaughter on

19 September 1997 and was released on bail. He was finally charged with seven counts of manslaughter on 17 April 1998, and was again released on bail. He was also charged, by the Health & Safety Executive, with offences under Section 7 of the Health & Safety at Work Act 1974. It was not until 1 December that GWT was charged by the HSE with 'Corporate Manslaughter' and with offences under the 1974 Act. No Director of GWT was named in these charges. The trial of the manslaughter charges began at the Old Bailey on 21 June 1999 and six days later Mr Justice Scott-Baker handed down a written judgement, the effect of which was to reject the prosecution's case of corporate manslaughter. On 2 July GWT elected to plead 'Guilty' to the charges brought under the Health & Safety at Work Act, and the Crown and the HSE decided to abandon its action on all charges against Mr Harrison. The Judge directed that 'Not Guilty' verdicts be entered on the seven charges against him. On 27 July 1999, The Honourable Mr Justice Scott-Baker sentenced Great Western Trains for its part in the disaster.

The Learned Judge opened his judgement with these words: 'Those who travel on High Speed Trains are entitled to expect the highest standard of care from those who run them. Great Western Trains Ltd failed to meet that standard, and in my judgement they failed to meet it by a greater extent than they are prepared to admit. Their failure was a significant cause of a disaster that killed seven people, injured 150 others and caused millions of pounds' worth of damage. The lives of many families have been devastated.'

He went on: 'The immediate cause of the accident was the passing of a red signal by the driver. But a substantial contributory cause was the fact that the defendant company permitted the train to run from Swansea to Paddington at speeds of up to 125mph with the automatic warning system isolated.

'The simple solution would have been to turn the train at Swansea. The Defence say the Company did not do so because:

    1. It was not required by the Rules.
    2. It was never suggested by either Railtrack or the Railway Inspectorate.
    3. It was not the practice of operating companies to do so.
    4. AWS isolation was a category 'B' failure and it was therefore permissible
    for the train to continue on its journey.'

The learned Judge said he bore in mind these arguments, but: 'The primary obligation to run its trains safely lies on Great Western Trains. The company should have applied its mind to the risk created by allowing a High Speed Train to travel a journey of this length and at this speed without the AWS operating. It may be that the likelihood of a driver passing a red signal at speed was relatively small. But if the event occurred, the consequences were going to be, as in the event they were, appalling.

'The Prosecution say that there are various other things the Company should or could have done, such as adding another power car or double-manning the cab. The Defence submit, with some force, that each suggestion was either impossible or impracticable.

'I do not regard these matters as relevant, since the Company admits the simple solution would have been to turn the train.

'There is one matter that requires mention, and that is Automatic Train Protection (ATP). At the time of the Clapham disaster it was envisaged that ATP would be introduced within five years, and an undertaking was give to that effect. There is every reason to believe that, had ATP been operating on this train on this journey, the accident would not have happened. The introduction of ATP is not a matter for GWT alone but for the whole rail network. ATP has been beset with technical difficulties which has been the reason for its non-introduction across the board. GWT broke no obligation or undertaking by not having ATP in operation on this train. They were, however, at the time of the accident, operating a pilot ATP scheme, albeit with little enthusiasm. It is to be noted that the pilot scheme was increased dramatically in extent immediately following the accident.'

Had someone at Great Western Trains had the drive to do so, this could have been achieved before the accident. It is ironic that Electrowatt Engineering reported in the month after the accident (and the work on this report was done before the accident Author's note):

'In the absence of ATP there is predicted to be a 26% chance of an ATP-preventable accident involving a GWT train during the next 10 years. The political consideration and the very real requirement for senior management effort that such an accident would bring cannot be disregarded.'

The learned Judge said that the fine he would impose had to reflect:

'1. The extent to which Great Western Trains fell short of the standard required of it and the risk that was thereby created. In my view it was a serious failure.

2. The extent of the disaster and in particular the number of people killed and injured.

3. The need to bring home the message to GWT and others who run substantial transport undertakings that eternal vigilance is required to ensure that accidents of this nature do not occur. In my judgement a substantial fine is required to emphasise this to a large and profitable enterprise such as the Defendant.

'It has not been suggested that the accident was the result of a deliberate risk in pursuit of profit. Rather, the thrust of the complaint is that GWT did not have in place a system for preventing High Speed Trains operating with the AWS isolated and no alternative in place. That in my judgement is a serious fault of senior management.

'In mitigation I take into account:

1. The Defendant's plea of Guilty, tendered not at the first opportunity but at what Counsel considered to be the first practical opportunity. I give full credit to the plea.

2. The fact that the Defendants have a good safety record and have never been prosecuted under Health & Safety legislation.

3. The fact that prompt action was taken after the accident to ensure that there was no further breach of the HSE Act.

4. That they did not break any requirement imposed on them either by Railtrack or the Railway Inspectorate.

'I am surprised that neither Mr George (who, it is said, is in personal charge of safety at GWT) nor any other directors of the company came to Court to express personally remorse for GWT's breach of the HSE Act and to allay any impression of complacency that may have been conveyed to the victims, their families and the public.

'That said, I accept [Defence lawyer] Mr Caplan's submission that Great Western Trains does very much regret its responsibility for this disaster.

'The fine I impose is not intended [to], nor can it, reflect the value of the lives lost or the injuries sustained in the disaster. It is, however, intended to reflect public concern at the offence committed.

'The Defendant will pay the Prosecution costs of the Health & Safety offence. There will be a Defendant's costs order in respect of the manslaughter offences. Those will be in the terms I have already mentioned. There will be a fine of £1.5 million.'

# Index

158

159